ON HAVING AN OWN CHILD

Martin Richards

2009.

ON HAVING AN OWN CHILD

REPRODUCTIVE TECHNOLOGIES AND THE CULTURAL CONSTRUCTION OF CHILDHOOD

Karín Lesnik-Oberstein

KARNAC

First published in 2008 by
Karnac Books Ltd
118 Finchley Road, London NW3 5HT

British Library Cataloguing in Publication Data

A C.I.P. for this book is available from the British Library

ISBN 978 1 85575 545 1

Edited, designed and produced by The Studio Publishing Services Ltd
www.studiopublishingservicesuk.co.uk
e-mail: studio@publishingservicesuk.co.uk

Printed in Great Britain

10 9 8 7 6 5 4 3 2 1

www.karnacbooks.com

CONTENTS

ACKNOWLEDGEMENTS   vii

ABOUT THE AUTHOR   ix

INTRODUCTION   xi

CHAPTER ONE
The wanting of a baby: nature, history, culture,
and society   1

CHAPTER TWO
The wanting of a baby: desire, despair, hope, and regret   39

CHAPTER THREE
The child that is wanted: perfection and commodification   77

CHAPTER FOUR
The child that is wanted: kinship and the body of evidence   117

CHAPTER FIVE
The child that is wanted: reading race and the global child   149

CHAPTER SIX
Conclusion: coming to grief in theory   179

REFERENCES   185

INDEX   195

ACKNOWLEDGEMENTS

This book, as with so much of my life and research, is part of my work with Patrick Casement. Esther Beugeling discussed many of the issues with me in the early stages, and importantly introduced me to Marilyn Strathern's prior writing in the field. My friend Harriet Kline helped me to formulate several of my core ideas about the "own" child. Lib Taylor, Naomi Segal and Roger Cook very kindly invited me to attend, and write a paper for, their "writers' workshop" on "Indeterminate bodies" at the University of Reading in 1999. It was this paper (later published as: "On 'wanting' a 'child' or: An idea of desire", in *Indeterminate Bodies* (2003)) which prompted me to formalize my ongoing research in the area. Some further writing (which was later expanded into Chapter Two) was published in 2005 as "The owned child and commodification", in *New Antigone*, 1(1), 20–27 (see: http://www.newantigone.com/ oscommercedownload/reproductive%20technologies.pdf).

Professors Rachel Bowlby and Sarah Franklin kindly offered encouragement and some important references. Several academic friends and colleagues have supported me in my career and inspired me with their intellectual integrity and depth of scholarship: Professors Erica Burman, Peter Stoneley, and Jonathan Bignall, and Drs Sara Thornton and Emma Francis. Sue Walsh crucially told me to leave the fetish alone, and provided, as ever, great thinking and friendship. Neil Cocks's enthusiasm and brilliance are always an inspiration. Stephen Thomson supplied me with a crucial article (Derrida's "Disordered families"). Dani Caselli was my first reader for this book: the speed of her feedback, the warmth of her encouragement, and her wonderful support and friendship kept me going.

This book was written at the home of Hoyte Swager, and it would have been much less of a pleasure to write without his support and the wonderful computer he gave to me. All my dear friends supported me in this work as in all my work, but here I want to thank particularly for their enduring friendship Ada Jongsma and Jannekemay Pheasant. Finally, my beloved family were there for me as they always are. But my thanks to them in relation to this book includes the special fact that they provided me with a ready-made panel of expertise to draw on: my sister Sarit and my brother-in-law Martijn, as an eye surgeon and neurosurgeon respectively, did not just clarify my understanding of medical issues, but demonstrate to me every day what being a truly compassionate doctor is about. This is equally true of my sister Saskia, and, as she is a practising clinical geneticist, my discussions with her above all illuminated for me many aspects of the issues I am concerned with here. Any remaining errors in the book relating to matters medical or genetic are truly my own. This book is dedicated with the deepest of love and the greatest of admiration to my sisters: Sarit, Saskia, and the memory of Maaike.

ABOUT THE AUTHOR

Karín Lesnik-Oberstein is a Reader in Critical Theory in the School of English and American Literature at the University of Reading, and the Director of the School's "Centre for International Research in Childhood: Literature, Culture, Media" (CIRCL). Her research is in the area of multi- and interdisciplinary critical theory, particularly as it relates to issues of identity. Her previous publications include *Children's Literature: Criticism and the Fictional Child* (1994), and, as editor and contributor: *Children in Culture: Approaches to Childhood* (1998), *The Yearbook of English Studies*, Special Section on "Children in Literature" (2002), *Children's Literature: New Approaches* (2004), and *The Last Taboo: Women and Body Hair* (2006), as well as numerous articles on childhood and gender.

Introduction

Ever since the development of forms of assisted conception,[1] from artificial insemination and sperm donation to IVF, from ICSI to cloning, important questions have been raised concerning such techniques.[2] When, how, and why should they be used? Who could claim the right to use them? Making possible the having of children that otherwise could not be born through the use of medical interventions and technologies has alternately been seen as a Frankensteinian corruption of science, an appropriation of the role of a god, the bringing of a boon to otherwise deprived and distraught infertile people, and of possible benefits to both those potential parents, society at large, and even the to-be-born child itself (for instance in terms of the elimination or prevention of diseases through genetic counselling and/or pre-natal diagnosis and/or intervention).

The issues around reproductive technologies are also placed at the heart of ethical and moral dilemmas in society. The formations of marriage, love and romance, and sexual identities, of the family, community, and social life, are all drawn into the questions about the use of reproductive technologies, by whom, and for whom, and when, and why. Several reproductive technologies, such as artificial insemination and IVF, are by now widely established and accepted in several societies, but questions around their use reappear even when their application has long been regularized in law and in medical practice. Sometimes this happens when mistakes are made, such as in recent cases of the accidental implantation of one couple's embryos into another woman[3] and sometimes when new applications of that technology are developed, such as with new forms of pre-natal diagnosis, or new methods of gender selection. As anthropologist Heléna Ragoné sums up:

> [artificial reproductive technologies] have served to defamiliarize what was once understood to be the "natural" basis of human procreation and relatedness . . . as the Comaroffs so eloquently said of ethnography, "to make the familiar strange and the strange familiar, all the better to understand them both". [Ragoné, 1998, p. 118]

Many studies have been set up and carried out into these questions, and they suggest an array of responses and arguments, supported by a range of moral, ethical, religious, scientific, philosophical, psychological, and/or political considerations. Yet fundamental questions to do with reproductive technologies appear to continue to be supremely difficult to discuss, and these are to do with why people should want to have "own" or "biological" children *at all*, and what these children are defined to be. That people wish for such children apparently seems so important, so self-evident, so obvious, speaks so much for itself, that it rarely appears in discussions of motivations and justifications for the use of reproductive technologies. Views that the choice to use reproductive technologies is merely a practical one, made when adoption is for some reason impossible, may apply to some cases, but clearly cannot account for the much more prolifically expressed desires for an "own", "biological" child, or definitions of adoption or fostering as a "second choice" or "fall back" option. Any questioning of these assumptions has certainly not affected the continued expansion and use of reproductive technologies. And yet these assumptions provide the single underpinning motivation and justification for these activities.

Furthermore, the definition of the child to be produced by reproductive technologies is itself rarely raised even in the extensive considerations of reproductive technologies that are available. Even if the technologies may be examined in terms of how people use and experience them, the outcome of the process seems to be seen as self-evident and obvious, beyond question: children are children. Where this topic is raised at all, it may be in the form of overtly psychological issues such as: do the prospective parents have too high expectations of this much-hoped for child? What are they investing in the idea of what this child will bring to them and their relationship? Related to this, perhaps most discussion of the status and definition of the child has to do with what are seen to be ethical problems in terms of selecting gender, race, or the prevention of illness or disability (pre-natal diagnosis or intervention; genetic counselling), with its attendant concerns about strivings to achieve a "perfect" child. But these questions only partially point to the problem that definitions of "childhood", as with any identity (gender, sexuality, ethnicity, and so on), change over time, and from place to place, and even from individual to individual. Ideas and definitions about childhood differ widely. The child may be seen, for instance, as innocent or anarchic, wise or ignorant, altruistic or supremely selfish, super-sensitive to the state of others or entirely unaware, purely imitative or truly original, freely sexual or not sexual at all. As theorist Jacqueline Rose argues:

> ... the idea of speaking to *all* children serves to close off a set of cultural divisions, divisions in which not only children, but we ourselves, are necessarily caught. . . . Class, culture, and literacy— divisions which undermine any generalised concept of the child. [Rose, 1984, p. 7]

As sociologists, Allison James and Alan Prout formulate this position: "childhood . . . is to be understood as a social construction. That is, the institution of childhood provides an interpretative frame for understanding the early years of human life" (James & Prout, 1997, p. 3).

This book will work with this argument that childhood is constructed, as French historian Phillipe Ariès first argued in his famous, and still controversial, book *Centuries of Childhood* (for an extensive discussion of the controversies around Ariès' arguments, see Lesnik-Oberstein, 1998a). Ariès asks "have we any right to talk of the history of the family? Is the family any more subject to history than instinct is?" (1960, p. 9) but argues that although

[i]t is no doubt true that since the beginning of the human race men have built homes and begot children ... the great demographic revolution in the West, from the eighteenth to the twentieth century, has revealed to us considerable possibilities of change in structures hitherto believed to be invariable because they were biological. The adoption of contraceptive measures has brought about both quantitative and qualitative changes in the family. [*ibid.*]

Furthermore, and crucially, Ariès goes on to argue that

[f]or a long time it was believed that the family constituted the ancient basis of our society, and that, starting in the eighteenth century, the progress of liberal individualism had shaken and weakened it. The history of the family in the nineteenth and twentieth centuries was supposed to be that of a decadence: the frequency of divorces and the weakening of marital and paternal authority were seen as so many signs of its decline. The study of modern demographic phenomena led me to a completely contrary conclusion. It seemed to me ... that on the contrary the family occupied a tremendous place in our industrial societies ... I accordingly looked back into our past, to find out whether the idea of the family had not been born comparatively recently, at a time when the family had freed itself from both biology and law to become a value, a theme of expression, an occasion of emotion. [*ibid.*, p. 10]

I would add, as Ann Anagnost puts it:

In framing my arguments in terms of the historicity of the sentimental life of the family, I do not mean to imply that middle-class parents in the late-twentieth-century United States simply love their children more than parents in other times or places or to criticize them for loving "too much". I seek to explore how this structure of feeling articulates with the sociohistorical and economic transformations taking place in the larger social world in producing the specific formations of a desire for children. [Anagnost, 2004, p. 142]

The questions of why children are wanted, and whom they are seen to be are intimately enmeshed. It is these issues that this book wishes to explore further: what accounts are given for the wanting of the "own" child, and what this child is seen to be. Because the child will be considered as a construction, and one that is, as Ariès suggests, at the nexus of ideas of family, my arguments will also draw in wider analyses of the relationships between, and definitions of, those ideas of family, and the attendant definitions of culture, society, history, and nature that are used in discussions and arguments to define that child and that family.

When the questions of the wanting of the child are touched upon, whether by medical experts, philosophers, or lay-persons, the answers can be roughly divided up into two kinds: the idea that people want children because of a "biological urge", because it is "natural", or "instinctive", or that they want them because of social or cultural habits. As Susan Lewis Cooper and Ellen Sarasohn Glazer describe what they see to be the assumption of "most people": "nothing could be more natural and more ethically correct than to want a child" (Cooper & Glazer, 1998, p. 15). In the UK, the *Warnock Report*, which made recommendations concerning policies on human fertility at the request of the British Government, declares: "In addition to social pressures to have children there is, for many, a powerful urge to perpetuate their genes through a new generation. This desire cannot be assuaged by adoption" (Franklin, 1997, p. 91).

Anthropologist Sarah Franklin, in her study of experiences of IVF entitled *Embodied Progress: A Cultural Account of Assisted Conception*, cites this statement as an example of "many popular representations of infertility [which] . . . draw on the idea that there are natural, biological or genetic pressures to have children which cannot be suppressed" (*ibid.*).

This idea of an "urge" returns repeatedly in discussions of why people want to have children. The pieces in Stephanie Dowrick and Sibyl Grundberg's *Why Children?* (1980),[4] for instance—all written from the perspective of engaged and active feminism—thoughtfully and lucidly articulate the idea that this "wanting" of children can in no way be, politically and ideologically speaking, a ("free") "choice". All the writers in the book make explicit a range of social, economic, and political pressures to have children. Judith Barrington, for instance, writes that "I felt a profound shock of recognition when I finally understood that society relies on the nuclear family and the dependence of women on men to maintain the division of labour" (Barrington, 1980, p. 149). All of the pieces also include comments on the way motherhood and the wanting of children are included in constructions of femininity: "I 'ought to have a child, if I was to fulfil myself as a woman, etc.'" (Dutton, 1980, p. 123). Nevertheless, in attempting to account for any final decision to have a child, most of the writers take final recourse to expressions such as "yearning" (Goodison, 1980, p. 30ff), "urge" (*ibid.*), and "I want to have a child . . . to please myself" (Dowrick, 1980, p. 67).

Counsellors Lara Deveraux and Ann Hammerman, discussing infertility and identity, see pregnancy and childbirth as "culturally significan[t]", but admit that they do not know *why* this should be so: "Perhaps it is the 'miracle' of reproduction or our desire to participate in creation that leads to part of our fascination. Whatever the cause, reproduction . . . is central to our identity as human beings" (Deveraux & Hammerman, 1998, p. 103).

Similarly, Thomas Murray, in his book *The Worth of a Child*, discussing new reproductive technologies from the perspective of moral philosophy, explicitly raises the question of why people want children, but he too rests on the conclusion that

> There are times when adults hunger for children. *Hunger* is the right word, for it can be felt as a need, a profound longing, not a mere appetite for something pleasant. . . . for many of us, our children are a vital part of our own flourishing. . . . [H]umans . . . need affection, trust, and, above all, intimate and enduring relationships in order to flourish. [Murray, 1996, pp. 2, 33, original emphasis]

Laurie Taylor and Matthew Taylor, in their book *What Are Children For?*, discuss a whole range of reasons for why people may be deciding *not* to have children, but clearly also find it difficult to formulate reasons for having them at all. Their suggestions include "our parental efforts can [now] be inspired . . . also by the knowledge that our genetic imprint will always be an essential part of our successors' distinctive perspective on a new and possibly better world" (Taylor & Taylor, 2003, p. 127) or "[o]ne plausible answer . . . is surely 'to grow into adult friends, and to give us the pleasure of being grandparents'" (*ibid.*, p. 125). These suggestions leave open, in turn, why genetics is understood, or seen to matter, in this way, as well as the question of what the pleasure of grandparenting may be seen to be and how it might be a distinct motivation for the having of children as compared to, for instance, the pleasure of being parents.

There are other factors mentioned in relation to this wanting of children, as with the "social pressures" mentioned also by the *Warnock Report*, and articulated in several of the pieces in Dowrick and Grundberg as pressures to conform to ideas of femininity, motherhood, and the family, but, I will be suggesting, the extensive considerations or articulations of why people want children remain problematic, raising as many questions as they answer. Furthermore, as a corollary, the question of why people want children specifically through the pregnancy of the female in a (usually heterosexual) relationship, and preferably with an embryo carrying the genetic material of at least one, if not both, parents, is also a continued site of problematic arguments. The *Warnock Report* asserts that the "urge to perpetuate their genes . . . cannot be assuaged by adoption". Writings on this subject seem very clear on the idea that caring for adopted or fostered children is *different* from caring for "biological", "genetic", or "own" children, but, again, the precise reasons for this difference, and how it expresses itself, prove more difficult to explain. Thomas Murray, for instance, even when overtly advocating the desirability of "reexamin[ing] our legal presumptions that powerfully favor biological over rearing parenthood", concludes that

> [Although] I have no doubt that powerful, loving relationships develop between children and adults with no biological relationship. . . . I also know the delight I feel when someone notes how much my child resembles me. . . . Just how biological similarity works its magic is not clear. [Murray, 1996, p. 67]

Barbara Katz Rothman, similarly, even when arguing that a "genetic tie" is not the issue which need make a difference to the feelings for a child, still sees that tie as meaningful for some people, but, like Murray, can not really account for *why* this should be so:

> Part of having a baby is reproducing part of oneself. Whatever it is that is genetic in who or what we are, part of that part gets passed on to our children. . . . [W]hatever it is, some of us want very much to reproduce parts of ourselves in this world. [Rothman, 2004, p. 26.]

Mary Warnock, in a recent book of her own, *Making Babies: Is There a Right to Have Children?*, further suggests that adopting a baby is for many people an intolerable risk. As we become more aware of the role of inherited genes in the character of our children, so the bringing up of children in no way genetically related to us has come to seem a quite different undertaking from that of bringing up a child who shares our own genes. It may be worthwhile, but it is not the same. [Warnock, 2002, p. 40]

Cooper and Glazer agree:

There is another reason why a genetic connection is important to many people: genes determine a great deal about a person. Although the exact formula of the nature/nurture debate has not been (and may never be) settled, it is increasingly understood that genes play a major role in who we are. ... Many people seek the familiarity and security of having a child who shares their genes. [Cooper & Glazer, 1998, p. 20]

This would seem to suggest that adoption has become less desirable as a knowledge of genetics has revealed a hitherto unknown "risk" that adopted children will somehow turn out in unpredictable ways, while the "own" child has a genetic predictability. However, as we will see, this idea of the predictability of character[5] is first of all contestable even in scientific terms. Sociobiologist Sarah Blaffer Hrdy, for instance, states that "[i]t is clear that genes are not puppeteers directing behaviour" (Hrdy, 1999, p. 57). Roger Lancaster writes about his research into sex and sexuality:

I had hoped to discover sophisticated new biological perspectives ... What I encountered instead was the same ... belief that complex social identities are scripted in strands of DNA. The notion that desires are coded, microscopically, in the genes. [Lancaster, 2003, p. xi]

Lancaster, then, instead of simply looking further at the scientific claims about his area of research in their own terms, goes on to look at how "scientific claims about gender and sexuality entered into public discourse" (Lancaster, 2003, p. xi).

Similarly, Sarah Franklin reviews in her article "Making miracles: scientific progress and the facts of life" how anthropologists have critiqued the "naturalizations" of "the facts of life", noting that "anthropology has long been centrally concerned with the social organization of what are seen as universal natural facts of human regeneration and heredity" (Franklin, 1998, p. 102). In the same way, one aspect I will be considering in this book is how claims are made on behalf, and through, science, about reproduction and reproductive technologies specifically in relation to the child and the desire for the child. Like Franklin and Lancaster, therefore, I will not be assuming that science has already provided—or may even be able to provide—definitive answers to "complex social identities" and issues. The involvement of science with reproductive technologies, therefore, will be one of the issues I will be considering, in ranging across a number of academic disciplines as well as areas of popular culture to examine how ideas of childhood are articulated in relation to reproductive technologies.

It may be helpful to explain at this point, in relation to this ranging across academic and popular writings, that I will be confining myself to the examination of texts, and, unlike many of the anthropologists, psychologists, or counsellors writing in this area, not using oral accounts derived from interviews I have conducted. This is because, as I will be continuing to explain throughout the book from a variety of perspectives, I am not here assuming that oral accounts or interviews are somehow necessarily a spontaneous and privileged source of a self-formulated and self-generated experience. This seems to me a point particularly worth making again[6] in relation to studies in the areas of childhood and reproduction where, as I will be arguing throughout, experience is in fact often defined as a privileged and primary source of meaning. Sarah Franklin, for instance, suggests that

> [t]he lived, immediate, and concrete dilemmas produced in one specific set of relations to the enterprising-up of life itself are indicated by the experience of the women and couples interviewed for this book, and it is for what their experiences can reveal about the other myriad variations on this encounter that it is entitled. [*Embodied Progress*] [Franklin, 1997, p. 10]

Although Franklin goes on, as part of her entire endeavour, to consider closely and rigorously how and why anthropology and ethnography operate, and certainly does not base her discussions on any simple claims for the priority of oral accounts and interview, my arguments nevertheless wish to take one step further back even in terms of not considering oral accounts as a necessary site of "rev-elation" or source. Instead, I will be examining here too, in terms of this quote from Franklin for instance, what might be understood as the "lived", the "immediate, and concrete", "experience", or "embodi[ment]", in relation to narratives of reproduction and the child. In this sense it is important to my arguments in this book that my use of texts is for these specific reasons, and not motivated by a certain eclecticism or relativism, as Dion Farquhar, for instance, proposes for her study *The Other Machine: Discourse and Reproductive Technologies* when she writes that "following a relative eclecticism in the selection of source materials, this study will look only at *writ - ten* textual productions—newspaper, magazine, and journal arti-cles, as well as popular and academic books" (Farquhar, 1996, p. 14, original emphasis). Although I, too, will be ranging across "acade-mic and popular books", and not seeing certain kinds of genres as necessarily in turn providing definitive or ultimate accounts in and of themselves, I do not relate this eclecticism to the choice to focus on texts. I will be interpreting what the possible meanings are that may be read in texts offered as the narratives of reproductive tech-nologies, including the stories they in turn include as recounted by participants in reproductive technologies—whether as patients/clients (two of the terms used) or as researchers (in whatever field) and professionals. What are those stories, in other words, seen to mean: how and why are they told? What claims are made for, and what status accorded to, the oral and experience in those texts?

Further potential problems with the claims about genetics and the adopted or "own" child are also already indicated within Warnock's own argument. For, just a page after making the argu-ment about the riskiness of adoption, she suddenly argues precisely the opposite: that

> the most obvious basis for the longing to have children is, perhaps, a kind of insatiable curiosity: what will the random mix of genes produce? What will be familiar, what unfamiliar? The amazing pleasure of each child is that he or she is new, a totally unique being that has never existed in the world before, seeing things with his own eyes, saying things that are his own inventions. [Warnock, 2002, p. 41]

The child who is supposedly predictable through genetics, is now also unpredictable, albeit in terms of an unpredictable "mix" of the familiar and unfamiliar. But not only will the mix be unpredictable, but the child will, at the same time, according to Warnock, also be "new, a totally unique being". Where does this leave the claimed fundamental difference between adoption and the "own" child, in Warnock's terms? For, as she herself states, the assumption and acceptance of that fundamental difference is what led to the

> Committee of Inquiry into Human Fertilisation and Embryology [in Britain] . . . [having] no difficulty in agreeing that for those who wanted children, infertility merited treatment, and that scientists and the medical profession would be right to continue to develop remedies through research and practice; and that those who need assistance in conceiving ought to be provided with access to such assistance. [Warnock, 2002, p. 40]

Therefore, the questions of why people want children, and why specifically children they define and see as "own", seem to me to be absolutely fundamental to the whole premise of reproductive technologies. The entire enterprise, as Warnock's arguments demonstrate, justifies and vindicates itself on the grounds of the claim that the wanting and having of "own" children is somehow integral, or of the highest importance, to human life, and that this desire, moreover, "cannot be assuaged by adoption". Reproductive technologies in many cases would have no validity, or a different validity at the very least, without these assumptions: that the having of children is of a paramount importance, and that these children need to be "biologically", and preferably also "genetically", "own" children.[7] Anthropologist Charis Cussins Thompson proposes in the introduction to her book *Making Parents. The Ontological Choreography of Reproductive Technologies*, in which she otherwise meticulously analyses a whole range of issues in and around reproductive technologies, that

> the single biggest problem with reproductive technologies in the United States is . . . a lack of access to health care based on need rather than on employment status and its identity-based proxies. . . . In the end, members of a biomedical society should have help in getting pregnant . . . if they wish to be pregnant and they cannot get or stay pregnant without help. [Thompson, 2005, p. 27]

But what is this "need" that Thompson assumes? It may be important to add here that asking such a question does not somehow necessarily entail arguing that reproductive technologies as such therefore are not legitimate or should not be used, as I will be explaining further throughout. As Sarah Franklin writes about her book:

> [*Embodied Progress*] is determinedly a project which moves away from the tendency in legal studies, bioethics, feminist criticism and many strands of cultural and science studies to take a position, or to argue for or against particular techniques. My interest is elsewhere, specifically prior to such judgements, at the level of the effort to make visible the accumulated practices, assumptions and constraints which inform most contemporary assessment and discussion of new reproductive and genetic technologies. [Franklin, 1997, p. 16]

This book shares Franklin's aims and endeavours in this respect.

It is these issues, then, that this book wishes to address: to explore how the ideas about the "wanting" of children, and the defining of those children as "own" or not "own", operate. In doing so, the discussion will not limit itself to reproductive technologies narrowly, as I will also argue that the ways in which the wanting of children are articulated are not necessarily different with respect to children born "naturally" and those born through assisted reproduction, but that a whole array of ideas around the having and wanting of children are bound up with the very existence of reproductive technologies, whether or not they are actually used. An example of this is the way in which, in Western society, as Sarah Franklin points out, the conception of children in general has come to be seen to be primarily a potentially fraught or emperilled activity: "[a] second consequence for conception models post-ARTs is that they are increasingly defined in terms of *reproductive risk*, that is, in terms of what can go wrong" (Franklin, 1998, p. 104). Instead of anxieties about unwanted pregnancy, anxieties are primarily articulated and circulated around what Gay Becker calls "the elusive embryo" (Becker, 2000).

In exploring these issues, this book hopes to help to clarify the debates and decisions around the uses of reproductive technologies, specifically in relation to childhood and the having of children.

In doing so, I will also be addressing wider issues to do with thinking around, and articulating ideas about, nature, culture, history, society, the family, the individual, and the child. Instead of largely taking for granted the idea that of course people want to have children, and of course they want them to be their "own", and, of course, they want these children because everyone knows what children are, this book will not take these ideas for granted, but argue, with Ariès and others taking similar approaches, that the child and the desire for the child constitute in particular and specific ways "a value, a theme of expression, an occasion of emotion". I hope here to offer a further examination of ways in which these values and emotions are articulated and defined, both in terms of the desire for children and the children produced by this desire.

Notes

1. Differing terms are used for reproductive technologies, including "assisted conception", "medically assisted conception" and "artificial reproductive technologies", as well as a range of acronyms, including those for the specific techniques involved. I will be using the term "reproductive technologies" myself within my own discussion, except where I am examining a text which uses a different term, where I will then follow the usage of that text, also in my own commentary.
2. In fact, as Susan Squier demonstrates in her excellent study *Babies in Bottles*, narratives of reproductive technologies, including these questions and problems, can be read long before the implementation of the technologies as such (see Squier, 1994).
3. Two famous incidents of this kind occurred, for instance, in Great Britain, in 2002: one case, reported in the press in July 2002, when a white mother gave birth to black twins as a result of IVF, and one case, reported in October 2002, when three mothers had the incorrect embryos implanted (the embryos were subsequently removed) at St George's Hospital, London (see for one press report of this: Hall, 2002, p. 2).
4. With thanks to Dani Caselli for drawing my attention to this book.
5. Ideas about similarity and difference between parents and children seem to be attached to either character or looks or both. Barbara Katz Rothman, for instance, writes that

> For myself, I feel that [the genetic part is] just the physical body that gets passed on to our children—the shape of a nose, body build, tendency towards diabetes, a bad back, strong legs. Other people feel that it is also intelligence, wit, sometimes even "character". [Rothman, 2004, p. 26]

I will consider definitions of "character" and "looks" and their roles in defining difference and similarity between parents and children at several points throughout this book, but at this stage want to comment specifically only on an aspect of the idea that "character" is somehow genetically predictable. As in Rothman's comments, "looks" are often assumed to be self-evidently genetically predictable anyway (particularly in relation to ideas of race and ethnicity), although this genetic self-evidence can be questioned in turn in terms of how "similarity" and "difference" are defined and perceived. In this sense, my comments here can be applied to both "character" and "looks".

6. Critiques of experience and the oral as primary, spontaneous and self-generated are, of course, manifold, but for some well-known examples see: Jacques Derrida, 1967; with regard specifically to the body Judith Butler, 1990 and 1993; and, with regard specifically to childhood, Jacqueline Rose, 1984.

7. Some writers, such as Barbara Katz Rothman, suggest that in some cases the motivation for wanting a "biological" baby, is "the actual act of bearing the baby. . . . 'Having' a baby is something a woman may want for herself, for her own experience, independent of her relationship with her child" (Rothman, 2004, pp. 25–26). This, however, poses in turn the same question of why women should want such an experience, and I will thus be addressing this issue as an aspect of my overall discussion.

CHAPTER ONE

The wanting of a baby: nature, history, culture, and society

I f the whole industry of reproductive technologies rests on the idea of the crucial importance of the having of children, and "biological" children at that, then the first thing to examine is what the accounts are that those involved with reproductive technologies provide about this wanting of a baby. How do they explain or see this single motivating factor behind the enormous investment of research, medical attention, and time, finances (governmental, insurance, or from the potential parents, depending on location), and all the efforts and expectations of the potential parents? Most familiar of all, perhaps, are the claims, already referred to in the formulations of the *Warnock Report*, that the wanting of a baby is somehow natural or instinctive, part of the much mentioned "biological clock". As Plato famously states in his *Timaeus*:

> The womb is an animal which longs to generate children. When it remains barren too long after puberty, it is distressed and sorely disturbed, and straying about in the body and cutting off the passages of the breath, it impedes respiration and brings the sufferer into the most extreme anguish and provokes all manner of diseases besides. Such is the nature of women and all that is female. [1949, p. 74]

1

This recourse to an idea of the innate, the animal,[1] or biology, has been questioned extensively in feminist critiques of accounts of gender as determined by innate factors or attributes (see Chodorow, 1978 for one famous example of such an analysis, which I will be considering extensively in its own right in Chapter Two). However, I would still like to examine some instances of ideas of the wanting of children as being biological, animal, or innate in order to discuss both what ideas of biology and nature may operate here, and why. What do these definitions and accounts achieve? What are they *about*? Moving on subsequently to ideas about the wanting of the child as not biological, but, instead, social, cultural, or traditional, I will then suggest that, in fact, it is not easy or straightforward to change, or even distinguish between, ideas of the wanting of the child as innate to that of it being a socially or culturally conditioned or implanted desire. This is in line with analyses such as that of Parveen Adams when she, in discussing approaches to gender, suggests that

> ironically, these two apparently opposed views which could be respectively called biologistic and sociologistic are in fact two sides of the same coin. The biologistic view assumes already constituted capacities, and while the sociologistic view assumes a *tabula rasa*, it also always has to rely on already constituted capacities of experience, cognition, and purposeful action. [Adams, 1990b, p. 104]

The questions that these shifts wish to address or resolve are not, I will suggest, necessarily thus resolvable or addressable.

In the first instance, then, there is a wide and familiar range of reasons that people may provide for wanting to have children; for instance, that they would enjoy it, or that they find it meaningful, or see it as some form of religious or social duty, or that they might rely on a child to support them when they are older or in need. But these answers do not address two central issues. First, why is there a need felt for these children to have issued in some way from oneself? If children are fun, or the raising of them is meaningful, or they could provide support, then why is this not felt to be the case for any children? Children in a teacher's classroom, for instance, or the nursery, or being fostered, or the children of neighbours? Second, why is the having of children—and the wanting that prompted the having—seen at all as "fun" or "meaningful" or "supportive" in the first place? What is seen to make it so? In the case of replies that may refer to forms of "duty", these questions are not necessarily resolved either, as "duty" requires an obedience to a rule or practice that is not always itself further accounted for or motivated.

Sylvia Ann Hewlett, in a recent best-selling book on career women and the having of children, writes that

> I believe I have a special understanding of the unfathomable—and unfashionable—depths of the drive to have children. This thing has a terrible power. If you're over 40, the desire to have a baby before it is too late can kick in with ferocious intensity. It can become a non-negotiable demand—a veritable obsession—that rides rough-shod over every other aspect of life. All of this must be hardwired. It isn't as though we get much support or encouragement from the culture these days. [Hewlett, 2002, p. 24]

In Hewlett's formulations, the depth and power of the wish for the child are evidence for its being "hardwired". This hardwiredness is something which triumphs over the resistance of culture, so that culture is not the product, or inclusive, of hardwired aspects, but a separate phenomenon, deriving from elsewhere. Likewise, fashion can be out of step with the hardwired. Therefore, the hardwired triumphs over a culture and fashion that are both separate from and in opposition to it. Also, Hewlett claims[2] levels of understanding of the unfathomable, which, as the hardwired, is also disproportion-ate, non-negotiable, obsessive, and riding roughshod over every other aspect of life. These comments include aspects that I will track through further ideas about nature, history, culture, society, and the wish for the child. Nature, as with Hewlett, can be defined as some-thing separate from history, culture, and society, existing beside or underneath it, or history, culture, and society can be defined as a product of the natural. In the latter case, they are regarded as expressions of the natural, or derivations of it. It is not my approach to discuss these issues with the claim that I will be offering a final answer or solution to them, such as which does indeed originate from which. Rather, in tracking the ways these terms move around in arguments, I hope to clarify how the claims are made at all, and which investments direct the underpinnings of the arguments. As with Hewlett, for instance, the idea of the hardwired or innate wish for the child sets up a paradox where hardwiredness implies, on the one hand, a constancy and ubiquity, while, on the other, being accessible to differing levels of understanding. In other words, why, if the urge for the child is so deep, strong, and inevitable, does it take Hewlett (or others like her) to diagnose it and to defend it? Moreover, why and how is this understood quite differently in other writings? This paradox is an aspect of the wider and complex issue that the natural can be claimed as a self-evident, transparent, and simple presence, while simultaneously, in the very process of being explained, described, catalogued, dissected, or analysed, requiring a privileged perspective, a "special understanding". (One of the classic texts involved in this paradox of the natural in this sense is Rousseau, 1762.)

The paradox of the natural, which is on the one hand present and experienced but nevertheless somehow simultaneously not known, is present too in the work of one of the well-known proponents of an evolutionary anthropological or sociobiological[3] view of motherhood, Sarah Blaffer Hrdy. As Hrdy writes,

> I found myself in the throes of cyclically experienced sexual feelings. At that time, such restless yearnings were a still largely unacknowledged primate legacy. Indeed, in some circles such feelings were assumed not even to exist in women. Hence I had no framework for interpreting them . . . at that point I had no idea how inextricably linked sexual and maternal emotions have been in the course of primate evolution. [1999, p. xi]

In this formulation, Hrdy does experience her cycles, but, in being unacknowledged or even denied by others (presumably science), the experience cannot be interpreted. It is therefore a knowledge that is not experience which makes the primate legacy available as such: the natural can only be known *as natural* once it is acknowledged by the non-natural. Experience here can only be made accessible, or interpreted, by non-experience, or the non-natural. Experience is, therefore, for Hrdy, neither an acknowledgment nor self-evidently natural, and nature cannot speak itself. Yet Hrdy also writes that:

> Gilibert and others like him looked to the animals not to make unbiased empirical observations but to use nature to confirm their

own and their society's preconceptions about how humans should behave. These men, who were more evangelists than scientists, imposed their moral code on nature rather than allowing creatures in the natural world to speak for themselves. [*ibid.*, p. 11]

In this case, creatures in the natural world can speak for themselves, and this can be observed by unbiased empirical observations. But Hrdy's experience of sexual cycles is not available to her own unbiased empirical observation, or even known to be natural as experience. Acknowledgement is first necessary to provide an interpretive framework, and for the natural to be recognized and confirmed as such. The animal therefore comes, in Hrdy's argument, as in much previous anthropology (also with regard to studies of tribal communities), to function as that which is—in its natural setting—available to unbiased empirical observation by humans. This is then translated to the human in order to provide the explanatory narrative that Hrdy wishes to compose. The unbiased empirical observation of the natural *as natural* here creates a non-natural that permits an access to the natural. Issues, then, around what can be seen to speak for itself, and what requires this interpretative framework of the non-natural, and why, persist through Hrdy's work, and affect—among many other topics—the ways she sees the wanting of the child.[4]

For Hrdy, animals reproduce, although in different ways and to differing extents, due to mating, which in turn is regulated by a range of evolutionary pressures. It is in revising certain assumptions about the nature of the mating and the evolutionary pressures through re-examining perspectives on gender that Hrdy develops a view of why women might choose to have a child or not, if forms of choice are available to them. Unlike Hewlett, Hrdy does not see the desire to have a child as a "hardwired" urge in opposition to culturally or socially determined career pressures. Instead, Hrdy sees aspirations to career and status success as *part of* female evolutionary strategies of mothering: both aspects are products of evolution. Throughout *Mother Nature* she stresses that the difference between male and female reproductive strategies is quantity, in the case of males, versus quality (of child survival and longevity) for females. Therefore, Hrdy argues, for women to strive to be successful in terms of hierarchy, status, or power, draws on evolutionary advantages in being able to raise their children better under such circumstances:

> When given the opportunity, many women value upward mobility over time devoted to rearing a family. . . . But if our evolutionary heritage has any relevance to what we are, how can this be? The answer is simple. In worlds where there was no birth control, and where no female was ever celibate, there was no possibility that female rank and maternal reproductive success could be *other* than correlated. Nature built in no safeguards to ambition run awry, as it were, to energies diverted to status ends that were not linked to the production, survival, and prosperity of offspring. Now that status and the survival of offspring have been decoupled, will there be selection against women who are especially inclined or driven to achieve? Probably, if our species survives long enough, and if circumstances in the workplace don't change. [Hrdy, 1999, p. 112. original emphasis]

Two points may be noted about this argument. First, the having of children on the one hand is assumed as an inevitable subsidiary consequence of a natural, innate drive to mate (either on the part of the male, or the female, or both), not chosen in and of itself. Roger Lancaster notes that

> the main thrust of these works was and remains starkly hetero-normative, and their social residue—the naturalization of gender relations and sexuality, however these might be conceived politi-cally—has contributed to the more familiar staging of arguments about female nurture and its role in male–female complementarity. [2003, p. 383, n. 15]

As such, the having of children is not a separate innate desire or need. The child is not conceived of when mating is an urge in itself as itself. Mothering is deployed only when the child arrives (or is on its way) in the service of maternal reproductive success. However, on the other hand, as having a child becomes formulated as something that can be chosen (or not chosen), the urge to mate seems to start to include, or produce, choosing to mother and to have the child to mother. In other words, "reproduction", in Hrdy's narrative, initially means, for females, only the mothering that follows on inevitable conception of offspring. But when choice starts to intervene in that inevitability, then reproduction seems to slide, willy-nilly, into meaning also the making of a choice to have a child. In this sense, the urge to mother can be said to produce the urge to have the child. It might also be said that mating without the choice for the child is then an unreflective animal or primitive act, while choice rests on a consciousness that is here the (modern) human. Choice, therefore, "splits" the urge to mate into the urge to mate and the wish to have, or care for, a child. Mothering and following a career are not formulated as necessarily in opposition to one another (in terms of hardwiring clashing with a hostile culture, as with Hewlett), then, but as "two ancient, pressing, and now incompatible urges" (Hrdy, 1999, p. 112). The choice to have a child here dwells somehow within the "urge" to mother. This is why I am referring to Hrdy as focusing on the "choice" for a child, and not the "wish" for the child. The wish can be taken, in this sense, as only a manifestation or outcome of the maternal urge as one of the bottomline, natural, evolutionary inheritances within the modern human female. This, then, creates a paradox for this argument. For the urges have no further meanings or forms. They are just there, and have always been there, "ancient, pressing". The urges are not themselves just an outcome of evolution, but one of the motors of it. But the advent of choice simultaneously can and does also change the urge to mother by creating within it, or as part of it, the choice to have a child. Somehow, a conscious decision has sprung from non-conscious[5] action, and an urge or pressure—as a drive to action—has transmuted into an ability to formulate alternate hypothetical futures and to make decisions on that basis in terms of a speculative weighing of outcomes. As Marilyn Strathern suggests, "there is a subtle shift from regarding naturalness as part of the workings of physiology to attributing it to parental desire" (1992, p. 56).

Second, if there is a choice not to have a child, it is only because the urge to mother is seen as being suppressed or obliterated by the second urge, which it is "*now* incompatible" (Hrdy, 1999, p. 112, my emphasis) with. In this way, the urge to mother has always previously had primacy, as the striving for status was in the service of it. The unavoidability of reproduction (if not for every specific individual, then for the species on the whole) was itself the "safeguard to ambition run awry". But now ambition has run awry and energies have been "diverted". In this sense, Hrdy's career woman without children is more like Hewlett's version after all. If her urges are innate and evolutionary inheritances, the direction and course of the energies and ambition are not. These are now the non-natural forms that oppose or overwhelm reproduction. For women, in this sense, the striving for status is now too much striving for too much status, at least in relation to reproduction. This does also, of course, determine quite specifically that women who do not have children do so because they prefer "ambition", "status", and "achiev[ement]".[6] Other possible reasons for choosing not to have children are not mentioned. Or, to put it differently, there is a requirement that every reason for not having children can be made to fall into the category of deriving from the maternal ambition and search for status.

In the light of Hrdy's reasoning, then, nature is that which strives to maximize reproduction. This process persists in the (modern) human in ways that mean that both the choice to have children and the choice not to do so are the results of maternal reproductive strategies. The wish for the child can therefore be said to appear after a gap in Hrdy's discussion that she never addresses as such: the issue of how an evolutionary urge (unreflected action) becomes decision-making. In other words, the animal or the primitive are constructed as not being the subjects of choice in terms of the child, in both the sense of not making choices about it—not being constituted as choice-makers—and in not being affected by choice. Yet the modern human is a choice-maker, albeit, according to Hrdy, in terms of both "conscious or unconscious 'decisions'" (Hrdy, 1999, p. 114). The tension in this area is marked by the quote-marks around "decisions". The evolutionary urge *as* urge denies a freedom of decisions, undoing the possibility of decision, and yet it is also what produces the decisions as decisions. Furthermore, in terms of Hrdy's premises, a certain circularity occurs, for the maternal urge can be seen to be only possibly dividable into two ancient urges by a later split into caring and ambition. It is only when, and *by*, becoming "incompatible" that the maternal reproductive strategies can be conceived of retrospectively as composed of a caring and a status urge. In this sense, Hrdy's narratives of the struggle of the modern human Western female between child care and career are charted in, and as, her evolutionary past. It may be asked in which sense this narrative is necessarily able to be more empirically objective than that of the biologists and anthropologists Hrdy critiques as merely confirming their own society in the past. I do not raise this question as a biologically or anthropologically authoritative judgement on Hrdy's work in turn, but in terms of noting the complications for Hrdy's arguments of her own shifts between claiming nature as self-speaking on the one hand, and as requiring interpretation on the other. That there is no attention to the fact that, in her discussion, the having of the child can seamlessly become a choice for the child, which in turn becomes a wish for the child, is part of this problem.

Jill Bialosky and Helen Schulman, in their introduction to their book *Wanting a Child*, write of their children watching a video of Disney's *Dumbo* while they talk. In their account, the animals in the movie have their babies delivered to them by a flock of storks, except for Dumbo's mother. They conclude that

> [w]hat becomes clear, as our young children watch this familiar story, is how early these desires—this desire for a child—is imprinted in our minds and hearts and imaginations, and how necessary it is for new stories to be told. [Bialosky & Schulman, 1998, pp. 7–8]

Here the desire for a child is imprinted from very early on, in the shape of a story that is familiar. It is the story that constitutes a desire not there in the child of itself, and a story that lodges in "minds and hearts and imaginations". This story also requires new stories, however, which indicates an idea that the story must both continue and also be modified. The stories that Bialosky and Schulman have assembled are to play the role of these new stories, their newness apparently having to do with ways in which people may become parents, families are configured, and children acquired. They write that "whatever their configurations, these families of one, two, three, or more are made up of brave people, eager to live their lives, fully embracing what it means to be human" (*ibid.*, p. 8). The struggle to have children, to create a family in whatever form, is constituted as central to an aliveness and humanity. The story and the family in Bialosky and Schulman's account may change, but not so much that the central factors are not retained: the desire for the child, and the child that creates the family that is recognizable enough as such.

Bialosky and Schulman's idea that the wanting of children is imprinted early on as familiar stories, which nevertheless also must somehow change as families and reproduction change, is repeated elsewhere in trying to account for the wanting of children. Susan Lewis Cooper and Ellen Sarasohn Glazer turn not to *Dumbo*, but to the Old Testament as the story about fertility and infertility. In retelling the story from Samuel of Elkanah and his two wives, Hannah and Peninnah, they conclude that "the story of Hannah is especially important because it illustrates the timelessness of emotions that surround infertility" (Cooper & Glazer, 1998, p. 13).[7] At the same time,

> although the feelings infertile men and women experience are timeless, there is also a timeliness to the ways in which these feelings are perceived and resolved ... advances in reproductive technology have offered new hope to countless couples, [but] these advances have also complicated their experience of infertility, adding new—and perhaps deeper—dimensions to a couple's suffering. [*ibid.*, pp. 14–15]

The pain and suffering of Hannah underpin the relevance and importance of reproductive technologies, even if, but also precisely because, they can somehow also make this suffering worse.

What is of relevance here is that Hannah's suffering is the grounding offered for the wanting of children, and the possible application of reproductive technology. In other words, the reason for wanting children, as with Bialosky and Schulman, is a story occurring from early on, either early on in personal history, or in human history. It is a story about desire and a desire that is reproduced and passed on, even if modified. It also demands its own reproduction in two ways. For Bialosky and Schulman, it imprints itself on the unwitting child, or the unwitting society, which carries the story further and implants it in turn. Like the embryo implanted in the womb, the story is implanted and reproduced in this way. For Cooper and Glazer, the story is carried through time by redescription and repetition, and is reproduced in this way. Moreover, as with Bialosky and Schulman, the longing becomes a central constitutive part of, or produces, a certain humanity and aliveness. If Hannah's grief is also the grief of the modern infertile couple,[8] then this is because the "importance" of her story lies in demonstrating precisely that this is an eternal, inherent, established situation: "theirs is a centuries old anguish that has been described and redescribed throughout history . . . [t]oday's infertile couples share the intense longings of Hannah and Elkanah and of Rachel and the many other biblical figures who struggled with infertility" (Cooper & Glazer, 1998, p. 14). The fundamental nature of "the intense longing" is both established and validated by its longevity and continuity. Humanity here, then, is that which expresses and reproduces a story about reproduction that is "described and redescribed". Humanity is that which reproduces reproduction, uniting Hannah, Elkanah, Rachel and today's infertile couples as one in their longing.

It is notable that for both Bialosky and Schulman and for Cooper and Glazer—although in somewhat different ways—the story itself has no cause or origin in turn. For Bialosky and Schulman it circulates as an external force or desire that encounters the individuals it imprints. For Cooper and Glazer the origin of the story is that humanity which produces or expresses it, but which, in this sense, does not function as a further origin itself: humanity and the longing for reproduction define each other in this account. These two accounts of story we are looking at are distinguished from each other by being either about a "social" story that imprints individuals as they encounter it, or as being about the expression of an aspect intrinsically present in the "human". In this way, these ideas of stories of desire for the child share with ideas of the wanting of a child as being natural, genetic, or instinctive, a concept of origin that itself has no prior cause or source. The story is simply present, just as the natural is. At issue is only where the story is located.

In several texts that also question an inevitable rootedness of the desire to have a child as simply natural, a story itself without origins also replaces the natural without origins. Gay Becker uses culture as the story that imprints, and also sees a need for the story of the desire for a child to be changeable, precisely through being seen as only a story; only one particular version of how a life might be lived, albeit a dominant story, one preferred and professed (imprinted) by the culture. As she writes:

> . . . in portraying women and men struggling with the problem of not having children when they want them, I explore complex ideas

about gender and normalcy. Such ideologies make it more difficult for people to deviate from widespread cultural expectations. When women and men aspire to parenthood and find themselves unable to live out this deep-seated cultural expectation, they initially cling to traditional notions about what constitutes womanhood and manhood. [Becker, 2000, p. 29]

There are several factors that may be noted here. First, "culture" here splits into several kinds of stories. Gender and normalcy are defined as "ideologies" that function as constriction and coercion,[9] as do "traditional notions" and "cultural expectation". Yet there are also other stories available outside ideology, tradition, and cultural expectation, which are the ones that might be deviated to, albeit with difficulty.

Defining the story of the wanting of a child in terms of particular types of coercive stories leads to Becker defining the stories that might be deviated to as "resistance to the power of cultural norms" (*ibid.*, p. 33). Here "normalcy", particularly in terms of gender, is what is seen to be the source of the wish for the child, and it has "power", because, Becker argues,

[c]ultural dialogues about reproduction are not simply about different means of reproduction: they reflect dominant views in the United States about what constitutes a person ... While people's stories and their actions are ostensibly about reproduction, the underlying issue is about fitting in—about fulfilling society's expectations. [*ibid.*]

The wish for the child is seen by Becker not to be about a wish for the child as such, but as a wish for something else: "fulfilling society's expectations". This sets up "society's expectations" as somehow existing *outside* of people, who must conform to them, unless they can deviate and resist. It also sees the wish for the child as only a means to another end.

In this sense, identity—gendered, as parent, or family—is part of an idea of selves as produced by coercive stories, but the coercion is, in turn, also somehow not coercion, for Becker writes that ". . . I refer to shared cultural assumptions about what is considered as normal as 'normalcy'. Women and men strive for normalcy in their daily lives; infertility disrupts that sense of normalcy" (*ibid.*).

Here, the stories are "shared" by women and men, not just external to them. On the one hand, the wanting of the child is imposed on the individual as a means of becoming an accepted part of a social group, defined *as* group by its obedience to a normalcy, but on the other hand that normalcy is created as shared assumptions, which are striven for. The difficulty with this argument is that normalcy must then be both imposed and shared simultaneously: both created by the group as group, and imposed on it from an external position. This would seem to be part of an overall struggle around the wanting of the child. This is perceived as having a central importance, but in order to be questioned at all in terms of that centrality, it must also be either removable and/or changeable. Hence the move we see in Bialosky and Schulman, Cooper and Glazer, and Becker, to describe a story which is, in somewhat differing ways for each of them, "familiar", enduring, or "dominant", and on the other hand subject to, or in need of, change.

Reproductive technologies, in this sense, are defined as connecting an unchanging component of humanity—the having of babies—to changing ways in which to have them. As Phillipe Ariès (1960) argues, contraception, seen as an introduction of *choice* or some level of control over reproduction, first introduces ideas of the child and the family as not inevitable, but as malleable or formable.[10] These ideas of contraception first, and then reproductive technologies subsequently, changing that which was previously unavailable to question, occur widely in accounts of the wanting of children or the use of reproductive technologies. As Sue Dyson also, for instance, suggests, in her book significantly entitled *The Option of Parenthood*:

> . . . parenthood is no longer the open-and-shut case it used to be. With the advent of reliable contraception, having children has changed from being an assumption, into a decision—a decision which is perhaps the most important that any individual or couple will ever make. . . . Parenthood, then should be the result of a positive, informed choice, and not an unthinking reflex. And choosing is what this book is all about. [Dyson, 1993, p. 1]

while Laurie Taylor and Matthew Taylor add that "Modern methods of birth control have created the possibility for all children to be chosen. Children are in theory, even if not always in practice, optional: every child can now be a wanted child" (Taylor & Taylor, 2003, p. 11).

In this way, the family is construed as unquestioned in the past, but made to change by the introduction of choice to the having of children, or not having them, leaving them altogether as an option, as Dyson and the Taylors point out. This account therefore retrospectively stabilizes the family of the past as set in its formulations and ways at least with respect to the having of children, and simultaneously posits that child as the keystone to that family. As Dyson states, "according to conventional wisdom, a family is not a family until the children come along" (1993, p. 13). In turn, that family is, inevitably, part of a stabilized culture and society, composed of these families. The having of children as inevitable is assumed as underpinning these structures. In this sense, the having of children as shifting from inevitability to being about choice can be said to produce the very notions of history, culture, and society themselves, where there is previously only a timeless humanity. Although history, culture, and society may be claimed to change and have changed in other ways, the family in this definition underpins a certain constancy, and limits the changes, or levels of change, which may, or can, take place. The idea of the having of children as choice, and therefore the idea of the changing—or even, then, disappearing—family, retrospectively splits history in this respect into a timelessness of that eternal family, determined by biological processes of reproduction, and an entry into history, culture, and society, released from an unchanging and unreflected-upon biology. (For an extensive parallel analysis of the way that assumptions of childhood as unchanging affect the writing and ideas of history, see Lesnik-Oberstein, 1998a, pp. 1–28.)

Becker's normalcy, which can be striven for, furthermore indicates that there is a self posited that is anterior to this struggle, that can choose to attempt to achieve normalcy. These selves are, therefore, not of themselves already normal: this specific kind of conformity must be achieved, as with Bialosky and Schulman's children watching *Dumbo*. The children already had "hearts and minds and imaginations", however, in which the story of the desire for children could be implanted. In that sense, the children are defined in terms of configurations and aspects of self already present, but these are not seen to be part of the desire for the child: that is a separate, and later, story. Culture, and society, in these uses, are confirmed as forces unifying disparate selves, who are initially outside of, or anterior to, these narratives, with the selves defined in turn in terms of aspects anterior to those narratives. This argument constantly re-works the splits between what is cultural or social and what is not, or differently so, attributing that which is not to a self somehow not cultural, not social (yet) in that way. Thus, the desire for the child is a *secondary* formation in arguments such as those of Bialosky and Schulman and Becker. It is a desire that is acquired by an anterior self, and that therefore can also, potentially, be relinquished in turn.

The problem of normalcy as both imposed and shared generates further issues. Becker returns to distinguishing the types of stories according to the level of their perceived strength or power, and divides them up into "cultural ideology" and "cultural dialogue" (Becker, 2000, p. 34). "Ideology" is the more coercive of the two, defined as being "repeatedly defined and portrayed within certain narrow limits" (*ibid.*). Immediately, however, these narrow limits also produce their own exceptions and qualifications, in this case "racism and class biases" (*ibid.*). The coercive story of "motherhood" only appears to apply to "white, middle-class women" (*ibid.*). There are alternative stories already available outside of the certain narrow limits, but they do not have the power of the dominant ideology over a certain group. Here a certain tautology is revealed as another aspect of the problem of stories that are both produced by, and imposed on, a group, for the group and the power of the story over it are thus defined in terms of the power that they perceive in their *own* story: the group is that which is produced by that particular story, and other groups have other stories. Both the account of coercion and dominance are limited in this way to the groups who succumb to these stories, for the other groups appear to be invulnerable to it. Falling outside of a certain agreed normalcy, they have either no normalcy, or a normalcy of their own. In this way, the group *is* its story, as the story is what defines the group. The range of culture and society is thus divided up and limited, in this case through racism and class.

But what is the coercive power of a normalcy that has power in one place but not elsewhere? These issues are part of a well-known wider range of issues with the way ideas of "society" and "culture" are mobilized in these kinds of arguments. On the one hand they are seen to be *causal* entities, creating identities externally, on the other they are seen to be themselves *results*; entities produced by, and as, shared views or practices. Do individuals tell stories that are seen to have a communality called "society" or "culture", or do individuals get shaped into "society" or "culture" by stories that have existed before them? Is this a diachronic or a synchronic process, in other words? And is the selfhood or individuality itself also a form of the cultural or social, or does it fall entirely outside it? The difficulty this situation creates for arguments such as the ones I have outlined above, is that these accounts of stories cannot explain the wish for the child any more than the claims of the natural or instinctive can; both nature and story can only diagnose that wish as existing, in the shape it is seen as having. Although the idea of stories may at first sight appear more liberal and flexible than the idea of a fixed and eternal nature, it too cannot, in the end, resolve the problem that the story is somehow both always already present, strangely similar to nature or instinct, or a story that is external and limited, attributed with a power that it then appears to be able to enforce only in tautological ways; powerful for the group it is powerful for. And the meaning of the stories, in either case, remains unclear.

A further question in relation to these arguments is also: *who* sees these groups as sharing, or being coerced by, a story? This is not a spurious question about the authorship of a given text, but to do with the perspective necessarily embedded in arguments about the social or the cultural. What perspectives are produced—and how—in a text in terms of the observations and arguments engaged in? For example, Gay Becker's text negotiates perspectives that might be called both confessional and external. Becker writes openly of her research resulting from her own encounter with infertility: "I began studying infertility after spending several years addressing my own", and her introduction is sub-titled "From personal experience to research" (Becker, 2000, p. 1).[11] This motivation for her research is centrally related to the striving for normalcy mentioned earlier: ". . . one important aspect has changed very little: the underlying cultural phenomena that conspire to make infertility so agonizing for many men and women . . . [t]hose issues revolve around questions of normalcy—for one's body and one's life" (*ibid.*). The own experience of infertility is written of as in the past, overcome through great effort and application, and leading her to decide to "study infertility instead of living it" (*ibid.* p. 2). This produces a position as "external" to the "present" of those studied in the text as still "living infertility". Such a perspective again becomes implicated in the consequences of the definitions of society and culture operating in the arguments. Culture here is expressed as phenomena that conspire, but also as underlying something else: it is a covert conspiracy. The position of the infertile person is to come to recognize and to resist this conspiracy. This resistance is not directed at the wish for the child itself, but at the normalcy that this wish is constituted as being subordinate to, or a part of.

Crucially, in relation to this, Becker writes that "[w]ith this insight I began to look at bodies and at illness in new ways and to ask myself how I could pass my newfound perceptions on to others" (*ibid.*, p. 3). It is this achieved "newfound perception" which can look from an outside perspective at the still ongoing processes of coercion into normalcy. The perspective of the narration is that of one who has already achieved the resistance to that coercion, and has overcome it: who has overcome the stories of culture and society. Personal experience is therefore here within culture and society, but the perspective of the researcher is outside of this, constituting personal experience as an object of study. This is the anthropology of this text. From a perspective of anthropological methodology Becker negotiates well-known questions around problems of interpretation—the anthropological discussions around the impossibility of "objectivity"—as being, on one level, about the status of emotion and empathy, where her account of her personal past experience positions her as personally involved:

> As the initial study began, I tried to distance myself emotionally. I was trained to keep a strict separation between my life and the lives of people involved in my research. Of course, anthropologists today acknowledge that such detachment is not possible or even desirable. And as soon as I started interviewing other people experiencing infertility I realized the futility—even ludicrousness—of such a position. I realized that this study was helping me to work my way through the personal issues infertility raised for me. Sometimes I was a few steps ahead of the people I interviewed,

simply because I was finished with medical treatment, but sometimes they were ahead of me. [*ibid.*]

Anthropologist and interviewees here are all subject to infertility,
albeit at differing stages of a process of understanding. On the other
hand, Becker has by definition written herself as the researcher
external to her interviewees' dilemmas, able to see the coercion of
normality that they are not—yet—able to see, or, in an other sense,
able to see what they may already know too, but have not yet
achieved an external position to.

Kaja Finkler, also an anthropologist, similarly calls her kind of
external position "the anthropological microscope", which is necessary according to her because

> Although the subject's perspective elucidates her own life, it is
> necessary to interject at least one caveat: human beings themselves
> do not always recognize the consequences of their own ideological
> beliefs. Our subjectivity restrains us from seeing our existence in its
> totality. There are, thus, limits to which we can understand our
> subjectivity. Hence, when people discuss their beliefs about genetic
> inheritance but could not elaborate on how their subjectivity
> connected with their actions or on the ways in which it affected
> their lives and their familial relations, I brought out the anthropo-
> logical microscope to assist in further interpretation. [Finkler, 2000,
> xiii–xiv]

The microscope "assists" in understanding a subjectivity that
cannot fully understand its own subjectivity *as* subjectivity. This
subjectivity is both split into differing subjectivities—like a Russian
doll, with dolls within dolls—and is something partial, not "our
existence in its totality". Our total existence is subjectivity, plus a
sometimes unobtainable understanding of that subjectivity, plus
ideology and its consequences, and a recognition thereof, plus
actions. Finkler's microscope helps to make it possible to "see" all
of these elements, unlike the participants themselves. The plot, or
movement, of Becker's text is also about the achievement of this
externality in one way or another, as she indicated from the start.
This is her deviant story.

On another level, the dilemma Becker is addressing may be
read as not being about internal/external positions, which may be

negotiated through an empathic sharing of experience, past or present, but about another kind of methodological issue. Becker overtly roots her analyses in theoretical ideas of narrative: identity, gender, and the body as being about stories, not about given, "natural" entities-in-the-world, noting that "many feminist scholars have examined the question of what is considered 'natural', especially with respect to women" (Becker, 2000, p. 266), and adding that: "People's stories express bodily experience. When someone narrates such a story, the story itself can be seen as the enactment, or performance, of bodily experience" (*ibid.*, p. 24).

Yet Becker also, apparently inadvertently, troubles this view of experience as narrative from the start. First, stories are here *expressions* of a bodily experience therefore situated as prior, and this recurs in the ideas of enactment and performance.[12] In her further arguments, however, it seems unclear to me where and how Becker situates bodily experience: is this experience in turn itself a narrative, or is it an originary natural entirely outside of narrative? Her own further explanation that "the main purpose of studies that begin with 'experience' . . . in my view, is to attend to the phenomenological foundations of cultural practices" (Becker, 2000, p. 273) also appears to attribute to experience simultaneously a status as foundational to cultural practices, and at the same time as derivative of them in their phenomenology. These questions recur when Becker elsewhere explains that

> I became especially intrigued by how people take power into their own hands and resist ideas that are undesirable or impossible to live out. Indeed, once I began working seriously to uncover the cultural elements of infertility and reproductive technologies, I found myself mining a rich vein of societal conflicts. This work dovetailed with my lifelong interest in how people define what is normal, how they fit themselves inside that definition—or do not—and how vast the difference can be between cultural ideals, or ideologies, and the realities of people's lives. What people do in order to live with this disparity is, of course, the most salient question of all. [*ibid.*, p. 3]

Becker here confirms a fundamental split between normalcy and the pre-normalcy individual as being "about the realities of people's lives". Culture in this sense is defined, as we have seen, as a coercion and a conspiracy, but here it is, furthermore, not the reality of people's lives. Unless, that is, the reality of people's lives is in turn itself assumed to be an aspect of the cultural, albeit not a coercive or dominant aspect. Either way, some stories of culture may endeavour to impose themselves on people, or even become part of people ("shared"), but, in the end, those stories are, after all, *not* their realities, and even "undesirable or impossible to live out". The realities and possible lives are either not cultural, beneath culture, or they are cultural in a non-coercive and non-dominant way: the culture of Becker's deviant story. The argument this therefore maintains is that the real and the possible—whether somehow cultural or not cultural at all—are the deviant, while normalcy is an oppression of culture as coercive.

These shifting splits between the personal, the cultural, the social, and their subsequent changing positions with regard to the forces and powers of culture, as here read, are centrally relevant as they direct and redirect Becker's arguments throughout her text. Most of all, this is expressed through her formulation of the analyses of her interviewees' narratives in terms of an external—coercive cultural, social—story that has to be recognized as such and then removed. This reading may offer, for instance, an alternative explanation to one Becker herself provides for a difference between her own research and that of Sarah Franklin:

> Franklin (*Embodied Progress*) has analyzed how new reproductive technologies are represented by organizations offering these services as "natural". She also found that women in England viewed these technologies as natural, but that finding was not echoed in this research. Instead, women in this study viewed these technologies as a necessary, but alien, means to an end. [Becker, 2000, p. 266]

Ostensibly this accounts for the differences between Franklin's observations and her own as being the result of a difference between Englishness and Americanness. In the light of my analysis, however, I suggest that these results might also be understood as resulting from different assumptions about the definitions and operations of culture. In assuming that the plot of herself and her interviewees is, potentially at least, that of a movement away from normalcy towards deviancy, with normalcy encompassing the wish for the child of reproductive technology, it is consistent for the women of this text to view those technologies as alien or part of an external coercion.

The self is, therefore, in Becker's text, as I have argued, composed of internal and external stories, and the text strives to diagnose which is which, and to achieve a resolution in extirpating the external. It is a goal that she also attributes to, or sees herself as sharing with, her interviewees:

> People who repeatedly attempt to live up to cultural ideologies, yet fail to do so, experience acute social discomfort and emotional pain. They may eventually come to see those ideologies as interfering with and delaying their attempts to find alternative ways of regaining a sense of normalcy and thus finding a meaning in life. I believe this is why so many people volunteered to participate in this research: out of a conviction that ideas about fertility and parenthood in the United States society need to change, and that, collectively, their voices might make a difference. [*ibid.*, p. 25]

For Becker, then, the wanting of a child is about the coercion of normalcy, and infertility constituted as a challenge to that normalcy, with the cause of the pain of infertility being the impossibility of achieving social or cultural normalcy. For Cooper and Glazer, as noted earlier, the wanting of a child, and the anguish of infertility are ancient stories, transcending culture and history, expressive of the eternally human. Their view of the issues and experiences of infertility and reproductive technologies is therefore correspondingly different to Becker's. Cooper and Glazer's

> would-be parents, regardless of whether they have struggled with infertility, believe strongly that the power of love can transcend all difficulties. . . . [W]e want to assure our readers that each of us knows countless happy, thriving families who were created by assisted reproduction and by third party parenting. These families are what make our work so satisfying—they are living testimony to the true miracle of creation . . . please know [the families we have known] are in the background, encouraging you onward. Virtually all would tell you that the outcome makes the struggle worthwhile. [Cooper & Glazer, 1998, p. 10]

Clearly, this is virtually an opposite account to that which Becker provides. The participants in Cooper and Glazer's work are seen to be encouraging the readers onwards, assuring that difficulties will be overcome by love and the miracle of creation. Infertility here is seen as a challenge not to culture and society, but to personal ethics: "the ARTs and, certainly, third party reproduction raise profound ethical questions for all of us and force us to carefully consider what it means to create families in new ways" (*ibid.*, p. 15). In this view, history, as with the Old Testament stories of Hannah and Rachel, justifies reproductive technology also within an idea of medical ethics that "supports beneficence when a long sought-after goal—parenthood—is achieved and a new life is created (*a concept that has historically been viewed by ethicists as positive*)" (*ibid.*, p. 16, my emphasis). Unlike Becker's coercive ideologies of culture and society, history in Cooper and Glazer constitutes and confirms the human as elements that are continuous and constant through time. Here choice seems not to "split" history, as with Ariès, Dyson, and the Taylors, because the having of children is hardly considered as having become an option (even if this is mentioned by Cooper and Glazer in their text, this optionality does not operate as an integral aspect of their narrative). The wanting of children is precisely what is seen to remain constant and consistent, even if infertility imperils the actual having of them. The ethical issues for Cooper and Glazer therefore are particularly pertinent to the creation of families in *new* ways, not to the having of children *per se*. The family, defined as and by the having of children, is not for them in danger of perishing. Having accepted, as established through, by, and *as*, history, the process of having children and attempting to overcome infertility as a given of the human, infertility as such is configured as loss. Here Becker's striving for normalcy is, in a sense, reversed. Here there is not a striving, but a series of existing and established factors of identity that infertility threatens to eliminate, remove, or weaken:

> loss of self-esteem, loss of bodily integrity, loss of privacy; loss of sexual pleasure, loss of time, loss of money, loss of comfort in friendships and family relationships, and the loss of spontaneous conception. .... [T]oday's infertile couples are threatened by the possibility of losses involving basic structures in their lives ... their marriage ... their relationships with others ... their religious faith ... their careers. Managing these primary structures becomes of paramount importance, since the stakes, in each instance, are high. [*ibid.*, p. 17]

It is notable that for Cooper and Glazer these losses are about "basic" and "primary structures". What for Becker was secondary and imposed is here fundamental. What this makes clear is how researchers all working on the basis of interviews and narratives from participants can and do arrive at crucially different accounts about infertility and reproductive technologies. It is positions assumed or argued with regard to seemingly disparate issues such as culture, society, history, and the self that both determine and are themselves also produced by and as the interpretations of the experiences and choices of infertile couples. My analysis therefore disagrees, for instance, with Sally Kohlstedt and Helen Longino's understanding that such discrepancies necessarily result from an opposition between a medical establishment and the women involved in treatments:

> If we listen only to the experts, a vista of expanding human control over nature is optimistically displayed. If we listen also to the women who are targets of the new knowledge, a more ambiguous future and a more and conflicted discursive landscape displace the clinical cheer. . . . We hear women's voices, in sometimes great variety, amid the institutional, often male, voices that seek to influence women's thinking and their lives. [Kohlstedt & Longino, 2000, p. ix]

Becker and Cooper and Glazer are defined in their texts precisely also as listeners to women's (and men's) voices, and yet their interpretations differ widely, as we will continue to consider.

In discussing the attitudes of infertile couples to these losses, Cooper and Glazer, like Becker, and Kohlstedt and Longino and many others, see gender as an important factor. Gender is also defined, in this context, as being about "expectations about motherhood and fatherhood" (Cooper & Glazer, 1998, p. 18), but these are not externally formulated expectations, but expectations generated internally in terms of personal and psychological dimensions:

> for women, expectations of motherhood begin with pregnancy. For many, the threatened loss of pregnancy and childbirth represents an immense loss . . . for some women pregnancy feels like an essential life event, one that cannot be missed. [ibid.]

These are losses of experiences and events that have not yet occurred, projected as a future that ought to occur. For women their expectations are defined as beginning with that not-yet pregnancy, leaving pregnancy to be understood here as either an initiator of expectations of motherhood, or as the initial part of women's expectations of motherhood. Either way, this future is lost.

It is notable, however, that even so, pregnancy is described as feeling essential only "for some women". This account, which relies on an established, trans-historical emotion, simultaneously wishes to maintain an idea of variability and *choice*. This points to a tension in argument resulting from, on the one hand, accepting infertility and the responses to infertility as timeless, but, on the other hand, wishing to maintain an idea of autonomy, included also under the schema of medical ethics adhered to by Cooper and Glazer. If the infertile couples have timeless emotions, thanks to the invention of ARTs they now have choices about how to cope with those timeless emotions. In line with the internal source of the expectations about the having of children, Cooper and Glazer's readers are directed *inwards* for guidance in the making of these choices. As the eternally human sources the stories of reproduction, so it also figures as a source of answers to questions and choices. Where Becker's plot-movement is towards the diagnosis and removal of the external, Cooper and Glazer's is a journey inwards to locate and confirm an already-present answer. The self here is in this way an autonomous entity that inherently carries within it its own stories:

> Once they have all this objective information, they must make choices that are based also on subjective data, that is, on what *feels* right as well as on what is logical. . . . The point is that couples differ in respect to what odds they feel make it worthwhile for them to proceed with ART treatment. . . . Each couple must search inside themselves to discover what they need to do—or not do—in order to avoid future regrets. [*ibid.*, p. 59]

The stories "deep [in] their hearts" (*ibid.*, p. 139) are about what the couples "feel", and feelings figure largely in Cooper and Glazer's text, with several sub-sections specifically entitled "feelings" or about specified types of feelings, such as "fears and expectations" (*ibid.*, p. 99). These formulations result in a double role for "feelings". Feelings about infertility are both eternal, continuous, and identical, and on the other hand feelings are the site of difference. This would seem to be another version of the contradiction between the timeless and the timely, or the continuous and the changing, were it not that this doubleness is attached to different aspects by placing the timeless and the timely on different levels: the eternal and identical feelings about infertility are maintained as funda-mental, while the variability of feelings is seen to be about differing choices within that framework. This separation of feelings into levels of the enduring and timeless and the variable and changeable works through Cooper and Glazer's arguments in a range of ways, moreover, although it cannot resolve the conflict between the time-less and the timely in every case.

One difficulty that is produced in and by this kind of argument, for instance, is that the established separation between the different kinds of feelings is neither consistently realized nor maintained. Because the ARTs are seen to create choices, they are also written of as coming to produce new ideas about parenthood and (wanting of) the child, and, as part of this in turn, different ideas and emotions about this than were possible in previous history. This can be observed, for instance, in Cooper and Glazer's formulation that

> prior to the arrival of assisted reproduction, the loss of the preg-nancy experience was inevitably coupled with the loss of genetic continuity . . . Because genetics can now be separated from gestation, many infertile couples weigh these losses carefully and make choices based on which losses are more tolerable for them. [*ibid.*, p. 19]

The losses that infertility initiates are further specified by Cooper and Glazer in terms of factors

> directly related to reproduction and parenting: the loss of the preg-nancy experience, of a genetic connection to one's offspring, of continuity with one's bloodline, of conceiving a child jointly with one's beloved spouse, and of parenting itself. [*ibid.*, p. 17]

These losses are summarized as

> the three components of parenthood—the genetic, the gestational, and the nurturant—[which] can be separated, so that the loss of one does not necessarily result in the loss of the others. [*ibid.*]

A contradiction is immediately introduced here: genetics can only "*now* be separated from gestation" (my emphasis), but at the same time this genetic continuity was also an inevitable loss "prior to the arrival of assisted reproduction". This formulation has to include the assumption that the loss of pregnancy was always understood and felt *as* a "loss of genetic continuity", so that this definition of genetics becomes historical and timeless in and of itself. At the same time, it is ARTs themselves that are seen to have created the awareness of a distinction between these types of losses, so that couples can prioritize what matters most to them.

In this way, ARTs written as contemporary, or of the "now", simultaneously determine the past and the history which they are seen themselves to be justified by. We have seen, and will continue to see, that this is a pervasive issue in discussions about reproduction. In order to motivate and justify the use of ARTs, or, conversely, to critique it, ideas need to be deployed that articulate either the need for, the functioning, or the misguided use of, ARTs. In doing so, the languages of ARTs determine the terms of history, society, culture, and the self, even as they are themselves determined by them in turn. As theorists Lay, Gurak, Gravon, and Myntti write: ". . . ironically, women's demand for these reproductive technologies has in essence increased the cultural value of having one's own child, thus reaffirming the reproductive function of women" (2000, p. 16). Women's demand here creates the processes that make that which already exists, the "own child". The "own child" is defined and known both in the past, prior to ARTs, and yet is, at the same time, defined in the present more strongly by the technologies produced by the demand for what is already known. The technologies in this way mediate a reduplication: they are needed to (re-) make the own child already there. Furthermore, demand can be read as reproducing itself. This reproduction is seen as accumulating, strengthening, that demand. The reproductive function that is here seen to define women problematically is also seen to be both already established, and yet added to by the existence of ARTs. This can also be understood as another variant of the idea that ARTs introduce change ("timeliness") to the "timeless" concepts of family, children, and the desire for the child.

In examining these very issues, Lay and her colleagues produce further positions within their own argument similar to those that we have noted with Becker, and with Cooper and Glazer. As Kohlstedt and Longino's comments indicated, Lay and her colleagues see the "expert" (usually male, or embedded in a male establishment) as the source of narratives which define and control the feminine as body and identity:

> Within these normalizing arguments, although women are certainly subjects or creators of knowledge, they also become objects of knowledge. Their bodies may be fragmented into mechanical parts, and their reproductive functions may become medical conditions, to be fixed or rehabilitated if they fall outside the norm. This fragmentation . . . ignor[es] other aspects of the self, such as emotions and personal relationships and support systems. [Lay, Gurak, Gravon, & Myntti, 2000, p. 5]

In this careful consideration of the experts' stories as determinate of identity and experience, however, there is nevertheless a simultaneous instatement of a body and self that exist outside of these stories, as and of themselves. Stories, as with Becker's culture, are external impositions, "internalized by society's citizens" (*ibid.*, p. 4), where the source of these stories here is explicitly and specifically located as issuing from the experts in control of knowledge. This, first, places those "experts" as themselves outside of the social in creating it and leaves aside how these experts themselves came to articulate specifically such a narrative. Also, beyond, or below, these external stories, the citizens possess a self which has "other aspects . . . such as emotions and personal relationships and support systems": Lay and her colleagues can know and define this self and its proper attributes. The body too "*may* be fragmented into mechanical parts" (my emphasis), indicating that the body may also not thus be fragmented, and that non-fragmentation is its prior state; a wholeness of, and as, the body is assumed.

The return to perspectives which can identify or know entities and identities prior to the imposed stories is also apparent in a judgement offered by the text:

> . . . the births of the McCaughey septuplets in 1997 and the Chekwu octuplets in 1998 (. . . both . . . conceived via fertility treatments) were primarily reported in wondrous terms, with the parents claiming that their successful multiple births were primarily acts of God, not science. Yet in reality these births are both wondrous and frightening—acts of God and acts of science and technology . . . [*ibid.*]

The narration here is able to claim a knowledge of a "reality"; a reality, moreover, which is itself determined as composed of the two alternate possibilities outlined: "God and . . . science and technology". Despite the argument, therefore, that Lay and her colleagues make that they are offering a "[r]hetorical analysis of arguments . . . [which] identif[ies] authoritative knowledge, within midwifery and within the medical community, as not true knowledge but instead as discursive constructs" (*ibid.*, p. 6), their formulations have already reintroduced such true knowledge in turn as available from their perspective. As with Becker, the splitting up of identity, the self, culture, and society into, on the one hand imposed narratives, and, on the other, autonomous and identifiable entities, reverberates throughout the subsequent discussions and conclusions of the text.

If, then, Lay and colleagues can be compared to Becker in terms of the externality and imposition of stories, they also turn to Cooper and Glazer's idea of an innate and internal story, which issues from and as the self. This internal story is, as is often the case in studies of gender and ethnicity across differing fields (literature, history, anthropology, sociology, psychology), situated in the women's "voice", privileged as the voice heard from the start of Lay and colleagues' text. "Voice" in many critical approaches constitutes the expression of the true self, or, as Lay and colleagues put it, "women's experiential and embodied knowledge . . . that is, their unique experience with birthing their children and their knowledge of their own bodies' signs and needs" (*ibid.*). Consistent with their splitting of identity and the self into external and internal stories, here "experience" is inserted on the side of a body that can provide women with a knowledge of its signs and needs. The body signals to the self to which it belongs, and these signs can be read and understood in a privileged way by the self; not signs available to other selves. The plot of Lay and colleagues' narrative lies therefore in

> examining the discourse surrounding reproduction and technology, [to] reveal, explicate, and even shake up that discourse. We can recall women's experiential and embodied knowledge; we can illuminate how language normalizes certain reproductive choices. [*ibid.*]

This plot requires that Lay and colleagues are themselves positioned outside that discourse, able to view it. At the same time, they
can recall something that must have been once forgotten in order to
necessitate retrieval, and yet they already know that which is to be
so recalled. It is the experiential and embodied knowledge which
women earlier were said to possess in and of themselves, not needing to be recalled, but an inherent aspect of their unique knowledge
of birth and their own bodies. Lay and colleagues' text is, then,
construed as itself a recollection in the face of the expert technologies which deny or repress the women's knowledge of themselves:
it is itself the women's voice.

The splitting of Lay and colleagues' arguments into that which
is story and that which is non-story experience, body, or voice,
stems from their understanding of "rhetoric" and what they call
"rhetorical analysis . . . a powerful critical tool" (*ibid.*). They scrupulously rehearse their approach in terms of "rhetoric" as the close
examination of

> word choice, arguments, warrants, claims, motives, and other
> purposeful, persuasive features of language, visuals, and various
> artifacts to understand how such discourse not only creates our
> social conceptions of women's bodies and reproduction but also
> defines the policies and knowledge systems that are available to
> women and men. [*ibid.*, p. 7]

Yet, within this definition, the possibility of an escape from
language and discourse is already resident in the qualifications
"purposeful" and "persuasive features" and, just further on,
"aspects which build credibility" (*ibid.*, p. 9), or, in Chloé Diepenbrock's chapter, "fairy-tale qualities" (Diepenbrock, 2000, p. 99),
which divide language up into features that are not effective
socially and those that are, which in turn assumes an area of the
social that is not constituted or affected by such effective language.
It is this division into features that allows the continuation of the
non-discursive in the midst of a discussion which explicitly and
overtly wishes to adhere to an understanding of the relevant issues
as discursive. Besides this division, there is also a further division
of stories into "determinist stories"—where the "determinist" is a
part of the idea of effectivity—and "subtexts that may not be
readily apparent to the casual reader, listener, or viewer but

nonetheless are part of the messages" (Lay, Gurak, Gravon, & Myntti, 2000, p. 7). Lay and colleagues' aim is to "tell the other side(s) of these determinist stories" (*ibid.*), so that here, too, they constitute their perspective as able to see beyond what the "casual reader, listener, or viewer" can see, not themselves determined by the stories. One of the difficulties with this position and perspective is that the narration has constituted itself as, in this sense, the very idea of the "expert" that it professes to question and resist. It positions the narration as exempt from the determining persuasiveness of the rhetoric, as immune from its credibility; like, or as, the expert, they are outside this idea of the determined society.

These are urgent problems for texts which articulate a wish precisely to provide information, guidance, analysis, and critique for a group of people—infertile people—they perceive to be, in various ways, vulnerable, anxious, pressured, intimidated, or desperate. To summarize the problems that Becker or Cooper and Glazer produce in terms of that wished for provision of guidance: in Becker's case, as the comparative reading with such a text as Cooper and Glazer indicates, those who are not aligned with Becker's perception of "normalcy" as oppressive or external can be said to be positioned in terms of that text's guidance as subject to another—Becker's—external "normalcy" in turn. In the case of Cooper and Glazer, those persons who cannot locate their inner truth, or distinguish their inner answer from external imposition, are left without resource in terms of that text.[13]

In the case of Lay and her colleagues, the definitions of the narration as, simultaneously, the women's voice and the expert outside of the social result in a stabilizing of an allocation to women of the "experiential and embodied knowledge", for instance in their role as midwives, and to the men an "anatomical knowledge" characterized by contributor Jeannette Herrle-Fanning by "hierarchization of detail, analysis of component parts, and the development of an abstract, standardized model of Woman that encouraged the development of a mechanical metaphor of parturition" (Lay, Gurak, Gravon, & Myntti, 2000, pp. 14–15). The underpinning of these distinctions is the assigned "uniqueness" of pregnancy, childbirth, and menstruation to women. Men are those who, by definition, cannot have these experiences. Women are here constituted by experiences that speak for and to themselves without the intervention of rhetoric. Hence the definitions of "experiential and embodied", which seem to assume a knowledge in, from, and to, the body without language. As self-evident and commonsensical[14] as these definitions may seem (men surely do not menstruate, and cannot—yet—become pregnant, etc.), two serious paradoxes are raised by them, part, on the one hand, of the self-contradictory self-defined narrational positions as simultaneously women's voice and (male) expert, and, on the other hand, of the fundamental theoretical problem of positing the possibility of a body that can "speak" without language. As critics such as Judith Butler have argued extensively, this view of the body relies on an assumption of a division of "experience" and "language", where language is taken as being derivative, expressive, or representative of, and therefore secondary to, a spontaneous and originary experience (see Butler, 1990).[15] First, contrary to Lay and colleagues' interest in, and commitment to, rhetoric, women are, willy-nilly, constituted in their text as *outside* of this rhetoric in terms of their bodies. This poses the question of the very necessity of the rhetorical analysis itself, when the woman's body is anyway available consistently as the resource of a knowledge counter to, or free from, rhetoric. Only the notion of "recall" intervenes to qualify this resource as, after all, somehow hidden, precarious or vulnerable. Second, there is also the question of how the female body remains free of rhetoric in some ways, and not in others. In terms of recall, rhetoric here is seen to be a cover, "selective" (Lay, Gurak, Gravon, & Myntti, 2000, p. 13), or "filtered" (*ibid.*, p. 4), thus in some cases obscuring or fragmenting the body of experience which needs to be, and, here *can* be retrieved (or "recalled") from this rhetoric. This, however, confirms a prior unfiltered, unselected, body as the already-present knowledge of the text. These problems are, moreover, part of the very issue that much feminist criticism has battled, and that Lay and her colleagues are precisely themselves also concerned with, which is a relegation of women to the merely physical, a body without—or separate from—a mind, an object of the knowledge of men through the offering up of their bodies as the site of the essential definition of femininity through, and as, physical processes:

> . . . chapters 6, 7, and 11 reveal how culture tends to define *woman* according to her reproductive abilities and to divide women's

bodies into parts, functions, and processes. The discourse that identifies the female body as a legitimate object of scientific knowledge,
scholars note, often defines the female body, indeed women's lives,
according to reproductive functions and abilities. Moreover, the
discourse tends to divide that body into distinctive parts and, to a
great extent, distinguish them from the activities of the mind. [*ibid.*,
p. 15]

Yet Lay and colleagues, despite themselves, end up relying in
their arguments on this very body, and this very underpinning of
the identity of femininity, as the grounds of their resistance to what
they define as the experts' rhetoric: Laura Shanner, for instance,
concludes that

'[a] man may therefore perceive himself as having transcended his
body when he controls his daily appetites, but even when women
perceive themselves as having transcended their bodies, intermit-
tent bleeding reminds them otherwise. [Shanner, 2000, p. 155]

Lay and her colleagues, throughout their text, shift continually
between a body-of-rhetoric and a body of experiential and embodied knowledge, free of, or resistant to, rhetoric. As with Becker,
this also necessitates an idea of levels of language (besides an idea
of rhetoric as language on top of experience), and here, too, "ideology" appears to mean a particular kind of effective—or a particularly effective kind of—language:

Visual and verbal messages reinforce or reflect the ideology of technology, its symbolic and social link to masculinity, and its application to the socially assigned place of women, including their
reproductive roles. [Lay, Gurak, Gravon, & Myntti, 2000, p. 11]

Other kinds of languages seen as possessing a particular power are
called, for instance, "fairy-tales", as we saw earlier, or "sensational-
ized narrative" (Diepenbrock, 2000, p. 104); positing the woman as
a reader who responds in predictable ways to certain kinds of
stories.[16] A further issue that this creates is the assumption of
women's specific vulnerability to these ideologies and messages
with the necessary joint assumption of the grounds of men's power
as experts and formers of the social for women. This point is not to
question widely and well-analysed ways in which patriarchy has

been understood as systems of power, but instead to examine how within these specific texts the power of the (male) expert is seen to be constituted and to function and what the implications of this are. In other words, to *whom* in this text are these languages persuasive and credible, and why? To Lay and colleagues, rhetoric as a particular kind of language is that power in and of itself, interacting in certain ways in turn with other perceived powers, such as institutions, technology, finance, and science, either to constitute them, or be constituted by them in turn. The uncertainty of this causality is part of the problematic definition of rhetoric as both power as such, and as only a level on top of a known and knowable reality (again, despite overt refutations of an idea of rhetoric as "[m]ere rhetoric" (Lay, Gurak, Gravon, & Myntti, 2000, p. 8)).

What, then, is the position of the assumed underlying reality seen to be in relation to its vulnerability to persuasion and belief? This question is pertinent, again, to the issue of the desire for the child. In Lay and colleages' text, as I quoted it earlier, the women's desire for the own child led to their demand for reproductive technologies. That assertion is the crux of the problem of the text assuming an underlying female body with an accompanying woman's voice, for here that body and voice express a demand for the technologies which are elsewhere in the text explicitly and repeatedly defined as the product of the male experts. The result is that the shiftings between the women's voice and the experts' story frequently create contradictions or collisions, sometimes within one sentence:

> Finally the woman who becomes pregnant while using fertility drugs may declare that the multiple fetuses she might bear are the result of both her physician's expertise and God's will—a characterization that assigns even greater authority to those who control reproductive technologies and greater identification of her body with its reproductive technologies. [*ibid.*, p. 16]

The results of reproductive technology demanded by the woman are nevertheless assigned by her to the expert physician and the will of God. This is formulated as the woman strengthening the characterization imposed on her by the experts. In this sentence there is an entire instability in terms who has created what, and for whom: the woman's voice speaks both her own demand, the role of the experts (and the will of God), and her own identity, which is, however, also an identity imposed by the experts. Lay and colleagues' understanding of rhetoric as at once crucial and secondary leads here to a woman's voice that is both originary and imposed, sometimes with respect to precisely the same definitions.

In any case, the desire for the child is located as both issuing absolutely from the woman as an innate wish and demand, and as an imposed, externally controlled and mediated story. Thus, after having introduced women's desire for the own (and healthy) child as the source of the demand for reproductive technologies, the following claim occurs just a few pages later on:

> Prenatal testing, contraception, and infertility treatment [are] . . . created or aided by reproductive technologies, [and] seem to reinforce the societal messages that most women want very much to become pregnant but that many need help to become so . . ." [ibid., p. 23]

This claim either assigns the wish for pregnancy to "societal messages", or it can be read in terms of splitting the statement into a desire for pregnancy as being innate, with the societal message being constituted solely as the imposition onto that natural desire of the conception of it as a difficult and fraught process, requiring help. Even this reading, however, sits awkwardly with the prior claim that it was women who demanded reproductive technologies: their demand in this way then somehow anticipated certain roles for these technologies, but not others. Furthermore, the women's demand presumably situates these technologies as the fulfilment of a need; a need that can only be conceived of in terms of problems with the "natural" production of the "own child". What otherwise could the demand be about or for? A problem is therefore simultaneously already there and known, and at the same time a later add-on or imposition. Similarly, Diepenbrock, whose rhetoric is the fairy-tale, claims that

> [t]he emotional and highly subjective language of the first-person narrative attracts the reader who, because she identifies with the storyteller, is more inclined to adopt the storyteller's unexamined belief in both motherhood at all costs and reproductive technologies. [Diepenbrock, 2000, p. 118]

Here it is a concept of identification which defines the woman reader both as a product of the text and at the same time as prior to that text: she is in it, and, encountering herself there, is in turn confirmed by it.[17]

The problem for all these accounts of the wanting of the child, then, is that they all, in the end, somehow establish or maintain a subjectivity that is already outside of culture or society. In order for culture, society, or the experts to impose their narratives, there must be a recipient of those narratives, who, fundamentally, is vulnerable to those narratives. That vulnerability, as with Diepenbrock's reader, is what constitutes the recipient as the *appropriate* recipient. And that appropriateness is, in these terms, what the natural is: both appropriate as self-identical, as innate, and as spontaneous. Gender, in these terms, is perhaps the most frequent specification of this natural appropriateness, but we have also seen that ethnicity is a possible other configuration. Bialosky and Schulman's children are also a form of this natural vulnerability, as watching *Dumbo* impresses the child's heart, imagination, and mind. The child here figures as an opened gate, defenceless to that which is directed at it. For Cooper and Glazer history provides evidence of a timeless and transcendent desire for the child. In Becker's case, a predetermined wish for normalcy generates the anxiety that provides the enduring pressure to pursue the family through ARTs. Finally, for Lay and colleagues, the stories of the experts impose on women ideas and goals about themselves which run counter to the truths they experience through and as their own bodies. The wanting of the child, in terms, then, of both the natural, the biological, the cultural and the social, is the encountering of an appropriate story.

Notes

1. For a thorough analysis of constructions of the animal and animality, see Sue Walsh, "Untheming the theme: the child in wolf's clothing" (unpublished doctoral thesis, University of Reading, 2001). My reading of the "animal" here is based on Sue Walsh's analysis.
2. I should emphasize that when I refer to an author in my analyses, my comments are not intended in any way to be a commentary on, or criticism of, authors as individuals. My interest here lies in looking at the

implications of certain arguments to do with power, nature, stories, society, and the individual, as I read them in texts. I do not assume my readings (here or anywhere else) necessarily coincide with an individual author, their intentions, or their view of themselves, in any way.

3. For further extensive considerations of problems in these fields see Rose and Rose (2001).

4. For a well-known analysis of the work of Hrdy and other primatologists that also reads the "natural" as a narrative and discusses the problems of positing nature as something that can be seen "correctly", see Haraway (1991).

5. I do not use the term "unconscious" here, because I am not following terms in Hrdy's argument, but attempting to formulate implications of her formulations. In doing so, I do not wish to insert an idea of an unconscious as a necessary complement to consciousness here. I am using "consciousness" only as a part of choice or decision, and "non-consciousness" as non-choice.

6. Just to be clear: I am not claiming here that Hrdy's text is antagonistic to career women or women who choose not to have children, only examining how her arguments involve ideas about the operation of the wish for the child.

7. This narrative of ancient or authoritative texts demonstrating the "timelessness" of infertility is ubiquitous. In a textbook on *Couple Therapy for Infertility*, to give just one other example, the authors write:

> From time immemorial, fertility has been a primal concern for human society. From the Venus of Willendorf, the plump fertility goddess of prehistoric Europe, through the Biblical injunction to "be fruitful and multiply", fecundity has been highly prized, ensuring the survival of the species and of the particular tribe or nation. [Diamond, Kezur, Meyers, Scharf, & Weinshel, 1999, p. 5]

8. Cooper and Glazer specify that it is outside the scope of their book to look at specific factors that may play for lesbian or gay couples, or single parents, and assume they are largely addressing heterosexual couples (p. 11). I consider the relevance of this later.

9. For extensive analyses of the issues involved in defining "ideology" on which I am drawing here, see Geertz (1973) and, particularly in relation to the problems of reading "ideology" as one particular aspect, part, or level of a story: Stephen Thomson, "The child, the family, the relationship. Familiar stories: family, storytelling, and ideology in Philip Pullman's *His Dark Materials*" (2004), pp. 144–168.

10. There are, of course, many other historians who also write of contraception as changing ideas about the family in some way. For one other
such account, for instance, see Gay (1984).

11. It is notable that quite a few books on reproductive technologies are
introduced by a confession of the author's own personal as well as
professional involvement with infertility and reproductive technologies. Charis (Cussins) Thompson, together with such a personal anecdote, also includes in the author photo on the jacket of her book *Making
Parents: The Ontological Choreography of Reproductive Technologies* (2005;
the anecdote is on the first page of the introduction, on p. 3) a child
(a girl) of perhaps some four or five years of age, leaning against her
upper body. Reading this against the personal anecdote, I would see
the child here as being implicated in the authorship of the text, suggesting that the child is indeed framed by the adult as the "source" as well
as aim of reproductive technologies, as I am arguing in this book. As
I state in Note 5 above, I do not claim for my reading the status of a
penetration or revelation of Charis Cussins Thompson's intentions.

12. It may be worth noting here that Judith Butler, to whom Becker also
refers, uses "performativity" as a term for her understanding of the
constructions of identity, where "performance" is precisely not secondary or derivative of a prior authenticity. I can see that Becker may be
deploying "performance" in this sense, but my argument here is
precisely that an idea of secondariness or derivation seems to me to re-
enter her discussion none the less. For Butler's definition and use of the
term, see Butler, 1990, 1993.

13. It is important to state here that I am here not describing or assuming
the responses of individual readers to any of these texts. I take the position that I cannot know, or predict, how other readers may respond to
texts, or whether they may find them helpful or not, or in which ways.
What I am addressing here is the constitution of the "reader in the
text"—that is, the position that is assigned by the text to an idea of a
readership in terms of the implications of its arguments.

14. I am here relying on, and referring to, critiques of the idea of "common
sense" as a self-evident and natural knowledge. See, for instance,
Geertz, 1983, pp. 73–93.

15. For an excellent collection of essays by other critics also arguing this
kind of view see: *The Woman in Question* (Adams & Cowie, 1990).
The equation of the body with the central site of suffering remains
ubiquitous, even in self-consciously theoretical texts that profess a view
of the body as constructed as in arguments such as those of Butler and

of Adams and Cowie. See, for just one further example specifically from the writings on new reproductive technologies, Elizabeth Ettore, who argues that

> I want to make sure that the stories I tell reflect the lives of people I study. Arthur Frank (1991, 1995) has argued that there is a need for an ethics of the body, shaping a sociology of the body. He equates ethics with a social science that empathises with people's suffering. . . . So for me as a feminist sociologist interested in reproductive genetics, ethics means offering true reflections that are empathic as well as attentive to reproductive bodies. . . . Simply, women's bodies and their corporeal experiences are the starting point for any ethical evaluations. [Ettore, 2002, pp. 8, 132]

16. Issues and problems around the constitution of identities in terms of vulnerability to particular kinds of languages or stories are also extensively discussed in, for instance, Rose, 1984; Lesnik-Oberstein, 1994.
17. For further extensive analyses and critiques both of "identification" as a supposed part of the reading process, and as assuming a reader both inside and outside of a text, see Barker (1989), and Cocks (2004).

CHAPTER TWO

The wanting of a baby: desire, despair, hope, and regret

I have read the accounts of the wanting of a child in the previous chapter as developing ideas of nature, history, culture, and society to explain this wish. But these explanations themselves might be said to have been aimed, in turn, towards accounting for the feelings, emotions, and desires of individuals. Nature, history, society, and culture, I have argued, function as part of attempts to define individual selves that are seen to possess and express the wish for a child, suffer the anguish of infertility, or are involved with the use of reproductive technologies. Often these selves seem to exist underneath, above, next to, or despite the wider narratives that are mobilized to account for them. These texts, therefore, are implicated in wider considerations of the complex problems of explaining where and how identities are shaped. I suggested in the previous chapter that these difficult issues of the shaping of identity might be formulated in terms of the location of story: where stories of identity and the self are seen to be coming from. They may be conceptualized as imposed and external, as generated internally and autonomously, or as shifting between these locations. Further questions arise in terms of where external and imposed stories themselves are claimed to come from. Internal stories, too, even when positing a spontaneous, self-generating source, leave this question open. I have pointed towards these ideas as "stories themselves without a source". As I implied in the previous chapter, my point is not to see this lack of an ultimate source or origin as the central problem for these arguments that must be resolved somehow (as if a final origin could be found), but instead to understand better how the location, and locating, of stories, has many implications for the way the arguments themselves develop, and the conclusions that are reached through them. Furthermore, examining the way these accounts are argued also can help us to understand that many stories without a source are in the area of the taken-for-granted that form the assumptions on which a discussion rests. In finding ways to make these assumptions visible *as* assumptions, an analysis can move forwards to asking how these assumptions are formulated: what their specific claims and assertions are about and for.

The area that seems to "bridge" the external and the internal self-generated narratives might be loosely termed psychology. I do not mean this term here as a designation strictly of an academic discipline, but only in general terms as ideas of ways in which the location of stories of identity are seen to transmute from an externality to an internality or vice versa. Feelings, emotions, and ideas of consciousness, subconsciousness, or unconsciousness may occur in texts about the wanting of the child as ways of thinking both about the nature and operation of that desire. They are seen to be shaped by certain ideas of nature, society, history, and culture, or to shape them in turn. In this chapter, I move to examining more closely the definitions and explanations of the wanting of the child in terms of these more "psychological" claims.

Nancy Chodorow, in her book *The Reproduction of Mothering* (1978), offers a classic critique of both biological and certain psychological accounts of mothering. In terms of problems with certain psychologies, she writes:

> Role training, identification, and enforcement certainly have to do with the acquisition of an appropriate gender role. But the conventional feminist view, drawn from social or cognitive psychology, which understands feminine development as explicit ideological instruction or formal coercion, cannot in the case of mothering be sufficient. In addition, explanations relying on behavioural

conformity do not account for the tenacity of self-definition, self-concept, and psychological need to maintain aspects of traditional roles which continue even in the face of ideological shifts, counterinstruction, and the lessening of masculine coercion which the women's movement has produced. A second deficiency of role-learning and social control explanations for the reproduction of mothering is that they rely on individual intention—on the part of socializers, of girls who want to do girls-things or be like their mothers, and on the part of men who control women. . . . However, social reproduction comes to be independent of individual intention and is not caused by it. [Chodorow, 1978, pp. 33–34]

For Chodorow, the problem of extant accounts of mothering she discusses here is that they cannot, to her, explain the perceived prevalent persistence of women's definition of themselves as mothers, and as wishing or needing to be mothers in the face of increased opportunities for women and a lessening of pressures to conform to certain domestic roles. Neither can it explain the "quality" of motherhood:

behavioral conformity to the apparent specific physical requirements of infants . . . is not enough to enable physiological, let alone psychological, growth in an infant. . . . This is because parenting is not simply a set of behaviors, but participation in an interpersonal, diffuse, affective relationship. Parenting is an eminently psychological role in a way that many other roles and activities are not. . . . Given these requirements, it is evident that the mothering that women do is not something that can be taught simply by giving a girl dolls or telling her she ought to mother . . . men in particular or society at large . . . cannot require or force her to provide adequate parenting unless she, *to some degree* and *on some unconscious or conscious level*, has the capacity and sense of self as maternal to do so. [*ibid.*, p. 33, original emphasis]

Chodorow's formulations seem to me particularly relevant in the light of the way that many accounts of reproductive technologies continue to describe the women (and often the men, too) who make use of them as "desperate", "anguished", and "in despair". The having of a child is often explicitly located as within a "psychological" realm in the terms Chodorow uses: as the fulfilment of an internal need or desire beyond an external social instruction or expectation. Cooper and Glazer state of infertile couples that "[t]heirs is a centuries old anguish . . . probably best captured in the words of another biblical woman, Rachel, when she exclaimed, 'Give me children or I die'" (Cooper & Glazer, 1998, p. 14). As anthropologist Charis Cussins Thompson notes, "one of the contested naturalizations of infertility medicine in contemporary culture stems from the view of infertility as a major life crisis" (Thompson, 1998a, p. 97, n. 22).

Even in accounts that are not simply accepting of these assumptions around reproductive technologies, the wish for the child may recur as of a particular importance. Sarah Franklin, for instance, explains in a footnote in her book *Embodied Progress*, that she prefers to characterize women undergoing IVF as being "determined" rather than "desperate", not only because this is "a more flattering description", but also one that "correctly identifies her active desires in relation to treatment as opposed to an image of near pathological need" (Franklin, 1997, pp. 226–227, fn. 9). There must be a question around the qualification "correctly" here, for the text allows at least a possibility that (near) "pathological need" is employed as a definition or description in some cases or at some times.[1] Furthermore, this is Franklin's footnote to a section of her text in which the very idea under discussion is how "these women describe themselves as *not* 'desperate' initially, and as *becoming* 'desperate' *as a result of treatment*" (*ibid.*, pp. 182–183, original emphases). Her footnote seems to blur an argument that the women she spoke to do not describe themselves as "desperate" when they *begin* the IVF, into one defending them against them being "pathologized" at all while "undergoing" IVF, even when this seems to be exactly what the account of the women's own narrative is seen to endorse: that IVF produces a pathology or "desperation" in them.

Marilyn Strathern, in her collection of essays *Reproducing the Future*, writes that "[t]he child is literally—and in many cases, of course, joyfully—the embodiment of the act of choice" (Strathern, 1992, p. 34). Strathern's almost off-hand introjection that the child of IVF is "in many cases, of course, joyfully" chosen also alerts us to a special status of the wanting of the child. The "joyfully" seems to operate as a defensive measure, upholding, in the midst of the analyses of assisted reproductive techniques, a "core" of motivation, validity, and justification articulated as "natural" emotion (and emotion as the "natural"). Michelle Stanworth inserts a similar qualification in her article on "Reproductive technologies: tampering with nature?", when she argues that

> [t]o call "natural" the energy and commitment involved in achieving a wanted pregnancy, in carrying it safely to term and in creating a sense of relationship with the child-that-will-be, is to deny the very human investment that some women make in "my baby". [Stanworth, 1997, p. 487]

In the midst of this anti-naturalization argument we find the "investment that some women make in 'my baby'" defended as "very human". "My baby", apparently reinstated as an object with pathos, effectively *renaturalizes* the woman and her "energy and commitment" under the guise of the "very human". The human only replaces, rather than disrupts, the natural as the continuous story.

Dion Farquhar, in her extensive discussion of what she diagnoses as "liberal" and "fundamentalist" views of reproductive technologies, works hard neither to reject reproductive technologies outright as imposition ("fundamentalist") nor to claim them as simple salvation ("liberal"). Farquhar writes

> [j]ust as the desire for a child must be explained and is overdetermined given the weight of natalism and the limited nonreproductive options available to most women, the desire to reproduce "naturally" must also be explained. [Farquhar, 1996, p. 124]

Farquhar wishes here to avoid polarities she diagnoses as either maintaining the wish for the child as natural, or rejecting the wish for the child as an external imposition merely. She concludes that "reproduction is . . . a social and historical process with multiple variations, contestations, and ambiguous gains and losses for women, depending on their particular circumstances" (*ibid.*, p. 126). However, she writes surprisingly little about desires for the child, and it seems to me that "reproduction" here refers primarily to the having of children, chosen or not. The desire for the own child is, in her arguments, I would suggest, situated across the middle of her two polarities in that it must retain relevance and some specificity of meaning, or reproductive technologies could be dispensed with.

The few remarks that Farquhar does make outright about what the desire for the child might be about—rather than the having of children, chosen or unchosen—do not seem to me to clarify the matter further. In discussing critiques of commodification, for instance, she asserts that "[w]hat such accounts miss entirely is the *exhilaration* and productivity—of identities, pleasures, and options—that are inherent in commodification" (*ibid.*, p. 125, original emphasis). If I take the "exhilaration" to be about the wish to reproduce (which is here identified with "commodification"), then this seems to me a displacement from the "natural" (this is similar to my reading of Michelle Stanworth's "human". It is perhaps relevant in relation to this that Farquhar quotes Stanworth repeatedly and with approval), rather than a disruption of it.

Farquhar also argues that

> [f]eminist dismissals of women pursuing medical treatment for infertility are contemptuous of people who are already suffering from their involuntary childlessness and polices desire by making abstract principle more important than contextual empathy. Margarete Sandelowski's article is unique in the literature in responding to fundamentalist moralist excoriation of female ARTs clients on the grounds of the legitimacy of their desires and feelings. [Farquhar, 1996, p. 137]

This statement seeks to place the desire for the child as legitimate, or worthy of respect, regardless of its composition or causes, but it still does not situate the place of that desire in turn in terms of the issues around reproductive technologies. It addresses a different level of discussion in rejecting the unkindness of denying someone's pain because you think they ought not to feel it. Nevertheless, the allocation of one view to an "abstract principle" and another to "context" points to an inherent overall difficulty with Farquhar's argument. For Farquhar simultaneously positions herself as wanting to read everything as discourse, and as possible—and legitimate—meaning, and as rejecting positions as being a particular kind of discourse ("abstract principle"). Despite Farquhar's careful and close analysis of many of the assumptions underpinning resistance to, or the use of, reproductive technologies, it is not primarily her *analysis* that ultimately produces her own position, for this rests instead on a moral assertion. This is her concluding wish to find a "third appropriation" (*ibid.*, p. 179) in which ARTs "change and challenge the fetishizing of blood ties, the nuclear romance of reproduction, and their concomitant sexual identities" (*ibid.*, p. 191). That understandings of ARTs and the children and the wishes for them may be read to be multiple, diverse, and contingent themselves, as Farquhar states repeatedly, does not alter that even within—and necessarily within—her argument, ARTs are defined specifically in relation to an own child, and an own child in relation to ARTs. In hoping that her reading of ARTs will release reproduction from specifications and limitations, I would suggest, then, that Farquhar cannot, ironically, release it from *relationship*.[2] Indeed, Farquhar's discussion is produced through—in relation to—her reading of ARTs.

Farquhar's wish neither to condemn nor to claim ARTs as salvation ends up celebrating them nevertheless. It is exactly a *wish* (not an analysis). Arguing that multiple meanings can be, or are, made about and through ARTs cannot support a wish or ruling that they *must* be read *as* "multiple meaning". This (re)constitutes an alternate directive on reading, where directives have been claimed to be rejected. An invitation to read Farquhar's readings slides into an order to read as she does. "I read this way" becomes "read this way!" Farquhar's wishes and hopes finally do not, then, after all, lead to a recommendation for the recognition of *all* possible meanings, understandings, and uses ("appropriations") of ARTs (many of which she notes in her book), but instead for a particular way to read them in turn (a "third appropriation"). Or, to put it differently, she, too, moves from a "contextual empathy" to the "abstract principle" she has previously condemned, albeit in an ostensibly different context. ARTs are to be read as a positively valorized proliferation of reproductions. Proliferations of reproduction are to be seen as "exhilarating". Proliferations of reproductions are wished for in and of themselves and in this sense the wish for the child, I suggest, is part of this position, and is, as I argued earlier, situated across the gaps of the discourses Farquhar defines.

The wish for the child can be seen, then, to be bound up with a range of special or exceptional tenacities and depths of investment, commitment, or emotion. Chodorow suggests that a different kind of psychology, or a different understanding of psychology, is appropriate to account for a tenacity and quality of motherhood and the wish for motherhood.[3] For Chodorow, having defined motherhood in terms of not primarily a set of behaviours merely, but in terms of a desire and a state of being, the questions of what this desire and state of being are, and how they are produced or shaped, are central. In this way her core question may be said to be: "what is a 'wish'"? With Sarah Hrdy's work, for instance, as discussed in the previous chapter, an activity (the having of offspring) is simply somehow transformed, or transmitted, through evolution into a conscious wish for a child, and an accompanying ability also to choose not to have a child. By contrast, for Chodorow the voluntarity of, and commitment to, such a desire and a state of being are precisely what produces the question: why and how should women *want* to carry out this role, when they are no longer necessarily coerced into doing so? What is "wanting" or "wishing" in this context?

One component of these complex issues may be considered in relation to a problematic diagnosed by Eve Kosofsky Sedgwick in her "Epidemics of the will". Sedgwick argues in relation to a boom in the language of "addiction" that:

> so long as "free will" has been hypostatized and charged with ethical value, for just so long has an equally hypostatized "compulsion" had to be available as a counterstructure always internal to it, always requiring to be ejected from it. The scouring descriptive work of addiction attribution is propelled by the same imperative: its exacerbated perceptual acuteness in detecting the compulsion behind everyday voluntarity is driven, ever more blindly, by its own compulsion to isolate some new, receding but absolutized space of *pure* voluntarity. [Sedgwick, 1994, pp. 133–134]

Sedgwick sees this as

> the ugly twisting point of that in the present discursive constructions of consumer capitalism, the powers of our free will are always already vitiated by the "truth" of compulsion, while the powers attaching to an acknowledged compulsion are always already vitiated by the "truth" of our free will. [*ibid.*, pp. 141–142]

In Sedgwick's reading, then, a mutual implicatedness of free will and compulsion are considered. For Chodorow, the persistence of a desire and state-of-being *as* "voluntarity" in the face of a release from coercion needs to be accounted for in terms of its also, to her, precisely not being innate, inevitable, or necessary. In other words: how do women come to continue to desire that which they are no longer required, or assumed, to desire (if such is thought to be the case)? Sedgwick's formulation can be read as parallel to what I am calling the issues of internality and externality, or the location of story. Chodorow's questions are situated within this same area of consideration: she sees desire and state-of-being as neither "natural"—spontaneously internal—or fully external as implanted or coerced.

The introduction of ideas of a psychoanalytic unconscious is crucial here. In the first instance, in Chodorow's case, in terms of the analyses I have offered so far, this unconscious can be said to be introduced as an area of mediation of the internality and externality of the wish for the child, or the location of story. In parallel with my reading of the diverse locatings of the wish for the child in the works of the writers on reproductive technologies in the previous chapter, Chodorow argues that

> Both "cultural school" psychoanalysts and object-relations theorists have taken an alternate position emphasizing the importance of society and culture. Cultural school psychoanalysts ... oppose Freud's theory of the instinctual determination of development and neuroses with an argument for the importance of culture in determining mental life, personality, and development. ... The cultural school contribution is important, but is limited in fundamental ways. It borrows from anthropological culture and personality research an unanalyzed, holistic concept of culture, and a view that development consists in the direct internalization of the social and cultural world. ... [I]t substitutes a simple unidirectional cultural determinism, a model of direct transmission of social reality to psychic reality, and total isomorphism between these, for the complex internal operations and emotions psychoanalysis has described ... [where s]ocial experiences take on varied psychological meanings depending on the child's feelings of ease, helplessness, dependence, overwhelming love, conflict, and fear. ... Internalization is mediated by fantasy and by conflict. [Chodorow, 1978, pp. 46–47, 50]

Individuality, in this argument, is constituted as differing states of receptivity and interpretation of the external. Internality and externality can form and transform each other:

> [i]t may involve identification where the self or sense of self is
> modified, or may involve continuity of the same self or sense of self
> in relationship to a new or transformed object . . . inner worlds and
> intrapsychic conflicts are imposed upon and give meaning to exter-
> nal situations. [*ibid.*, p. 50]

It can be noted directly from these quotes, however, that notions
of externality and internality, or the location of story, are not so
much removed or dissolved as shifted. Rather than a "unidirec-
tional" internalization, the internal can shape an external, or an
external vary in its impact and shape upon being internalized.
Nevertheless, these are still externals and internals, albeit acted
upon. Similarly, the complexity Chodorow sees in and as internal
operations has to do with a splitting into various internalities and
externalities, rather than a dissolution of these categories. This
raises ongoing questions around, and has ongoing consequences in,
Chodorow's argument for how motherhood can be conceived of as
the voluntarily desired role that she perceives it to be.

This is pertinent to Chodorow's understanding specifically of
the psychological wish for the child. In the first place, mothering is,
in her work, overall still seen as a socially defined—and therefore
external—identity. It is a role Chodorow sees as exclusively
assigned to femininity, where her aim is to argue against the exclu-
sivity and specificity of this social assignation. The wish for the
child in the *Reproduction of Mothering* is therefore explicitly part of
discussing how the wish for mothering is seen as particularly a
female wish, whereas in the other works I have looked at so far, the
wish for the child may either be seen as that of "a couple" (usually,
but not always, heterosexual), or of a single parent (either male or
female, and often, but not always, homosexual). Even when the
wish of the parent concerned is considered as differentiated according to gender, this is, as with the overall arguments, subsumed
within the internal or external factors that are seen to constitute the
wish for the child (for instance as with ideas about normality as
applying differently according to gender). For Chodorow, the

> [c]onscious aspects of development—the barrage of oughts about
> having babies and being a good mother from television, toys, story-
> books, textbooks, magazines, schools, religion, laws . . . reinforce
> the less intended and unconscious development of orientations and

relational capacities that the psychoanalytic account of feminine development describes. [Chodorow, 1978, pp. 51–2]

The social, then, "reinforce[s]" issues "less intended" and "unconscious", whereby the "less intended" introduces a qualification of intentionality (presumably of the social or cultural) as a differentiation between the conscious/social and the unconscious it reinforces. Reinforcement simultaneously fulfils intention and is weakened in the unconscious. The "total isomorphism" attributed to the cultural psychoanalysts, like the externalities and internalities, is here therefore subject to qualification rather than to revision or dissolution, and this persists in Chodorow's further discussion.

In a sense, this qualification of what Chodorow has previously herself critiqued, rather than an entire revision, is inevitable in terms of her overall position. If mothering is seen from the outset as incorrectly or unnecessarily allocated exclusively to femininity, then this diagnosis includes a rejection of an innateness, at least as restricted to women. Therefore factors that are seen to be part of a determination of motherhood as feminine must also be demonstrated not to be innate or predetermined. If they are not internal, however, they are here located as external, and as an internalized external, however acted upon in this case. In fact, the necessity for this external to constitute a removable or changeable component is what supports in this argument the maintenance, after all, of a division between an externality and an internality, for if this division were not sustained, then the question of removability or gratuitousness might be seen to be under question (within the terms of this argument, at least). The limitations on revision are therefore built in by an initial acceptance of an external that must be removable or changeable. The tenacity or persistence of the forms of motherhood diagnosed by Chodorow is therefore nevertheless also limited within her position by the possibility of—*and wish for*—change. This can be related to Juliet Mitchell's critique of Chodorow:

Chodorow's subtitle to her first book . . . was *Psychoanalysis and the Sociology of Gender*. This is an accurate description, for here the Anglo-Saxon feminist meaning of "gender", as socially inscribed by learning and identification, both unconscious and conscious, is a term appropriate to a sociological use of Object Relations theory.

> A girl identifying with her mother who in turn identified with her mother is one important aspect of the transmission of gender roles. Such a realistically based identification is the basis of the proposition associated with these theorists, that if we had shared parenting there would be less gender differentiation. . . . The question not addressed by a reference to identificatory processes is: Why is something that is not realistically encountered—for instance, Freud's observation that a sense of guilt does not necessarily relate to an actual crime—nevertheless a transmitted, common and necessary experience? [Mitchell, 2000, p. xxiv]

What is at stake here is both ideas of an external as "realistic" and ideas of "identification". The "realistic" for Mitchell is not necessarily a causal factor for psychic experience, while she sees it as such for Chodorow: changes in the gender of child-caring individuals will change the gender-roles of the child in turn. Similarly, identification, as I discussed also in the previous chapter, involves a recognition of sameness, or oneself in another, while Mitchell raises the question of how that self (and that other) becomes established in the first place. Identification, therefore, can be either initiatory and causal, as in the case of Chodorow (it produces an identity), or it can be secondary, as with Mitchell, only possible after other processes of production of identity. As Mitchell argues further,

> In [Object Relations] . . . the focus is on fantasies, identification and behaviours, not symptoms. Unconscious processes are regarded as though they follow the same logic and appearance as consciousness. . . . Nancy Chodorow . . . used psychoanalytic Object Relations theory to explain sex/gender divisions as arising from processes of differential identification. . . . In Freud's concept there is an economic dimension, the human drive wants satisfaction and the release of tension—it is indifferent as to the object through which this is attained. Object Relations proposes that there is an urge towards a particular human object, such as the mother, or part thereof, such as the breast ("object" so called because it is the object of the child's drive). [Mitchell, 2000, pp. xxiii–xxiv]

Mitchell here sees, as I also do, the maintenance of an isomorphism rejected by Chodorow initially. Parveen Adams, too, in a critique of Chodorow that I am closely parallelling in my reading here, argues that "[for Chodorow] there is to be no isomorphism between social reality and psychical reality. However, this is not to say that ultimately she herself avoids the dangers"[4] (Adams, 1990a, p. 324). "Symptom", then, understood as something standing in for something else, related to it in some way, but not directly traceable to that "other", disrupts isomorphism for Mitchell and Adams in a way that Object Relations' reliance on "fantasies, identification and behaviours" cannot.[5] Furthermore, Mitchell sees Freud as postulating a "human drive" towards satisfaction that may require the involvement of an other, but not a specified other, even as "other". In other words, the satisfaction could also be achieved by the person by themselves, or by parts of themselves either experienced as self or other, or by the involvement of another person either experienced as self or other. In these terms, Mitchell is asking, how does the child come to know the object as object in the first place? Different definitions of "drive" here either engage a concept of directionality in terms of an outcome ("satisfaction"), regardless of how achieved, or the idea of a compulsion ("urge"), including an ability to locate and recognize an appropriate fulfiller of a need.

These issues arise in relation to the account specifically of the formation of the wish for the child in Chodorow. She writes:

> ... assumptions of the primacy of maleness distort the Freudian view of gender and female psychological life, especially by downplaying anything associated with motherhood and refusing to recognize that desires to be a mother can develop other than as a conversion of penis envy and a girl's desire to be masculine. The baby, Freud says, is to a woman a symbolic substitute for a penis, which she really wants more. Freud here is again not simply reporting empirical observation, nor discussing a possible psychical component of a wish for babies. He admits that there are other ways that women come to want babies but then makes it clear that any baby will not do, that a girl does not have a properly *feminine* wish for a baby until her femininity includes as a fundamental component the wish to be masculine. [Chodorow, 1978, p. 147]

For Chodorow, what matters here is that the wish for the child should not be part of "assumptions of the primacy of maleness", which presuppose that the wish for a baby is part of a striving to recapture a lost masculinity, but part of a just assessment of the centrality of the identification with the mother. This identification itself, however, is in turn seen by Chodorow as problematic, and to be disrupted by demonstrating that motherhood and gender can and should be unlinked. In these terms, the wish for the baby for Chodorow is diagnosed as passed on by identification with the mother, but to be disrupted in turn through that understanding.

This is where the isomorphism that Chodorow critiques earlier after all underpins her argument:

> Adolescent girls in our society tend to remain attached to their mothers and preoccupied with preoedipal and oedipal issues in relation to her even while becoming "heterosexual". These pre-occupations persist not for biological reasons, but because their mother is their primary caretaker. Her father has never presented himself to a girl with the same force as her mother. He is not present as much, and is not involved with his children in the same way. . . . he is not the same primary, internal object as her mother and therefore cannot, finally, counteract his daughter's primary identification with and attachment to her mother. Mothers, especially in isolated nuclear family settings without other major occupations, are also invested in their daughters, feel ambivalence toward them, and have difficulty in separating from them. [Chodorow, 1978, p. 140]

Reality here, as Mitchell points out, is that seen as instituted as a capitalist, gendered division of labour, which in turn is established as causal in terms of the reproduction of mothering. The proximity of the mother constitutes here a "force" for the child, and specifically the female child in terms of the reproduction of mothering. Identification here works as the recognition and transferral primarily of and as gender. It is this in which the child is seen to know itself always already as female, and at the same time to see its mother as that identity, and to link the two. Gender, in this sense, *is* force, in being the aspect that is identified, identified with, and transmitted willy-nilly. As Adams summarizes:

> Parenting capacities, then, are different in children of different sexes [for Chodorow] because given the nature of the masculinity of fathers and the femininity of mothers, identification processes are different for the two sexes. The girl's identification is predomi-nantly *parental*, based on a "real relationship" with the mother. This

determines what it is like to be womanlike. The boy's identification is predominantly a *gender-role* identification. [Adams, 1990a, p. 326, original emphases]

It is difficult to see how this provides the escape Chodorow initially claims to provide from cultural uni-directionality and an isomorphism assumed between social and psychic reality. This does, however, confirm how and why Chodorow's wish for change in gender roles and the assumptions around caring for children necessarily directs her view of the unconscious. Although she initially argues precisely that the unconscious is not isomorphic with the social, and that it transforms meanings in unpredictable ways, this unpredictability must be limited in so far that the production of gender as unconscious meaning must have a predictable enough outcome for Chodorow's hopes to become possibility. As Mitchell and Adams argue, this is how and why a "reality" in Chodorow's argument must remain a stable and predictable influence on the unconscious, to some extent at least, in order to affect the meanings and definitions of gender produced therein. The unconscious, therefore, is here a factor that guarantees a tenacity and quality of a socially defined role, but that nevertheless can also adapt as the social role adapts, in line with the way that social role adapts. Its content is, in this respect at least, that social role. It is because of this that Adams therefore also concludes,

paradoxically, it is what Chodorow retains of the psychical that makes it impossible for her to consider *social relations* in any but the most simplistic way. By conferring the status of unquestionable truth on some aspects of the parent's relation to the infant, she narrows the domain within which the social can have effects. [Adams, 1990a, p. 326, original emphasis]

In this sense, Chodorow may be said to share this aspect of her work with Dion Farquhar, in that, in both their cases, a specifically predictive impulse in their works—a wish for, and vision of, change—determines definitions and directions within their arguments.

It seems to me that Chodorow's own further arguments around the wish for the child struggle with these tensions in her position, for, increasingly, albeit uncomfortably and tentatively, Chodorow starts—in the face of her own repeated explicit rejections of ideas of determinacy, innateness, and the natural with respect to gender roles—to turn to biological accounts to confirm the primacy of femininity in opposition to what she reads as Freud's assumptions of the primacy of maleness:[6]

> Although we might dispute the extent to which feminine biology shapes psychic life without mediation of culture, it does seem plausible to look for drives towards pregnancy and lactation in femininity, rather than defining away anything which is not the result of blocked masculinity. Biologically, also, there is no justification for ascribing superiority or inferiority as a general feature of masculine or feminine genitalia or reproductive organs, though these organs have different capacities for particular functions (penetration, parturition, lactation). [Chodorow, 1978, p. 149]

Chodorow, apparently in her anxiety to negate claims of female inferiority, now contradicts her own initial rejection of biology in terms of a gendered innateness of mothering to re-establish it as a meaning after all available outside of a culture seen as imposing value-judgements or hierarchies on a value-free or neutral "biology". That innateness and a teleological determinacy are revalidated along the way appears to be of less relevance at this point, and a "plausibility" is inserted as generally and self-evidently recognizable. Furthermore, we are also, by this route, returned to the "drive" that we have encountered in earlier claims, which is itself not available for further analysis or explanation. It may also be noted in this context that Chodorow's bracketed terms may be understood as an effort to use appropriately biological terms, but that the allocations of differential functionality to organs as being to do with "penetration, parturition, and lactation" may themselves be read as neither necessarily self-evident, natural, biological, or "neutral", even if—or precisely because—underpinned by specifically the biological views of sex that Chodorow elsewhere repeatedly repudiates.[7]

In Chodorow we find, then, two main accounts of the wish for the child: her suggestion that the wish for the baby is part of the female child defining itself as female in terms of identifying itself with its mother, which in turn is the result of the mother's greater role in child-raising: "[w]omen mother daughters who, when they become women, mother" (Chodorow, 1978, p. 209). The second account is her reading of Freud as seeing the wish for the baby (at least in its most "feminine form") as a result of the wish for a penis. One aspect that can further be noted here is that Chodorow's theory therefore accepts the baby as something self-evidently continuous with, and appropriate to, a desire. In this sense, this idea of the baby is consistent with the acceptance of an object as known and know-able *as* object elsewhere in Chodorow's arguments. Drive and object are appropriate to, and continuous with, one another, and the drive "knows" its object. The object is, it may be said, inherent to the drive. This may, paradoxically, support a reading that the wish for the baby in Chodorow's discussion is about the wish of the daugh-ter to be a woman and mother as her mother was, rather than a wish *for* a baby. This baby—precisely in not being questioned and questionable further itself—is a means to attaining the identity of mother. That is its status and identity in this argument. In this sense, it can be said that Chodorow's account is indeed very precisely concerned with the reproduction of *mothering*, and only secondarily, as one component of that, with a (re)production of babies. In Chodorow's account of Freud's theory, the baby instead is not wanted as and in "itself", and is therefore also not accepted as the "natural" object or aim of this wish. Instead, the desire for a baby is the result of a desire for something else, which is knowable as itself: the penis. The wish for the baby is, here, not continuous with its object, while the wish for the penis is. Chodorow seems to rest on this acceptance of the penis in Freud as being a physical self-identical object when she writes that "[o]thers hypothesize physio-logical bases for the *wish for a child*—Kestenberg's vaginal sensations or Freud's symbolic penis–baby equation (when a girl cannot get a penis, she substitutes the wish for a child)" (Chodorow, 1978, pp. 88–89).

I will return shortly to considering in Freud the wish for the baby as a wish for the penis, but first want to examine further some psychological accounts of the wish for the child. As with the accounts of people using reproductive technologies by Gay Becker, Susan Cooper and Ellen Sarasohn, and Mary Lay and co-authors that I discussed in the previous chapter in terms of ideas of the social, the cultural, and the personal, I am here continuing to trace ways in which some assumptions about, and definitions of, "psychology" determine the development of arguments and their possible conclusions.

Juliet Miller defines herself as a "Jungian psychoanalyst" in a chapter "Mourning the never born and the loss of the angel", where she describes a therapy with a patient, Frances, with "unexplained infertility". For Miller, the wish for the child is a subset of "creative drives", which in turn are "part of the experience of being alive" (Miller, 2003, p. 47). She quotes Jung as seeing women who are unable to become pregnant as in

> a special kind of hell. For a woman there is no longer any way out; if she cannot have children, she falls into hellfire because all her creativeness turns back to herself, she begins to eat herself. [*ibid.*, p. 51]

Therefore, here, creativity is an aspect of a gendered antecedent self; in Jung's formulation, a force specific to the having of children, and it turns from an autonomous productive force into an autonomous consuming force if not used in this specific way. For Miller, aliveness or death are not therefore themselves primary either, but in turn are the result of either being in touch, or losing touch, with a "spiritual life":

> To be fully human it is necessary to acknowledge our connections to a spiritual life without believing that we are also angelic . . . The Angel has to be acknowledged but not embodied in our creative acts. To be touched by spirits is one of the ways we experience our humanity. What happens, however, if we feel cut off from this connection? If, through trauma, body and psyche are experienced as unrelated and as a result conception is identified as miraculous. To be infertile is to experience such a disturbance. [*ibid.*, p. 48]

The wish to have a child is part of a creativity that is inspired by "spirits", or, to put it differently, this creativity is a kind of inspiration leading to a full humanity. In this way, as with several of the writers I have considered previously, the wish for the child is formulated as not a wish in and of itself, but instead a wish as part of, or for, something else. In Miller's case, the creativity postulated is itself a source as well as being a possible achievement when retrieved from loss. Because the creativity can be lost and found it is not fundamental to that self which can possess, lose, or retrieve it, but within that self functions as an autonomous, *sui generis,* entity or force. It is a meaningful "spiritual life" that is the aim or achievement of the creativity as source.

Moreover, it is significant that this creativity and life are, in Miller's formulations, "experiences" or "experienced". Experience, as we have seen in other writings, may either be a spontaneous, autonomous source, or it may play a mediating function between ideas of the external and internal, or between various internalities. In Miller, experience works to release meaning to some extent from determinacy. Objects, acts, or emotions are modified by "experience", not necessarily in terms of a progression of time or a rite of passage, but in terms of how they are perceived and felt. In line with this, Miller's view of ARTs is that, on the one hand, they may help to make families possible where this would previously not have been the case, but, on the other hand, "To live within this medically vibrant age not only opens up new solutions to making babies but it can also become a defence against other forms of creative awareness and understanding" (*ibid.*, p. 51). It is the creativity that is linked to an idea of meaningful life that is primarily at stake for Miller, not the own child, an adopted child, or even necessarily a child at all. As she writes:

> The medical consultant and ART can be seen as the saviours and can be pursued at all costs. The fertile spirit then appears to reside with them and not with the couple. The hundreds of photographs of babies emblazoned on the walls of infertility consultants' offices appear as signs of the fertility of the consultant or his magical powers and offer up the hope of the infertile couple being included in this abundance. For the couple, sex and reproduction are separated from each other and conception fantasies may involve ideas of parthenogenesis rather than a creative male and female sexuality. Sometimes, to regain a sense of control, and a belief in their own powers, infertile couples who are going through infertility treatments will create their own rituals in an attempt to make conceptive meanings for themselves. [*ibid.*]

It is not ART as event, but the way that event is used and experienced, or interpreted—within certain parameters—by the couple that matters. The risk of ARTs is that the couple will relinquish a control and "belief in their own powers", which are in turn expressed through, or bound up in, "a creative male and female

sexuality". "Parthenogenesis" is not creative, but a result of a separation of sex and reproduction. Thus, creativity is flexible, found in
a range of modes of expression, but there are limits or particulari-
ties to its manifestation, too: a male and female sexuality is creative,
while parthenogenesis is not.

Also, the couple may perceive photographs as signs of the infertility consultant's "magical powers", which are not creativity, or at
least alternative to fertility as creativity, while body and psyche also
belong together, and are separated by "trauma". And "[i]f, through
trauma, body and psyche are experienced as unrelated . . . as a
result conception is identified as miraculous", where the miraculous, as with the magical powers, is not creativity (*ibid.*, p. 48). The
body and psyche are the premises for creative conception.

> Conception is one of the facts of our humanity which still holds
> mysteries for us. It inhabits a place between psyche and soma,
> somewhere between the Angel and the corporeal body. It is an
> issue both grounded in the physical world and yet rich with
> symbolic meanings; an area inhabited by gods and angels and yet
> made concrete by the conception and birth of human babies. . . .
> Our responses to birth and death may be one of the few ways we
> still allow ourselves to acknowledge that we are connected to a
> spiritual life. [*ibid.*, pp. 48–49]

These statements are outside the realm of experience or interpretation: birth and death, despite the range of expressions of creativity,
still have a privileged status as a "fact of humanity" that is nevertheless a "mystery", and which holds a status of a privileged "place
between" an existing "physical world" and a non-physical spiritual
life, and which is both "rich in symbolic meanings" but also "made
concrete". Conception and birth, perhaps understood as a certain
physicality, transform a spiritual realm of gods and angels into a
concreteness. In this way the mystery lies in the uncertainty of
precise location, but it is known nevertheless to be characterized by
being situated "somewhere" between a spiritual psyche in opposition to a "corporeal body".

Miller's schema of emotional functioning depends, then, on a
stable and known set of oppositions that are the innate structure of
an internal, mental, life, and, as a corollary of this, on a known and
gendered body. The oppositions include masculinity and femininity,

a spiritual realm that is bound up in an (here) appropriate heterosexuality of the gendered body, and creativity and destructiveness.
Beyond these stable factors, acts, events, and objects are experienced, and, being so, are assigned a shifting range of meanings,
albeit limited by the parameters of the factors outside of experience
or interpretation. The roles of the gendered body demonstrate these
vicissitudes of the known and experience.

> Conceiving and miscarrying, or suffering from blocked tubes, or
> ovarian failure, or any of the many medically recognized reasons
> for infertility, presents the patient with reasons for and realities of
> loss. There is a failure to conceive and this can be painful to accept
> and to mourn. But there is a loss which can be thought about and
> pictured in bodily terms. [*ibid.*, pp. 50–51]

The body "presents" "realities of loss": a knowledge that is determinate and fixed, and that can be "pictured in bodily terms". In a
tautologous sense, the known body supplies its own knowledge of
itself, and this stalls or stops loss by constituting it as real. The real
body presents real loss. On the other hand,

> For those who have unexplained infertility there is no loss but
> rather a void. No embryos however young, no damage however
> guilt-ridden can be focused on, there is simply a space into which
> a child cannot or will not come, and about which it seems that
> *nothing* can be known. [*ibid.*, p. 51, original emphasis]

The lack of explanation leads to a void, or a space about which
"nothing can be known". That "nothing" can, none the less, already
be read as a knowledge or experience as, and of, a void or space.

In other words, I can (and do) read void and space, and nothing, as in turn a knowledge or experience. This reading, in fact, is
itself directly confirmed when Miller, just a few lines later, quotes
Erik Erikson:

> "in female experience an 'inner space' is at the centre of despair
> even as it is at the very centre of potential fulfilment" . . . The womb
> is both a container for a healthy baby or a coffin for a dead one. It
> is an organ that is preparing itself for a child or emptying itself out
> because of the lack of one. . . . For a woman who has unexplained
> infertility, this active duality, in her conscious life, appears to be

absent. Her womb is neither a container or a coffin, simply an empty space. [*ibid.*, p. 53]

In the quotation from Erikson, femininity is, at least in this context, characterized by the experience of an "inner space", which is a space of potentiality, both for despair and fulfilment. I should note, by the way, that this can be linked to the many ideas of femininity as constituted by and as lack.[8] In the way that Miller reads Erikson, that inner space is identified as the womb, and is defined in relation to roles to do with (potential) pregnancy. In the woman with unexplained infertility, however, the womb is seen to be a space that is "simply empty", not a container filled with either a healthy or a dead baby, or even potentially a healthy or a dead baby. Moreover, "[t]his space not only separates the woman from her creativity but also from her destructiveness" (*ibid.*, p. 53). For Miller, this space constitutes a gap or broken link, in relation to which she quotes psychoanalyst Joan Raphael-Leff:

A connection may be helpfully reactivated if she does become pregnant: "Pregnancy, like all transitional phases, reawakens earlier unresolved conflicts and anxieties. The archaic clash between her inner imagined life-giving and death dealing forces is now relocated in the arena of birth, a test, culminating in proof of whether she is destructive or creative". [*ibid.*]

Raphael-Leff's oppositions of "life-dealing" and "death-dealing forces" seem at this point to be accepted by Miller as equal or closely related to her creativity and destructiveness. In any case, they are archaic and imagined inner forces, "relocated" to "the arena of birth". Birth is a clash and a test, which culminates in "proof of whether she is destructive or creative". Although it is not stated explicitly in Miller's discussion, this culmination seems to hinge on the birth of the (live) child, which then constitutes the proof of creativity over destructiveness. The pregnancy and birth therefore connect the forces in and through a battle for victory, where the baby is the required proof of the victory of creativity. In other words, feminine creativity is constructed as the giving of life (for classic considerations of ideas of a feminine creativity as "giving life" as opposed to a masculine creativity such as "writing", see, for instance, Sandra Gilbert and Susan Gubar, *The Madwoman in the Attic: The Woman Writer and the Nineteenth Century Literary Imagination* (1979), or the writings of literary critics such as Elaine Showalter, Luce Irigaray, or Helene Cixous): "an infertile state may confirm an earlier impotent state where there was either a lack of a struggle or a fear that destruction had won" *ibid.*, p. 54).

I am not trying to reject or avoid Miller's important point that explained and unexplained infertility may well be defined and, indeed, experienced, differently by people.[9] But, at the same time, I still want to examine how the assumption of certain stabilities of the body and knowledge seem to militate against, for instance, people with explained infertility equally perhaps experiencing *that* as a "void", or as a "space into which a child cannot or will not come". The idea that a medical narrative of the body constitutes a necessary thing-which-can-be-known may be put into question. Medical narratives may well, in many cases, be seen to be subordinated to, or rejected in favour of, after all, focusing on "embryos . . . damage [or] . . . guilt". In other words, the body need not be bounded or defined (only) by medical accounts.[10]

In Miller's schema of emotional functioning, a wish for a child is not itself originary or original, in that it is secondary to creativity, even if it is a privileged form of that creativity:

> Most infertile couples who seek treatment are not successful in producing a child. . . . Any suggestion that there might be other ways of looking at this deathly state to help warm it into life, apart from a birth, can be experienced as an additional unbearable wound. . . . Studies of infertile couples who attend infertility clinics are now beginning to acknowledge that protracted medical interventions can become anti-therapeutic and anti-healing. Acknowledging an infertile state as permanent can help a couple to adjust. . . . For some infertile women, for whom reproductive technologies have not turned out to be the answer, an acceptance of their failure to conceive may not release them but may keep them imprisoned in a state of permanent failure. In this prison there appears to be no escape, no space for psyche and soma to talk to each other and no possibility of other creations. [*ibid.*, p. 52]

The possibility of a discussion between "psyche and soma" and the "possibility of other creations" are seen as a way forward which ARTs may block if they are experienced as the only solution, the only route to the child, and only to the child, and therefore the ultimate unresolvable ending if unsuccessful in producing that child.

Miller, therefore, does not formulate a specific investment in an own child and a wish for an own child: on the one hand conception and birth are privileged expressions of creativity, but, on the other hand, adoption may also be such an expression. It is a process—experience—not a product in and of itself, which figures as primary in Miller's therapeutic narrative. A child, whether "own" or adopted is not necessarily either a solution or not, but can only be this if produced creatively. The process partly determines the product: definitions of the child shift in terms of the meaning they are assigned in relation to creativity:

> If acceptance of an inner world alive with creativity and destruction was never strongly established as a child then an infertile patient may feel confirmed in her inability to work through this void and in her own worthlessness as a result. . . . the desire to show that previous losses have not destroyed creative capacities can make procreation seem like an essential healing task. The desired baby may then become symbolic of the rebirth the woman wants for herself, and as a result it can be doubly painful if no baby arrives. Yet to experience a rebirth in this way, whether through the birth of a child or not, it seems that there has to have been enough concrete proof that there has been a good enough relationship both to and between the parents and that a creative union could have happened and therefore could now happen in the present relationship. [*ibid.*, p. 54]

The limits of the variance of meanings of the child, as we have seen previously in other writers, lies in repetition and the idea of the symbolic: both are predicated after all on a transcendent child who can be recognized either as repetition, or as non-symbolic. The repetition is a rebirth that is therefore not a precise repetition, as it is to include a retrieval of what-never-was as a "healing", or at least that was there only as "enough concrete proof" in order that the repetition knows what there is to aim for as a retrieval: the (potential) multiplicity of the experience of such a rebirth is again predicated on, or a consequence of, something outside the realm of experience, namely "concrete proof".

That child which is to be reborn as the woman who was and is that child, moreover, is a being that has to have "accepted" an "inner world alive with creativity and destruction", so that this being can either accept this, or become filled with a "void" to work through. The child that had to accept this inner world therefore knows if it is not strongly enough established, and that this constitutes a void to be addressed. She has a knowledge of what she does not have, and how potentially to obtain it, although she already knows, too, of the possibility of failure. In this way, a prior self is posited as in a process of becoming where it is both aware of its own lacks with reference to how this process ought to proceed, and how to address and heal these lacks, although this may also fail. Finally, a creativity under threat from loss attempts to defy this threat by acting out itself as the production of a baby. In this respect too, then, a production must figure as a repetition in order to defy or neutralize loss and both be able to modify a past in and as a future. In either case, the child is the repudiation of the present as the moment of lack.

It is, further, a split between a symbolic and a non-symbolic realm that negotiates the meanings or experience of the child and the wish for a child in Miller's text. There is a "real" child who, minimally, is constituted as a body, as an object, "externalised" (*ibid.*, p. 58), and there are children of the non-symbolic:

> For those parents whose child dies, the pain of loss may be warded against by attempting to replace the child rather than facing the unbearable feelings of guilt and pain. Attempting to replace the child before the mourning process has been completed is to confine the experience to the non-symbolic realm. This is similar to the infertile woman's desperate attempts in the IVF clinic to achieve a baby at all costs. But without the symbolic a psychological balance between destruction and creation cannot be rediscovered and the experience of the loss of the Angel is a trauma without hope of rebirth. The symbolic cannot be retrieved if the death cannot be mourned. . . . This loss of soul may be retrieved if the lack of procreativity can be mourned and space made for other creative possibilities and the arrival of the Angel. [*ibid.*]

To replace a dead child before mourning is completed confines the experience to the "non-symbolic realm", as if the child as object or body is eternal, identical, and replaceable, which, therefore, it must not be experienced to be in the symbolic realm. A replacement would be as if there had not been a loss: the loss of the child and the having of another child after mourning may therefore be part of an experience in the symbolic realm, and in this way the symbolic seems to mean something like a depth, multiplicity, or transformation of meaning as opposed to a concreteness of a literality of a non-symbolic. Experience remains the transformative medium, as perspective, meaning, interpretation, albeit within the limit of being, after all, rooted in a concreteness, or non-experience. A problem I read in Miller's type of work, therefore, is constituted by where and how definitions of the concrete (or the non-symbolic) and experience (or the symbolic) are drawn up, resting on assumptions of the known body, innate forces, and their inherent dynamics.

Joan Raphael-Leff, like Nancy Chodorow, links unconscious desire to an external "reality":

> *for those who grew up in nuclear families*, the reproductive act draws part of its emotional current from a childhood source, replete with the mystery of secret activities behind the parents' bedroom door. Reproduction is what children originally understood sex to be about—the archaic mother and father bringing their parts together to create a baby—themselves, or a sibling replacement. Once partners decide to have a baby . . . no longer excluded from procreative activity, they now *become* the copulating couple of origination. [Raphael-Leff, 2003, p. 36, first emphasis mine, second original]

In this account, the "nuclear family" is that which is already always there, at least for those who encounter it as their environment: the origin and the end, the thing that creates and is in turn aspired to be created, that which is "originally understood" as the origin of both the self and itself as the aspiration in turn of that self. The "copulating couple" is eternal, as the anguish of infertility in Cooper and Glazer is eternal, and it is a difference that is overcome by repetition as motherhood is in Chodorow: reproduction is reproduced in and of itself.

Raphael-Leff further wishes to expand on the ideas in relation to the wishes for the baby in Freud and Klein as she reads them:

> While Freud deemed the woman's desire for a baby as substituting for the coveted penis, Klein saw the desired penis as a means to an end of having a baby. However, clinical experience reveals that

unconscious motivation for childbearing is multifaceted far beyond the baby wish:

- cheating death of its finality
- emulating progenitors
- providing proof of undamaged fertility
- cultivating urges to repay old debts of generosity
- pressure to meet (or refute) internalised parental ascriptions
- becoming "fully" adult
- renegotiating incomplete developmental tasks
- articulating further maturational growth
- rewriting history by actively guiding the passively encountered
- vicariously recapturing lost aspects of the (baby) self
- conjuring up the partner's unknown childhood
- physically releasing pro-generative capacities
- fleshing out the longstanding unconscious fantasy baby
- and, in some cases, resolving incomplete childhood mourning.
  [*ibid.*, pp. 36–37]

Two related points may be made here. First, (almost) all of the aspects of a wish for childbearing that Raphael-Leff lists above can be said to be about *repetition*. Raphael-Leff therefore may be seen, on the one hand, to elaborate "motivations for childbearing . . . beyond the baby wish", but, on the other hand, these ideas can in turn be read as collapsing back into "the baby wish" itself in terms, second, of the baby *as* the repeated, or the figure of repetition, as in Miller's analysis, too. (I take this idea from an analysis made by Neil Cocks in his PhD thesis "Reading repetition and difference in the boy's school story", 2002.) This list of elaborations is, after all, an enumeration of babies past becoming babies future; past babies produce (the wish for) future babies and *as* the future baby. The present self is that which serves as a passage for the past baby to produce the future baby which is the past baby. The baby, then, is also eternal, as the wish for the baby is seen to be eternal in so many writings in this area. The child is, here, reproduction as the eternal, as the constant, as the repetition of the "real" and the "real" as repetition. (I am reading the "real" here in terms of Jean-Francois Lyotard's definition of it, in, for instance, *The Post-Modern Explained to Children. Correspondence 1982–1985*, 1992.)

Raphael-Leff concludes that

if, unconsciously, sexual intercourse often carries imaginary hermaphroditic completeness . . . conception promises its realisation. A melding of the partners' genetic material, in *actuality*, creating a real hybrid of male/female unification. [ibid., p. 37, original emphasis]

This formulation refers again to a return to an origin as a desired repetition, but also links this "unconscious" desire to another idea of an "actuality" or "real", despite Raphael-Leff's earlier assertion that "psychoanalysis has informed our understanding that sex is not merely a meeting of bodily parts or their insertion into the other but *flesh doing the bidding of fantasy*" (*ibid.*, p. 33, original emphasis). "Genetic material" here constitutes that actuality which both overcomes the male and female to create a "real hybrid", and which coincides with, or even "realizes", an unconscious wish for "imaginary hermaphroditic completeness". I find it difficult to understand which perspective Raphael-Leff is putting to work here: am I to understand that she is claiming a scientific account in genetics that sees reproduction as "creating a real hybrid" in terms of gender? If so, then is not every human a "hybrid" in this sense (composed of both "partners' genetic material"), reproducing further "hybrids"? How is the creation of the "real hybrid" also then an overcoming of a previous male–female origin? Or is this a way that fantasy conceives of genetics? Am I to conclude that both the separateness of male and female, and the overcoming of this separation through the hybrid, are fantasy and genetics-as-fantasy? And if this is the case, then what is the role of the "actuality" and the "real" of the hybrid?

This same question arises for me when Raphael-Leff discusses efforts at conception in terms of

however egalitarian a heterosexual couple has been, once sex is geared to producing a baby, they shift into a register of sexed factuality which may or may not include cross-sex identifications and envy of the other. He is the male—virile, impregnating . . . [s]he is quintessentially female, doing what only members of her sex can do. [*ibid.*, p. 38]

If "cross-sex identifications and envy" "may or may not" occur, "sexed *factuality*" at least guarantees here the maleness and femaleness within the couple, doing each what only the male and female can do. Fantasy here is, after all, limited in its power by the "factuality" of sex, and the sexedness of factuality; by the "flesh" which is maintained as the thing that exists for fantasy to control. This equivocation between an idea of a constructedness of gender and sexuality, also as unconscious processes, and an attachment after all to gender-as-flesh repeats itself when Raphael-Leff goes on to note that "under repeated impact of lovemaking geared to reproduction even a hitherto egalitarian couple often become sexually polarised" (*ibid.*, p. 39). Where this may seem to state that the couple were previously "egalitarian" in terms of not being "sexually polarised", it subsequently becomes clear that the notion of egalitarianism here has instead to do with ideas of a lack of coercion or confrontation between maleness and femaleness, rather than a lack of differentiation or "sexual polarity" between them:

> she might feel . . . helplessly and angrily dependent on her partner to fertilise her . . . [a] man who once delegated the trajectory of his ejaculate to seek its womb-home may now feel trapped or suctioned into the dangerous womb. [*ibid.*]

In Joan Raphael-Leff's psychology, then, fantasy and the unconscious are rooted in and limited by a real, which is in turn constituted by gender and genetics, as Chodorow's is by the social, or Miller's by the body and innate forces:

> the infertile person sees themselves as the end . . . of a genetic chain . . . feeling that those who have had children cannot possibly understand what it is like to be faced with genetic extinction . . . unable to fulfil the most fundamental requisite of the human race. [Raphael-Leff, 2003, p. 41]

As the equivocation over what is maintained as a real, and what is assigned to fantasy continues, it remains unclear what Raphael-Leff—in her accounts of her understanding of her patients, as well as in her overall discussion—considers to be meanings and narratives ("fantasy"), and what she assumes as an unquestionable and inevitable real ("flesh"). Finally, this unconscious cannot here keep step with the reality that feeds it:

> within the last few decades, eternal and seemingly immutable facts of life have changed dramatically *in reality*, blurring fact and fiction,

as science races ahead changing the story of origins faster than the unconscious can keep up. [*ibid.*, p. 44, original emphasis]

This, despite a claim just a few lines earlier that "[h]uman narratives reflect individual fantasy elaboration . . . often rebelling against the limitations imposed by generative identity" (*ibid.*). Rebellion here may challenge, but also confirms, those limitations that are "fact", even if now proved changeable to the point of fiction.

In my reading, then, both Chodorow and Raphael-Leff depend on an idea of an unconscious to account for transformations of, or deviations from, their external reality—with this deviation often also being called fantasy—as well as for a tenaciousness or importance of the wish for the child (or maternity/parenthood), which is linked to a definition of the wish or desire as voluntary and somehow internal. Despite this, however, I have read these definitions of the unconscious as nevertheless rooted in, and shaped by, the externalities as defined in their arguments. The child, too, is subsequently part of these external realities, as it remains coupled to the external shape of the desire for it, even if in this unconscious. In Miller's work, there is a shift to allocate the wish for the child to a wider, overall "creativity", which is *sui generis*, although also not primary to the self. The child there returns too as repetition, if not the only expression of creativity. I have therefore so far charted some vicissitudes of the wish through ideas of internality and externality, spontaneity and imposition, timelessness and contemporaneity. I have suggested that Chodorow and Raphael-Leff engage ideas of an unconscious, and I want now to turn to Freud, the primary theorist of the unconscious, to examine how the unconscious may be read there, as well as the child and the wish for the child. I also wish to return to Freud because it is remarkable to me that his theories are so little mentioned or considered in discussions around the wish for the child (also specifically in the context of reproductive technologies), especially when, as I stated in my introduction, there are so few detailed or extensive analyses available (or even thought to be necessary or possible) of this wish anyway.[11] As Germaine Greer concludes in an "Afterword" to the volume in which Raphael-Leff's chapter appears, "[t]here can be little consensus on just why people want to have children because the evidence is both contradictory and impressionistic" (Greer, 2003, p. 207).

We have seen that both Chodorow and Raphael-Leff refer to Freud's famous formulation, that "in girls what is an entirely unfeminine wish to possess a penis is normally transformed into a wish for a baby" (Freud, 1964, p. 101). Chodorow repudiates this idea as a denigration of women and an inadequate and implausible account of femininity, while Raphael-Leff suggests that it only provides one possible explanation (with Klein's reversal as an alternate), and that there are several other reasons people bear children. Furthermore, Chodorow assigns the penis to the realm of the "physiological". The first point that I therefore wish to suggest, is that, in my reading, Freud does not define the penis, or the wish for the penis in terms of the wish for the baby, as being about a physiological given.[12] Instead, the penis is something which must attain its "affective cathexis" (its importance of/or meaning) in turn from an "ancient interest in faeces" (Freud, 1933a, p. 100). What is crucial here is that the idea of a "wish" or "desire" is here constituted in a different way than in any of the arguments I have discussed until now. Where the wish or desire (for the baby) was in previous arguments either internal or external, or somewhat external and somewhat internal, but in any case *a priori fully formed* externally or internally, here the wish and the baby are that which must be created, and which is not (therefore) self-identical, or entire in and of itself. Instead, the wish and the baby are assemblages, dispersals, or displacements, in line with an unconscious that can only be interpreted back from dispersed, displaced, or assembled ("condensed") meanings. This is what Mitchell refers to when she distinguishes between Chodorow's unconscious and Freud's unconscious in terms of arguing that "[i]n [Object Relations] . . . the focus is on fantasies, identification and behaviours, not symptoms" (Mitchell, 2000, p. xxii).

To be clear, this wish-which-is-not-one is different from, for instance, Becker's view that the wish for the child is about "normalcy" (something else than the baby as such): this is about the way these wishes can be conceived of as composed of a range of *conscious* strivings and expectations (these are all formulations that Becker hears from her interviewees, and that she presents as their accounts and motivations). Similarly, Freud's wish is different from Joan Raphael-Leff's listing of other reasons "beyond the baby wish" that people give for bearing children. Not only did I read those reasons as largely collapsing back into an eternal child, but the reasons are (therefore) also not about an (unconscious) *formation* of the wish for the baby, but outcomes in turn of those formations (and not all necessarily unconscious in Freud's terms). In short: there is a difference here between proposing a plurality of wishes, and seeing the wish or desire as divided-in-itself. As an aside: we could read a confusion of this kind between conscious and unconscious (albeit probably in the service of an acerbic irony) in turn in a comment in Greer's "Afterword", when she writes dryly that '[t]he reasons suggested in this book for desperately desiring a child, such as "cheating death of its finality" . . . are not reasons at all" (Greer, 2003, p. 207).

For Freud, then, the penis is not a thing, but a meaning (or, to put it differently, an object or body is not a speaker of its own meaning in Freud). A meaning, moreover, transferred from elsewhere—the faeces—"for faeces were the first gift that an infant could make, something he could part with out of love for whoever was looking after him" (Freud, 1933a, p. 100). The infant assembles and extrapolates its self from an initial everything, and continues to refine ideas about a "self" and an "other", whereby these do not ever settle into entirely stable categories. Body parts may either be seen to be, or feared to be, detachable. Here, a gift is a voluntary detachment (I am influenced also in this reading by the classic analysis by Marcel Mauss, *The Gift. The Form and Reason for Exchange in Archaic Societies*, 1950), and the faeces are the first such. Furthermore,

> It is a universal conviction among children, who long retain the cloaca theory, that babies are born from the bowel like a piece of faeces: defecation is the model of the act of birth. But the penis too has its forerunner in the column of faeces which fills and stimulates the mucous membrane of the bowel. When a child, unwillingly enough, comes to realize that there are human creatures who do not possess a penis, that organ appears to him as something detachable from the body and becomes unmistakably analogous to the excrement, which was the first piece of bodily material that had to be renounced. A great part of anal erotism is thus carried over into a cathexis of the penis. But the interest in that part of the body has, in addition to its anal–erotic root, an oral one which is perhaps more powerful still: for when sucking has come to an end, the penis also becomes heir of the mother's nipple. [Freud, 1933a, pp. 100–101]

Cathexis thus moves around, transferring in the developmental process as Freud theorizes it from a fundamental basis of oral and anal erotism to later genital erotism: "[t]he genitals are the latest of these 'erotogenic' zones" [*ibid.*, p. 98). In this sense, the body and sense of self are assembled from the primary "building blocks" of oral and anal erotism and the pleasure-principle, which for Freud are the first sites of development of stimulation, due to feeding and defecation. This theory of development therefore radically disrupts ideas of the self-present body and conscious sexuality as a *sui generis* set of impulses, instincts, or drives. Instead these are all secondary formations, deriving their meaning and affect from (unconscious) primary stages.

The wish for the child and the child are here not a desire for an object, but composed of, and derived from, ideas about the detachable and the non-detachable, the self and the other. In this way too, this theory of processes disrupts divisions of externality and internality of the kind I have been reading previously, by positing bodies not as containers of an interiority located within an exteriority of non- or other-body objects, but instead as divided-within, where, one might say, various "internalities" interact with one another, as well as with what is differently conceived of in a variety of ways as an "external real". Ideas of internality and externality are continually created and recreated, as well as shifting within themselves. As has been often pointed out, but less frequently followed through in terms of its consequences in my view, Freud's idea of the unconscious therefore disrupts identity and the self as coherent, continuous, and singular units. There is, then, in this reading of Freud, no wish for the child in and of itself, and no child to be wished for in and of itself. The child and the wish for it are conscious end-results of unconscious processes. As Juliet Mitchell writes,

> There is a further concept that must be integrated into this theory of desire; this is the notion of the lack of an object which in itself provides the very genesis of desire. At every level the relationship between the mother and child is mediated by an absence or lack. . . . In its [whatever is needed by the child] absence, need changes to demand (articulation), and if unsatisfied or unreciprocated, to desire. [Mitchell, 2000, p. 396]

There are two reasons that I have explored this position: first, this understanding of desire and the child as not self-present and self-identical allows me to read other texts in the way that I have, and will continue to do, here. It allows me to ask questions about how the child and the desire for it occur in other texts because it does not assume that they are self-evident, and therefore must have a self-evident meaning. As I have said earlier, I hope that this questioning helps to open ways of thinking for those involved, in whatever way, with reproductive technologies. This opening is achieved by demonstrating that what seems determinate—even within texts that do also address extensively issues around choices in and around reproductive technologies—can be read as not determinate, or inevitable. In other words, *further questioning is seen to be possible.* And this, in turn, may offer outcomes or decisions of different kinds than might have seemed initially appropriate or related. Second, it seems to me, following also my analysis of positions such as those of Chodorow, Miller, and Raphael-Leff, that it is still only Freud's account of the unconscious and its role in the desire for a child and the child itself that for me provide a way of thinking about these issues that reinstate neither an external or social—which we might say here falls together with the conscious—as determinate of these desires and that object, nor some spontaneous "biological" internal; an external, moreover, which must come from "nowhere", has no origin, but functions as pure imposition or cause in relation to an individual which is not ever (fully) part of it.

To be clear, then: it is not my aim in this book, having confirmed a reliance on this reading of Freud, now to continue by somehow speculating on the unconscious motivations of participants in reproductive technologies, or to base further discussion on assumptions of some Freudian "content", such as the specific ideas of femininity, or the connection faeces–penis–baby. This would merely constitute a lax, popular version of Freudianism that assumes this unconscious can be divined and controlled. Instead, I will continue, in the way I have done up until now, to question the ways in which I read texts as constructing the child and the wish for the child in relation to each other. This "Freudian reading" is, therefore, of the kind that Shoshana Felman, for instance, proposes when she writes (in her case in relation specifically to literature) that

> ... the traditional method of *application* of psychoanalysis to [textual analysis] would here be in principle ruled out. The notion

of *application* would be replaced by the radically different notion of *implication*: bringing analytical questions to bear upon [textual] questions, *involving* psychoanalysis in the scene of [textual] analysis, the interpreter's role would here be, not to *apply* to the text an acquired science, a preconceived knowledge, but to act as a go-between, to *generate implications* between [text] and psychoanalysis—to explore, bring to light and articulate the various (indirect) ways in which the two domains do indeed *implicate each other*, each one finding itself enlightened, informed, but also affected, displaced, by the other. [Felman, 1977, pp. 8–9, original emphasis]

Having thus considered various ways in which the wish or desire for the child may be read, I will now turn in the next chapter to considering further the ideas of the child that reproductive technologies are to deliver.

Notes

1. It should be noted that Franklin is elsewhere scrupulous in her disclaimers of any straightforwardness of generalizing representation, for instance when she warns that "[e]thnically, the interview pool was not representative of the wider IVF consumers . . ." (Franklin, 1997, p. 81).
2. In this context, I find it helpful to note that psychoanalyst and developmental psychologist Daniel Stern writes of defining relationship that it is "among other things, the remembered history of previous interactions (Hinde, 1979). It is also determined by how an interaction is perceived and interpreted through the many lenses particular to the participant of the interaction" (Stern, 1995, p. 12).
3. That the search for a different kind of psychology to account for a perceived tenacity and quality of motherhood is by no means over is demonstrated by more recent publications of books such as Daphne de Marneffe's *Maternal Desire. On Children, Love, and the Inner Life* (2004). De Marneffe, however, simply accepts an innate, female experience of birth and lactation as proposed by Karen Horney (a view which is both critiqued and accepted by Nancy Chodorow—see my discussion above pp. 40–55) as the reason to want to have a child, and then directs the rest of her discussion to considering why mothers want to care for (be with) their children.

4. As indicated, my readings of *The Reproduction of Mothering* are closely influenced by both Juliet Mitchell's and Parveen Adams's critiques, as well as the closely similar ones by Jacqueline Rose in her *Sexuality in the Field of Vision*, 1986. It may be noted that in other respects, however, Adams and Rose offer a critique of Mitchell's overall theoretical position, where Adams argues that "the theory of ideology Juliet Mitchell sets up itself demands an explanation of the opposition men and women, and psychoanalysis is employed to reproduce precisely these divisions" (see Adams, 1990b, p. 104).

5. For one specific discussion by Freud, which helpfully illuminates this understanding of the "symptom" through a parallel consideration of the definition of the "symbol", see Freud, 1916–1917.

6. I will turn to my own reading of Freud's writings on the wish for the child later. At this point I wish only to refer to Chodorow's (and others') readings of Freud, without assuming that these necessarily coincide with other interpretations of Freud's writings, including my own.

7. There are many further, often (inadvertently?) amusing, examples of how a supposedly neutral language of biology simultaneously contradicts or negates its own neutrality. One of these—also pertinent to the discussions around Freud in this chapter, by the way—is when the well-known geneticist Steve Jones manages to assert that "Freud's antique notion of women as diminished men is quite wrong. Biology reveals instead every man's battle to escape the woman within" (Jones, 2003, p. 62)!

8. I am noting this neither approvingly nor disapprovingly in this context, but merely to acknowledge the extant breadth and range of discussion in relation to this kind of idea. See, for one of the classic considerations of the issues and disputes in this area, Juliet Mitchell, *Psychoanalysis and Feminism* (1974).

9. Indeed, I note that Miller scrupulously qualifies many of her statements as being possibilities, or being the case for certain specific cases, but I remain interested in *how* her (and all, including my own) narrative is none the less determined by particular ideas of the concrete and experience, and the consequences of this.

10. Anthropologist Jeanette Edwards, for instance, writes that a woman whom she interviewed about ARTs gave the following account of her own pregnancies and miscarriages.

> In fact every one I've lost were boys. I can't equate that with anything at all. I mean they always say it's the father who sort

of makes the gender of the child. You know, it's the father who determines what gender it is, but I don't know whether that is true or not.

Edwards comments on this that

Mrs Bates was told that the reason she had so many problems was that she had a "tilted and twisted womb", but she clearly thinks it no coincidence that the one foetus which did survive was a girl. . . . Responsibility for so many miscarriages and stillbirths is, thus, spread beyond her own body and its short-comings. [Edwards, 2004, p. 760]

11. In some cases there are methodological reasons why Freud is not included in such discussions, such as in the work of critical anthropologists who are not attempting interpretations of possible unconscious motivations, but Freud is also rarely mentioned in writing which does express an interest in understanding or analysing overall why people might want children.

12. Juliet Mitchell, for instance, also discusses the whole issue of the role of the penis, penis-envy, and the wish for the baby, in her classic defence of Freud, *Psychoanalysis and Feminism* (1974), but does so primarily to elaborate her view that several feminist critics of Freud are most of all involved with resisting Freud's ideas of the unconscious. My reading here is indebted to Mitchell's and overlaps with her readings, as well as with the explanations and considerations of other writers on psychoanalysis, but I wish to concentrate here further on the details of Freud's ideas of the wish for the child specifically, for the purposes of this discussion.

CHAPTER THREE

The child that is wanted: perfection and commodification

"But what exactly is a wanted child?"

(Taylor & Taylor, 2003, p. 11)

W e have seen in the previous chapters that the development and deployment of reproductive technologies are motivated by people's postulated desire to have a child. We have considered some instances of how this desire is defined and formulated, and how the varying understandings of this desire direct and shape wider arguments about reproductive technologies. In the previous chapters, I have also started to argue that, and how, the desire for the child and the child that is desired are mutually implicated categories. I proposed that both these ideas can be examined further by not assuming that they are self-evident, autonomous entities. In this chapter, I want to consider further how the discussions around reproductive technologies produce childhood and the child. What children are produced by reproductive technologies, or what children are they supposed (in both senses of the word) to produce?

As I have remarked throughout, one of the curious issues around reproductive technologies is that its ostensibly desired product, the child, is little mentioned. In many ways, it is even less considered than the desire for the child, which is at least seen to be implicated in the choices available around reproductive technologies. The child of reproductive technologies is most of all referred to as the "hoped-for" child. In this way, the child is postulated in relation to ideas of temporality, as potentiality and futurity (see for an extensive consideration of the child as futurity, Edelman, 2004). This positions it as an anticipation, projection, or hallucination. It is there, and yet not there. It is both known and unknown. Because reproductive technologies enter into the area of a problematic production of the child, or, one might say, what is seen as a deferred production of the child, issues that arise in relation to any ideas of expectation are brought to the fore. This can also be seen in Charis Cussins Thompson, for instance, describing the embryo as *constitutively promissory*, and its value stems from its life-creating potential" (Thompson, 2005, p. 255, original emphasis). Expectation and hope engage both the known and the unknown, or, to put it somewhat differently, ideas of the knowable and the unknowable. As French theorist Louis Althusser writes:

> That an individual is always-already a subject, even before he is born, is nevertheless the plain reality, accessible to everyone and not a paradox at all. Freud shows that individuals are always "abstract" with respect to the subjects they always-already are, simply by noting the ideological ritual that surrounds the expectation of a "birth", that "happy event". Everyone knows how much and in what way an unborn child is expected. Which amounts to saying, very prosaically, if we agree to drop the "sentiments", i.e. the forms of family ideology (paternal/maternal/conjugal/fraternal) in which the unborn child is expected: it is certain in advance that it will bear its Father's Name, and will therefore have an identity and be irreplaceable. Before its birth, the child is therefore always-already a subject, appointed as a subject in and by the specific familial ideological configuration in which it is "expected" once it has been conceived. [Althusser, 1971, p. 176]

We saw something also of this already in my reading, in the previous chapter, of Joan Raphael-Leff's list of "other" reasons to have a child in terms of an eternal, timeless baby. In this sense, the issues we will be considering here, as in prior chapters, can also be turned back upon the question of the child in general.

When the child is involved in considerations around reproduction, it is largely in relation to two issues: disability and the search for the "perfect" child (or "designer baby"), and, closely related to this, ideas of the child as "commodity". In terms of the hoped-for child, these aspects are invoked to define and outline that child-to-be in advance, and yet therefore by definition in turn define a child of the past, from whom the future child is drawn. In so far as I am arguing that every identity is variable and various, it is also the reading of any identity *as* an identity that, willy-nilly, transcends temporality. (There are, of course, a range of philosophies which consider the problems of identity and repetition as simultaneously the same and not-the-same. I am drawing here on several such considerations, but a useful discussion is presented by Martin Heidegger's *Identiteit en Differentie/Identität und Differenz*, 1957.) It is in this sense an insuperable paradox: that assuming the child as changeable and variable at the same time still produces ideas of childhood as a transcendent category. Where claims are made for the individuality of the child, these are always still constrained by outer limits of understandings of the child *as* child. Childhood, then, encompasses all possible variation in, or individuality of, the child. The very category itself, however, and its boundaries, are in turn also variable and subject to interpretation and redefinition.

The complex implications of working from this position can be seen, for instance, where Claudia Castañeda suggests in her writing on the child that

> In using the terms "child" and "adult", I do not mean to imply that there are no differences between adults or between children, nor that all adults hold privileged positions in relation to all children. What I am trying to describe here, instead, is that relation of privilege that can and does obtain between some children and some adults, and in so far as this relation is constituted in and for theory as an "adult" domain. So, too, the general term "child" does not in itself suggest differences of race, class, gender, sexuality or historical and cultural location. ... Where the child appears in a more differentiated manner in a theoretical formulation, I use the term given ... However, my analysis suggests that such differentiation

> does not solve the problems I identify with regard to the child's use
> as a theoretical resource. In other words, a particular differentia-
> tion, such as gender, does not in itself necessarily undercut the
> child's invocation *as* a resource. [Castañeda, 2001, p. 51, n. 2 and 3]

(See Chapter Five for some further discussion of theoretical issues
in Castañeda's extended examination of the child in her book
Figurations. Child, Bodies, Worlds, 2002.)

Castañeda is here negotiating scrupulously the difficulties of
generalization, but not, in fact, the theoretical problems of identity
that I am arguing above. For, in her statement, Castañeda relies on
two aspects to establish her view of the definition of identity: qualification and an implicit split between "theory", or the theoretical,
and non-theory, or the non-theoretical. It is possible for her to state
that she does not mean to imply that "*all* adults hold privileged
positions in relation to *all* children" (my emphases), and that this is
instead the case with only "some". Likewise, her "differentiated"
child is still identifiable above all *as* child to her, even as Castañeda
herself diagnoses the way that such a child is invoked as a "theoretical resource". I would argue, instead, that, in so far as a holder
of privilege does so in terms of being adult, they then hold that
privilege over the child *inevitably,* as adulthood and childhood are
mutually defined from the adult position as a position of hierarchy
with the adult as dominant. If this is not the case, then they are not,
at that point, an adult and a child. We can see an example of this in
Valerie Walkerdine's analysis, in *Schoolgirl Fictions* (1990), of some
very young boys who call their woman teacher sexist names.
Walkerdine reads this as a gendered relationship, where as males
they perform a dominance over the female, regardless of age. In
other ways, the boys also are children, for instance with respect to
their ultimate containment within the space of the school, and the
teacher's authorization to exercise other forms of control over them.
In this sense, there is, in this argument, no "theoretical" and "non-
theoretical" adult or child, but a production of identity within a
given context that does not cleave to a "body". (See, for an extensive discussion of the, in my view, misreadings in children's literature criticism of Jacqueline Rose's arguments around the child in
The Case of Peter Pan or: The Impossibility of Children's Fiction (1984),
my article "The psychopathology of everyday children's literature

criticism", 2000.) An adult, or a child, is not always an adult or a child, in this way. As Parveen Adams writes (in this case in relation to gender):

> Thus there is a difference between analyses that explain the persistence of representations in terms of a general structure of the subject and its conditions and analyses that emphasize the importance of definite practices and their conditions. Is it not the case that in operating with unified entities we are kept busy explaining unities while the effects of practices of representation are *not*, in fact, unified? . . . It is only by examining the workings of particular practices that it can be shown that the concept of subject is inadequate to them. [Adams, 1990b, p. 108]

This is how the child—or any reading—is intimately enmeshed in the questions of re/production. Re/production relies on the possibility of repetition that is in turn only guaranteed by a return of the same, and the child is called on as one of these guarantees. And yet it cannot be that guarantee, in so far as, regardless of such claims made, nothing can be that guarantee, in terms of the position I am following here. As Jacqueline Rose writes: " '[r]epetition' . . . because of what it implies by way of something uncertain which therefore has to be constantly re-enacted" (Rose, 1984, p. 141). We will continue to see the implications and consequences of this argument as I follow my analyses.

Polemics concerning the child as "commodity" include wellknown books such as Naomi Wolf's *Misconceptions* (2001), or Germaine Greer's "Afterword" to Jane Haynes and Juliet Miller's *Inconceivable Conceptions* (2003). (For an interesting discussion specifically on the embryo and commodification, related to my further examination of the child and commodification here, see Thompson, 2005.) The concern of arguments such as those of Wolf and Greer is that the child be viewed as something more or other than a commodity. Wolf writes, for instance,

> . . . I couldn't help but wonder why we could not see babies for themselves, rather than seeing them as extensions of ourselves, our lifestyle preferences, our heritages, our fantasies. I became scared by what appeared to be a distorted value system in which fetuses and newborns were mere commodities. And if they were commodities, who "owned" them? [Wolf, 2001, p. 54]

The commodity, and commodity-ownership, here is a diminish-ment of babies, who should be seen for "themselves". This way of being seen is contrasted with being considered as "extensions . . . lifestyle preferences, our heritages, our fantasies", but at the same time is the result of Wolf claiming a double vision, both of how babies are seen, and how they should be seen. Babies are consti-tuted in the present as "extensions of ourselves", but are already also knowable as "themselves", apart from "ourselves", even if this is also projected as a vision of the future. Wolf continues:

> I started to see eggs, fetuses, and babies as little coins, little chits used in a modern currency system; they had the meaning and value we assigned to them. Healthy or unhealthy? Mother's or father's? White or black? Related to you or unrelated? The baby's value seemed to shift, to rise or fall accordingly. The economy was based on what adults longed for and needed. But what about the babies, I thought. What about what they needed? . . . What is lost in a market economy of "best" and "seconds", in a society where babies are a form of currency, is the central paradox of true parenthood, which should be defined as our absolute commitment to a creature of whom we can claim no rights of possession. Is there any other relationship in which we have to love not for ourselves or the return on our investment, but for love's own sake? [Wolf, 2001, pp. 55–56]

There is a temporal reversal here. Where the child previously needed to be divested of a commodity status it already had, here it is introduced into that commodity economy. What can be noted, then, is that the child and parenthood are consistently defined as inappropriate to "a modern currency system", but also therefore defined in relation to, or as already part of, this system. The babies are part of a "value system", but it is "distorted" in terms of seeing them merely as commodities. Wolf can "start to see" babies "as little coins, little chits", where the diminutive seems to merge, by quali-fying jointly, money and babies. Nevertheless, this is what the babies are not to be, although they can be seen as such. Babies are not the coins of a modern currency system, because "value" is something "we assigned", but inappropriately. The assignment is done by "we" adults, in terms of our longings and needs. But babies have their own needs, are not to be owned by their parents as money is owned, and ought to be loved "for love's own sake". Thomas Murray, in his discussion of new reproductive technologies from the perspective of moral philosophy, agrees with this when he concludes that

> We recognize that thinking of children as property . . . is a grievous distortion. . . . Economic analysis may help us to understand how families interact with the larger world of markets. But it remains a fiction, not an insightful description of how families function or, more important, why people live in families. . . . [T]here is [a] . . . sense in which having children is profoundly liberating. The kind of liberation I have in mind is not the liberty of the marketplace. It is, rather, the sort that comes from knowing what genuinely matters, what carries real meaning into my life. . . . A market in gametes . . . is a threat for us humans who need affection, trust, and, above all, intimate and enduring relationships in order to flourish. [Murray, 1996, pp. 19, 20, 33]

As Sara Thornton notes of such views, "the child is seen as a sacred object, outside of the market . . ." (Thornton, 1998, p. 131),[1] and Viviana Zelizer suggests that

> [after] the nineteenth century, the new normative ideal of the child as an exclusively emotional and affective asset precluded instrumental and fiscal considerations. . . . The economic and sentimental value of children were thereby declared to be radically incompatible. [Zelizer, 1985, p. 11]

Rachel Bowlby, in her discussion of reproductive technologies, childhood, and consumerism in *Shopping with Freud*, further argues that

> What is interesting . . . is that the attribution of consumerly qualities, unlike the attribution of a language of individual choice, is assumed to be automatically damning. . . . This also . . . has the effect of implicitly separating the choice to have children into two classes, the pure and the impure. If some people want babies the way they want cars, then somewhere else there are genuine parents-to-be, whose desires, whether rational or natural, remain untainted. In neither case, the genuine or the consumerly, is the wish taken as requiring any further analysis. [Bowlby, 1993, p. 90]

Although it may be clear, then, what Wolf (and many other similar writers) is pleading for on one level, the difficulty is to know exactly what this means, and how such recommendations are to be implemented. For Wolf's baby, on the one hand seen by Wolf from her perspectives, is for her ultimately self-constituted, apart from adult definition or interpretation. It can be known as itself, in terms of itself, and—and *although*—these terms are in relation to, and part of, the terms of a certain contemporary money economy. The baby, then, declares itself as not a commodity, not merely to be owned or valued in monetary and property terms. This positions Wolf as a privileged viewer of the baby's selfhood, a privileged reader of that which, on the other hand, is self-declared by the baby. As such, babies are no longer owned and interpreted by Wolf, but can be seen by her through an unmediated, direct vision. This is "true" parenthood, but it is also a parenthood to which so many are blind that Wolf must instruct others into it. Wolf is both part of the "we", and outside of it. Like Gay Becker in the first chapter of this book, Wolf begins by also not being able to see the baby for itself, and becomes able to do so through her personal journey of conception, delivery, and child-raising. And, also like Becker, she wishes to introduce others to this new or other vision. A paradoxical pedagogy of experience therefore operates here, too, in that the having of a baby is at one and the same time the revelation of a unique and minority vision, and part of a universal experience of the having of children. We can see that this dual view of the having of children that we have already encountered before occurs here too: it is formulated as both unique and ubiquitous, highly personal and the ultimate shared experience. In these terms, the having of a baby is both an ultimately private act, a personal pursuit of a private aim, and the underpinning of a joint humanity. Wolf's narratives of family and friends, who are alternately either in opposition to, or confirming extensions of, her own experience, act out this oscillation between isolation and commonality.

Wolf's self-declaring baby, then, announces itself only to the few, who are true parents already. True parents and the true baby, who is neither property nor money, nor a production of adults, go together and recognize each other. Further, the baby, which is not to be property, or necessarily related, or the mother's or the father's, or white or black, still has "parents". A "parent" must be not an owner of the baby, nor necessarily related to it. A true parent, then, is no more than the perfect student of the true baby, which it already knows in order to be such a true parent. This true baby, known in and of itself, and the true parent defined in relation to its ability to know such a baby, is self-evidently distinguishable from "our fantasies". This baby, as I suggested before, is an aspect of a real that is known as the real, distinct from "unreal" things such as money, or value, or fantasies. It is reality itself, speaking itself, simultaneously self-evident, and yet known to only a few. We may see a similarity here too to Sarah Hrdy's "nature", which is both self-evident and yet can only be known and recognized through the non-natural science. Experience here is the access to the real, but experience, at the same time, can only be accessed in turn through non-experience: the texts of science, in the case of Hrdy, or about childbearing and raising, in the case of Wolf.

Germaine Greer, like Wolf, sustains her view of a real child both in terms of a better past in opposition to a corrupted contemporaneity, and in terms of a child of fantasy as opposed to a child not of fantasy:

> In traditional societies children are full members, and may be seen everywhere. In post-industrial society children are segregated inferiors . . . The notional child can serve as a container for all kinds of fantasy goals, for reliving the past, especially the relationship with the mother, for reliving one's own youth, accomplishing one's defeated ambitions, and so forth. The infant who is expected to play some such constellation of roles for a parent will rapidly become a child in trouble. [Greer, 2003, p. 211]

Greer's traditional child remains a child, regardless of its full membership of society, and its existence depends on its visibility as such to the adult. Attempts at "differentiation" are trumped by the persistence of the child, as in Castañeda's formulations. Further, Greer's fantasy goals, for which the "notional" child is a container, interestingly can be noted to overlap with the legitimate "other reasons" that Joan Raphael-Leff (and many others) proposes for having a child. Besides the problems, then, of who is to be arbiter in separating legitimate reality from illegitimate, child-harming, fantasy, including the legitimate real child from the fantasy child, the difficulty is further raised that there are differing views on whether such fantasy itself is indeed harmful anyway.

Stephen Levick, for instance, in his book on the possible psychological and social consequences of cloning children, also touches on these difficulties when he writes that

> psychological research on motivations for parenthood has centered mainly on people having difficulty achieving it. We might wish to look beyond their socially acceptable explanations, such as wanting "to give and receive love". Whether or not a person is conscious of them, some motives may not be so noble. Alice Miller warns that "the urgent wish for a child . . . may express among other things the wish to have an available mother. Unfortunately, children are too often wished for only as symbols to meet repressed needs". [Levick, 2004, pp. 25–26]

Here, too, the anxiety around the child as a production of adult (repressed) needs—and in this sense a fantasy—rather than wanted for "noble" reasons, relies on the possibility of the real child: a child that is wanted in and of itself. We can see here again shiftings with regard to an altruism of "love" as the terms of the "noble". How is the wanting of the child ever to be formulated as entirely altruistic? How can any notion of desire ever ward off entirely that it is a desire *for*? The real child is introduced in an attempt to guarantee this warding off. The child is to be wanted as itself. Autonomy and self-constitution negate both ownership and production. The fantasy child therefore is only a "symbol". I find it difficult to know how to understand this term here. If nothing else, at least, this symbol is inadequate to the child ("only"). Yet this inadequacy is suited to the meeting of repressed needs, however it may do so. In any case, "love", given and received, here forms an economy, but, as with Wolf, constantly differentiated, and held at a distance, from an economy of money which accompanies it regardless.

Wolf's, Murray's, Greer's, Levick's, and Miller's separating of the child from a money economy or fantasy by identifying their real child are part of their efforts to value equally all children or "any child". But it is the already included acceptance of value that dogs their attempts in several ways. Even within their own discussions, children are already split into differing kinds of children, some of whom are wanted, some of whom are not; some, therefore, valued (more), and some not (or less). The value that they attempt to ward off as appropriate only to money, not to the child, which is not to be a commodity, or part of an economy, makes a troubling constant return. Just to begin with, Wolf's narrative of her own pregnancy and delivery rests on her acknowledged wish for an "own child". Greer, similarly, recounts her efforts to conceive a child, conceding an inability to account for the wish for such a child, even when she forcefully condemns that "[o]ur world already manifests a dangerous degree of contrast between the fertile rich and the fecund poor" (Greer, 2003, p. 208). (As noted in previous chapters, my references to Wolf and Greer, for instance, are only in relation to biographical narratives, and their meanings, that I read as such in texts.) As Rachel Bowlby argues:

> the psychological and social conditions of consumer choice are anything but obvious: the problem is rather in the way that consumer choice can come to function rhetorically as a category taken as being both simple—in need of no more discussion—and negative, if not corrupt. [Bowlby, 1993, p. 90]

We can consider the problem of the value of the child further in relation to a rare instance—which we have already previously encountered briefly—where commodification is seen as a positive process. Dion Farquhar, whose work I previously discussed in Chapter Two, argues that opposition to commodification is based on a

> [f]undamentalist feminist contempt for the liberal market model [which] is parasitic on a fantasy of an unproblematized edenic pre-market unmediated maternal body. The market, in this view, sullies and cheapens an essentially true or real transcendent reproduction by abstracting its functions and dividing its elements for exchange and economic compensation. Donors are paid; body parts are alienated. This critique of commodification is essentially a softened-up version of the Marxian account of reification. As such, it is not exhaustive, but quite one-sided. What such accounts miss entirely is the *exhilaration* and productivity—of identities, pleasures, and options—that are inherent in commodification. "'Commodification' of reproduction refers to the processes by which economic relationships of various kinds are *introduced* into the social patterns of human reproduction." The implication that before the development of reproductive technologies, reproduction . . . did not entail

oppressive political and economic relationships of dependency and
exploitation . . . is ludicrous. [Farquhar, 1996, pp. 125–126, original
emphasis]

I have already suggested, in relation to the wish for the child,
that one difficulty that arises from Farquhar's points here is that the
"exhilaration" seems to me a displacement from the "natural",
rather than a disruption of it. This rests on Farquhar's acceptance
of exhilaration as "inherent in commodification". This in turn seems
to me to result from an equating of economy with proliferation,
which, as I also argued earlier, is then valued as exhilaration and
productivity. For me the problem lies in both the assumed equation,
and the claimed inherence of such a valuation. Furthermore,
Farquhar's critique here of an opposition to the market relies on the
assertion of the market as also having these positive aspects, rather
than primarily on questioning further the way the market is
involved in identity. Farquhar does propose that a true or real
maternal body is produced in opposition to the market, but she
then, in critiquing Christine Overall, does not further consider the
construction of the market in its own terms, instead inserting that
market, or economics, as having been always present anyway as
oppressive political and economic relationships of dependency and
exploitation. Motherhood and parenthood to her have therefore
always been implicated in an economy. In terms of Farquhar's prior
positive evaluation of commodification, it is a release from ("social
and political") oppression for women that differentiates her exhilarating commodification from economies of dependency.

Farquhar's argument, in formulating identities (gender, in this
case) as involved in economic relationships, does not clarify how
any identity could necessarily be read as economic or not economic.
If economies have always, to her, mediated reproduction, primarily
in terms of oppressive gender relationships, then this still does not
address how women or children, for instance, are themselves seen
as commodities. Reinserting economy into the past can only further
confirm that babies have always been commodities. I can assume
either that Farquhar intends such a status as commodity to be the
product of oppression, or that this commodity-baby has also always
been part of the exhilaration of commodification. In the first case,
this surely re-instates commodification as a problem, a production

of oppression. But this would reinstate a true or real identity beyond the status of commodity that Farquhar rejects, at least with respect to the maternal body.

Metaphor is often brought in to discussions as the perceived mediating connection between identities and economies. Janelle Taylor, for instance, argues that

> One reason, perhaps, that these two streams [consumption and motherhood and reproduction] have tended to run in parallel is that the body metaphors of eating and digesting food remain implicit in theories of consumption, which mix rather badly with the metaphorical associations of procreation, making it difficult . . . to bring theories of consumption to bear specifically upon motherhood. . . . This metaphor [of eating] shapes—and, I would argue, hinders—our understanding [of pregnancy and motherhood]. [Taylor, 2004, p. 10]

But I would suggest such deployments of metaphor, as with Farquhar, raise the questions: what does it mean to say that an identity is either *like* an economy, or that it *is* (part of) an economy? Note, for instance, Zelizer's definition of the child as an "emotional and affective *asset*" in the midst of a formulation attempting to diagnose the extrapolation of the child from an economy of the "instrumental or fiscal" (Zelizer, 1985, p. 11, my emphasis). I read this problem as an ongoing determinant of arguments in Taylor's further discussion when she would seem, interestingly, simultaneously to be rejecting (or avoiding) and restating Freud's theories of the wish for the child (as I discussed them in Chapter Two) when she continues further by asserting that

> The fetus . . . may . . . "satisfy human wants of some sort or another", [but] it is difficult to imagine these wants as "springing from the stomach". This makes it rather difficult to conceptualize pregnancy, and by extension motherhood, in terms of consumption. How can the bearing of children be likened to the ingestion of food? The very suggestion seems to invoke that most frightening of all monsters, the mother who eats her own children. [Taylor, 2004, pp. 10–11]

Taylor therefore attributes her field's (anthropology) "ideological opposition" (*ibid.*, p. 10) of two topics (consumption and motherhood) to its difficulty in conceptualizing or likening motherhood to consumption, although she then promptly does so conceptualize motherhood, as, moreover, "that most frightening of all monsters, the mother who eats her own children". In other words, I can read "metaphor" here—even, or especially, in Taylor's own formulations—not as a source of the separation of motherhood and consumption, because they "mix rather badly" (*ibid.*, p. 10) with one another, but as a source of separation because they mix *rather too well*. Indeed, the very formulation of "ideological opposition" itself suggests this: as a warding off, as a *keeping* separate of that which belongs or belonged together and threatens to re-merge. Or, to put it differently, and in line with my overall arguments here, the question is what constitutes "metaphor" when it can be read *itself* as the very reality it is supposed to have only an indirect, derivative, or secondary, relation to? At stake in this discussion, again, are ideas of *relationship*, simultaneously in terms of ideas of "economies" (markets, consumption) and the child and/or mother as being "related", and ideas of kinds or levels of languages and the real as being related, or about relationship. As Taylor herself writes,

> Scholars of consumption ... have given the topic of motherhood comparatively little consideration. One reason for this, perhaps, is that consumption studies have tended to be cast as studies of "material culture", exploring the social and cultural role of material *objects*—while motherhood is understood to be a relationship between *persons*. The dividing line separating people from objects would seem, in this perspective, to be quite clearly bounded, fixed, and stable: the question is merely how they affect one another. The task of the analyst, then, becomes one of specifying relationships. Reproductive technologies and the controversies that swirl around them clearly suggest, however, that such distinctions—between persons and objects, bodies and commodities, mothers and consumers—are not so clear-cut. [*ibid.*, p. 11, original emphases]

Relationships, it would seem, are ready to collapse, or be collapsed, in on themselves. It is notable, however, that in Taylor's argument the foetus (among other things), after all, is reconstituted as outside of metaphor, as must inevitably occur in terms of metaphor's own relationship with non-metaphor: "the consumer of social theory inhabits a body that, if not necessarily male ... is at least not as easily imagined as a specifically pregnant body. The foetus is emphatically *not* 'an object outside us' " (*ibid.*, p. 10, original emphasis). This seems to situate the foetus as, inevitably, in a "biological" sense, "within" the body, while it may be (and has been) read in several ways as either not part of a (maternal) body— as an autonomous "object" or "subject"—or not "within" a body.² Linda Layne and Ann Anagnost, among others in Taylor, Layne, and Wozniak's *Consuming Motherhood*, make similar moves in the midst of self-consciously theoretical discussions when they argue, respectively, that "Shopping is one of the strategies used by mothers and their social networks to transform an anonymous mass of cells into 'our precious baby' " (Layne, 2004, p. 136) and

> Perhaps we might want to consider whether commodification is necessarily a dead-end. If it is one way of appropriating a sign or object, does this exhaust its possibilities? Of course, the object here is a child—not an object but a subject with its own possibilities of agency—and this, of course, is the source of unease, because we can never be sure that the child will grow into what we wish it to be. The child always holds forth the possibility of indeterminacy in the contingency of social reproduction. [Anagnost, 2004, p. 150]

The child is retrieved as, after all, "an anonymous mass of cells" or as "a subject with its own possibilities of agency ... [which] always holds forth the possibility of indeterminacy in the contingency of social reproduction". In both cases this extrication of a transcendent and universal child from the vicissitudes of production or consumption rests on ideas of innate qualities, either in terms of an atomizing scientific biology, or as a psychology that maintains the child as an entity growing into subjectivity and agency according to a universal trajectory of development. This trajectory, moreover, locates the child as apart from, or autonomous with respect to, the very culture and society otherwise diagnosed as implicated in the production of the international adoptee in Anagnost's analysis (see, for an extensive analysis of psychological models of (child) development as specifically cultural and historical, rather than universal and transcendent, Erica Burman, *Deconstructing Developmental Psychology*, 1994). Subjectivity and agency as characteristic elements of the unpredictable child in turn rely on specific conceptions of individuality, action, and consciousness. Lynn Morgan, for instance, refers to Monica Casper's work to argue

that "agency is not an already existing fact (ontological or otherwise) to be discovered or revealed but is rather a social project"
(Morgan, 1996, p. 54). The universal child maintains that consumption which is not it, but with which it is read as having a relationship. The reaffirmation of relationship as, then, after all, a necessary
mediation preventing unification is confirmed, moreover, as in
many writings, by Taylor's perceptions of the limitations of theory:

> The relationship between motherhood and consumption is,
> however, far more than merely a theoretical question—it is a vital
> matter with which ordinary people struggle on a daily basis: What
> must I (and what *can* I) do and have and buy in order to properly
> love, value, educate, nurture, provide for, raise—in a word, *mother*
> my child(ren)? *Consuming Motherhood* takes this up through ethno-
> graphic and historical explorations of how ordinary women, striv-
> ing to build and maintain relations of kinship in the context of
> globalizing consumer capitalism, live out motherhood in and
> through, as well as against, ideologies and practices of consump-
> tion. [Taylor, 2004, p. 12, original emphases]

The split (re-)introduced by metaphor is here elaborated as the split
between the theoretical and the vital, ordinary, and daily, where
motherhood is apart from consumption, whether positively or
negatively: "mere" theory against, or apart from, life as it is "lived
out".

Farquhar's argument, too, seems to me to leave this kind of a
question unresolved. It is relevant in this respect that her section on
these issues is entitled "Demonology of the consumer and the
market". This confirms certain understandings of these terms (as
with Janelle Taylor's formulations), while critiquing an enmity
towards them. Where a possibility is introduced of questioning
what and how commodities and markets are constructed in relation
to, or *as*, motherhood, reproduction, and the child, Farquhar's argument halts at confirming the market and economics as positive
proliferation, as long as the woman is free to choose (how) to
consume. Farquhar quotes Michelle Stanworth approvingly in
conclusion:

> . . . it is not technology as an "*artificial* invasion of the human body"
> that is at issue—but whether we can create the political and cultural

conditions in which such technologies can be employed by women to shape the experience of reproduction according to their own definitions. [Farquhar, 1996, pp. 126–127, original emphasis]

Much as I sympathize with the critiques that Farquhar and Stanworth are making of a polarity between a "natural" and a "technological", in which either one or the other is privileged, an approval of the market as a liberal, non-oppressive mechanism where women can freely choose their definitions of reproduction seems to me problematic in the ways that I have noted previously.

Finally, it is notable that Farquhar elides, at the start of her discussion, a shift from a mention, in a quotation from Barbara Katz Rothman, of the *baby* as commodity, to her own addressing of motherhood. Farquhar's overall discussion, as I have noted earlier, hardly mentions the child that is wanted. If her point, then, is to retrieve commodification as proliferation for women, this does not account to me for the baby as either commodity or not commodity. And this returns me to my critique in Chapter Two of Farquhar's attempts to see ARTs as proliferating reproduction to the point of the dissipation of relationship. Where this may conceivably be formulated as such a liberation from the point of view of gender in Farquhar's terms, it is anyway stymied, as I argued earlier, by the underpinning of ARTs by the own child. Farquhar, then, in endorsing the market, can no more account for the child as commodity than can Wolf, and many others, in their attempts to ward off the market. Instead, I want to pursue the complex idea that the child is constantly brought in relation to the market and commodity, and yet is not simply equated with commodity. When and how is the child a commodity and not a commodity?

Jacqueline Rose illuminates several aspects of this complexity in her discussion, in *The Case of Peter Pan*, of children's literature as a field that defines the child as knowable for its own purposes. The child in children's literature, Rose argues, is assumed as an autonomous reality, in that it is to be known as the appropriate recipient of a book to which it is equated. The child as the book reads itself, and this is seen to constitute the ultimate in education without force. A disinterested and "noble" altruism is upheld here, too, with the adult knowing the child in the child's best interests and on its own behalf. Rose instead reads the adult as that which creates the

child: in producing children's literature, it produces the child for
that literature as well as in the literature. Rose suggests further, in
parallel with my discussion above, that

> in the case of children's fiction, this relationship between the busi-
> ness of the trade on the one hand, and the self-generating body of
> the innocent child on the other, is of an essential, rather than a
> contingent nature. [Rose, 1984, p. 90]

For Rose, the relationship of the commercial value of children's
books and the value of the child is one suppressed in the service of

> a wholly generalised concept of culture which cannot see the divi-
> sions on which it rests. The aestheticisation, the glorification, the
> valuing of the child ... act as a kind of cover for these differences
> ... If we look at the children's book market, its identity falls apart,
> exposing the gaps between producer (writer), distributor (book-
> seller or publisher), purchaser (parents, friends and/or children)
> and the consumer (ideally, but only ideally, the child). These
> spaces, missed meeting points, places of imposition, exploitation
> (or even glorification of the child) are not entirely different in kind
> from those which characterise other aspects of the literary life of
> our culture. They are not exclusive to the world of children's books.
> [ibid., p. 134]

Nor, I would add (as Rose herself also does later), are they exclusive to the literary life of our culture, even if the gaps might be
located between slightly shifted locations. Where Rose notes how
the child in children's literature serves to gloss over differing values
in terms of class and literacy, the child in reproductive technologies,
I am arguing, serves to gloss over differing valuations according to
ideas of the own and not-own, which in turn are manifested in a
variety of ways, as we shall continue to explore. The warding-off of
the market through the child, which is to be exclusively self-constituted as a reality apart from, or in opposition to, a symbolic or
fantastic currency, fixes the child as existing in and of itself for itself.
In this respect, the market is established as paradoxically constitu-
ent of, and inherent to, culture and society, and at the same time as
marking, in these cases (as we saw in Wolf's, Murray's, and Greer's
comments, and, in an opposite but complementary way in Taylor's
and Farquhar's), a suspect encroachment on, or degradation of, a

purer private life, demarcated by the family and the sphere of emotions. As Rose adds,

> [*Peter Pan*'s] material success . . . and corresponding status . . . say something about the fantasies which our culture continues to perpetuate—about its own worth, its future and its traditions—through the child[;] . . . the whole question . . . of what—in general—*can* survive, of what *is* endurance, perpetuity, and eternal worth. [*ibid.*, pp. 109–110, original emphasis]

The wish for the child, and the child that is wished for, are called up as guarantors of the eternal and endurance of repetition: true re/production, undiluted or contaminated by other interests or investments. The credit is to belong wholly to the child. In this way, the parent is released, as Wolf wishes, from property ownership, and is simultaneously retrieved dialectically as merely the servant of the child. And this all is to be due to the child. (I am not a fan of punning for its own sake. I hope it is clear that I am here elaborating the, apparently automatic or inescapable, appropriateness of the terminology—its ability to suit the issues under consideration in a range of ways.) As Rose concludes, drawing on the same reading of Freud that I discussed in the previous chapter,

> Freud's theory of the unconscious is a challenge above all to just this sameness in that it undermines the idea that psychic life is continuous, that language can give us mastery, or that past and future can be cohered into a straightforward sequence, and controlled. Above all it throws into question the idea that the child can be placed at the beginnings of this process (origins of culture, before sexuality and the word), or, indeed, at the end (the guarantee of a continuity for ourselves and our culture over time). [*ibid.*, p. 134]

I also understand this problem of the child as both commodity and not-commodity to be parallel to, or part of, the argument by theorist Judith Butler, in her consideration of kinship, *Antigone's Claim: Kinship Between Life and Death*, that

> [t]he Hegelian legacy of Antigone interpretation appears to assume the separability of kinship and the state, even as it posits an essential relation between them. And so every interpretive effort to cast a character as representative of kinship or the state tends to falter and

lose coherence and stability. This faltering has consequences not only for the effort to determine the representative function of any character but for the effort to think the relationship between kinship and the state . . . For two questions that the play poses are whether there can be kinship—and by kinship I do not mean the "family" in any specific form—without the support and mediation of the state, and whether there can be the state without the family as its support and mediation. And further, when kinship comes to pose a threat to state authority and the state sets itself in a violent struggle against kinship, can these very terms sustain their independence from one another? [Butler, 2000, p. 5]

For "state" read also "market", and, in terms of "character", read also: child. Butler is here questioning these terms as autonomous and separable entitities, caught up in a politics of representation which presupposes language as a transparent conveyor of prior "images", "structures" or "objects". Further, the possibility of *relationship* is at stake (related to how it occurs problematically in both Farquhar and Taylor, for instance). What is read as legitimized and legitimating relationship, or what constitutes relationship at all? Legitimation is dependent on authority, but here is unstably constituted as the state or family, or family as/through the state and the state as/through family. Butler suggests that

although Hegel claims that [Antigone's] deed is opposed to Creon's, *the two acts mirror rather than oppose one another*, suggesting that if the one represents kinship and the other the state, they can perform this representation only by each becoming implicated in the idiom of the other. [*ibid.*, p. 10, original emphasis]

Or, as Rose concludes,

For *Peter Pan* has appeared not just as a part *of* history, but equally it has served as a response *to* history . . . No divisions of culture and literacy (the cry of a literature asserting its freedom from the world), no impingement on the family by the state (the reaction of the state to its earlier policies), no differences finally between children (the same the world over—no class barriers here). Instead the eternal child. [Rose, 1984, p. 143, orginal emphasis]

Linked further to this, Butler suggests that there is a possible reading of Antigone "in which she exposes the socially contingent character of kinship, only to become the repeated occasion in the critical literature for a rewriting of that contingency as immutable necessity" (Butler, 2000, p. 6). Thus, I read Rose's child and Butler's Antigone as the occasion of a parallel critical practice, with parallel aims and ends. Specifically, in this context, the own child of reproductive technologies is to shore up a division between—or rather, a dividability of—the state and the family, and kinship and the state, at the same time as it establishes the mutual implicatedness of the state (and the market) and reproduction, family, and kinship. In doing so, the child underpins, through and as the family, gender, heterosexuality, and nationality. The "right" child is the child of the Western market, even, and because, it is not itself only or simply a commodity. Or, to put it differently, it is precisely a condition of this market that there is a non-market which is implicated in it, and in which it is implicated. I do not think it is coincidental, then, that Butler's text echoes a phrase of Rose's from the quotation above, when she notes in her discussion of Hegel's reading of Antigone that the "public sphere, as I am calling it here, is called variably the community, government, and the state by Hegel; it only acquires its existence through interfering with the happiness of the family" (*ibid.*, p. 35).

Attempts, then, to reclaim the value of any child as a noble altruism, while continuing in every other respect to rely on the validated and validating desire for the own (or "right": for one example of the use of this term specifically see Rachel Shabi's article on reproductive technologies "Baby chase" (*Guardian*, 2004)) child create ongoing struggles and complications across the board. First, as we have seen, reproductive technologies are perceived to be motivated and justified by a desire for the child that is defined, as Stephen Levick puts it, as "highly intentional, as it must be with reproductive technologies" (Levick, 2004, p. 36). This child is, in this sense, more wanted than wanted, more intended than intended. This formulates an intensification of the problem of the desire *for*. If the child is only appropriately desired as itself, then an intensification of this desire is nevertheless seen to create difficulties of its own.[3] An intensification of intentionality carries with it an intensification too of determination. It might be said that what is more highly intended is pursued with greater determination, and is also more (pre-)determined. The child of reproductive technologies is already, then, by definition, not "any" child, and it is also always anyway precisely a *child*. Greer comments on two aspects of this when she asks:

> ART acceptors clearly want a child, but do they want any child? Will a sick or a disabled child do? If recourse to ART for a child of one's own is primarily driven by narcissism, the birth of a damaged child could have more than usually catastrophic consequences. [Greer, 2003, p. 212]

Greer queries not just the limitations around what kind of child is seen as an acceptable child, but also allocates the reason for wanting an own child specifically to being "driven by narcissism". In doing so, she is interpreting the wish for the own child as a wish for reproduction in terms of a similarity to, or duplication of, the self. This leads, however, either to the question of how the child conceived without ART would *not* be narcissistic, or to the conclusion that Greer accepts all wanted, conceived children as produced by a narcissistic drive. And this is a difficulty that pervades Greer's entire spirited discussion, in fact. Where she rejects ARTs on the basis of narcissism, and the attendant wishes to defeat mortality, for instance, she is also, willy-nilly, rejecting the conceiving of (wanted) children *tout court* (rightly or wrongly), as her argument offers no distinction between the children of ART and not of ART in these terms.

Wolf's, Murray's, Greer's, and Levick's writings, do, in any case, include the own child as a specific kind of child produced by reproductive technologies, even if they subsequently may lose track of the implications of this inclusion. For this own child challenges directly the refutations of ownership and production in their texts. John Robertson, in considering legal and social aspects of reproductive technologies, suggests that

> New reproductive technologies are also often seen as a further cause of the disintegration and breakdown of the nuclear family, even as they serve family interests by allowing infertile or at-risk couples to have healthy, biologically related offspring. . . . The most often cited threat to family integrity arises from the collaborative reproductive techniques that separate genetic, gestational, and rearing parenthood through the use of gamete donors and surrogates,

which have the potential to undermine traditional notions of paternity and motherhood. The wife–husband dyad may be altered in significant ways, either imploding under the extra pressure or expanding into a novel kind of blended family with multiple rearing partners whose precise relation to children and each other is unknown or bitterly disputed. [Robertson, 1994, p. 13]

Many of the writings on reproductive technologies report such views of these technologies as a threat to a nuclear family as a heterosexual unit of reproduction. The "family" of the past is here constructed in the light of a family of the present and future, as both challenged by changes and also perpetuated by them. A continuity of family interests is anchored by the having of children, and specifically "biologically related" children. "Biology" *is* relationship, therefore, as it underpins the categories of "genetic, gestational, and rearing parenthood" that both constitute and threaten family integrity. The paternity and the motherhood of the past are retrospectively accorded a definition of (at least a desired) biological unity and linearity, while future parenthood is dangerously prolific, in biological terms. The logic of this biology is that it both defines and contains the family of the past, while also generating a multiplicity that threatens "unknown or bitterly disputed" relationships to children. The child of the past is the legitimate own child, defined as such by a biology that constitutes a linearity and singularity of legitimacy, while the biology of the present or future generates a proliferation of relationships that attenuates or dissolves relationship altogether. The child is then disputed property. Robertson adds that

[w]ith the nuclear family so battered by illegitimacy, divorce, and single and gay life-styles, the feared effect of reproductive technology on the family is the recurring ethical theme in the reception of these technologies. [Robertson, 1994, pp. 13–14]

The own child, and ownership of this child, which in turn constitute a certain family, are at stake.

This struggle over a biology that both underpins the family and threatens it, which constitutes both the family of the past, of the present, and the family of the future, can also be read in Rachel Bowlby's "The constancy of kinship" (2003), a review of Butler's

Antigone's Claim.[4] At stake in Butler's and Bowlby's discussions are what Rose negotiates through the child: the status of language, history, and the family; the family *as* language and as history (and vice versa). Bowlby concludes that

> Butler wants to argue against the fixity of a symbolic order linked to kinship and to language: it is not so and it should not be wished or cursed upon us. Her challenge proceeds from the evident mutations of familial and sexual relationships at the present time. . . . Butler is right to point to the need for thinking about new forms of relatedness and commitment in the light of changing norms and practices. She is mistaken, though, in implying a history of relative (in both senses) stability until recently. Until the mid-twentieth-century's nuclear moment of marital stability and spousal longevity, the frequency of early death made second marriages a commonplace, with their accompanying complexities, as now, of step-parents and half- and step-sibling relationships. Kinship has always, or almost always, been muddled. But Butler also fails to mention the recent radical changes in the conditions of kinship: the new reproductive technologies. As well as socially (via adoption or step-parenting), it is now biologically possible to have more than one mother (the egg-bearer and the one who carries the child), while it is also now possible to identify positively a biological father. Paternity is no longer unprovable, while maternity has acquired a new vagueness. Along with the many new kinds of couple and family grouping, the dual and multiple connections and cohabitations, what will the new technologies of childbearing do to the way we imagine our ties and our origins? [Bowlby, 2003, pp. 79–80]

Time is of the essence in Bowlby's consideration. Butler, for her, is right to argue against a fixity of kinship, while, at the same time, that fixity is already anyway denied by the "evident mutations . . . at the present time". A first question here is to whom this is evident. Is the evidence in the now the achievement of a form of acknowledgement that Butler is looking for, or is it evident only to the positions held by Butler and Bowlby, outside of the state or public realm, not yet acknowledged? In any case, the wish for a refusal of fixity has been superseded by the demonstration of the lack of that fixity anyway. "Mutations", further, introduces a mediation that links a past and a present, building the one from the other, but reproductive technologies are "radical changes". Bowlby's Butler, therefore, on the one hand implies a ("relative") stability, while on the other hand her argument is seen to proceed from evident mutations. Change is both seen and not seen, while what exactly constitutes this "change" at all is unclear. In Bowlby's own views, this doubleness persists. "Kinship has always . . . been muddled", and the muddledness she notes is suspended only at "the mid-twentieth century's nuclear moment of marital stability and spousal longevity", returning subsequently in the "now". Mutations and muddle both rest on fixities that are somehow affected or mixed, but fixities initially, none the less. This is clear from the continuity of forms of muddledness that Bowlby lists pre- and post the twentieth-century nuclear moment. The continuity may be read, too, in the ability to write the muddledness as a list in the first place. It may be muddled, but it is still dividable, definable, and listable, and these components of the muddle are recognizable across time. Only the moment of stable and long-term heterosexual marriage constitutes "non-muddledness", apparently as guarantor too of the legitimate child. What would a muddledness be that is always muddled? It is only that moment of stability that can define an otherwise constant muddledness.

The "radical changes" introduced to the "conditions of kinship" by reproductive technologies are all linked to new "biological" possibilities. Kinship, therefore, at its most non-muddled, is non-biological—the paternity of the past not yet being "biologically provable". At the same time, the introduction of biologically provable paternity is part of "radical changes" which will cause as yet unimaginable changes in the way we "imagine our ties and our origins". Biology, therefore, intervenes into a situation of clarity to repeat that clarity, or, to put it differently, to introduce a new, other, clarity. The legitimate child of stable heterosexual marriage becomes the legitimate child of the biologically proven. Biological legitimacy is therefore implicitly both of the past and the present: lacking in the past for paternity, no matter how non-muddled otherwise, and supplemented in the future developments. This, as in the earlier examples, formulates biology as a knowledge and concern of all time, albeit lacking for fathers. The knowledge of the lack is in the past, if not the knowledge of the solution to that lack. The unprovable father is unprovable biologically. Yet the advent of the always lacking biological proof is also the coming of radical change. The coming into knowledge of the solution to the known lack constitutes radical change. In this way, biology is always known and present as the lack addressed by heterosexual contract-marriage. It is just the biological solution that is long-awaited, but also previously unimaginable.

Similarly, maternity, always socially potentially multiple, is "now" also biologically potentially multiple. Here, too, multiplicity is a "new vagueness", as multiplicity constitutes "muddledness" elsewhere. As in Robertson, for instance, a biology of the past (which coincides with the social and the legal) is held to align with unity and linearity, while the biology of the present is aligned with a multiplicity which, in many discussions—not just Bowlby's—quickly slips into ideas of confusion (for thinkers like Farquhar: potential liberation) and change. The shifts in time and the locations of the legitimate parent and the legitimate child therefore can equally be read to rest, in this type of argument, not on a necessarily "evident" change but on a repetition of precisely that term which does *not* change: the own child (and its attendant family). Whatever their "many new kinds", both the social and the biological can be read as operating to confirm a continuity of "childbearing" as the underpinning of the family and its legitimate ends. As I argued in the first chapter, biology, or the natural, and the social, are in this sense not separable entities, but collapse into each other as the terminologies of relationship. As Sarah Franklin notes in her readings of popular narratives of reproductive techniques:

> It is significant that the "happy couples" stories present both a continuity and a commensurability between biological science and the biological family. The achieved route of conception stands in for conjugality and family as *social* achievements, "after nature", though in this context, "after technology" as well. In sum, it is the substitutability of natural, social and technological "facts" these narratives demonstrate which indexes particular features of the kinship universe within which they are operative, and of which they are also transformative. [Franklin, 1997, p. 95, original emphasis]

In this reading, I am suggesting throughout this book, reproductive technologies, entirely based on the wish for the own child, are not, and cannot be, inevitably formulated as the harbingers of change, or as the harbingers of inevitable change. Instead, taking the child at and as the start of considerations, reproductive technologies are constantly reconstituted as the production of the eternal child: as the return of the same.

In Bowlby's formulation, the newly vague maternity was once not vague. Maternity becomes produced as the only evidently "provable" kinship of the past. The emergence of the baby from the body of the mother is constituted in the past—and, importantly, reconstituted in the "now"—as the fundamental biology. Both the egg donor and the "carrier" mother are "biological" mothers. Biology is, thus, the witnessed emergence of the own child from the body: the egg as body or the "carrier" as body. No wonder that change is "evident": here, the visual defines the "proof" and constitutes the continuity of the "own". A baby that is seen or witnessed as emerging from the body of the mother is here the most "own" child, both in this past, and in the present and future. As Marilyn Strathern also claims, "[i]n traditional Euro-American thinking, the mother's identity is created *by her offspring* in the act of her (*visibly*) giving birth ... *to see* a mother is thus to *recognise* a natural connection" (Strathern, 1992, p. 149, my emphases).

Reproductive technologies' "own" child does not advance away from this model in these arguments, it regresses into it. The evidence of the own child may be seen everywhere. The own child is the product of the vision of the meeting of sperm and egg in the glass test-tube, of the doctors implanting fertilized eggs in a womb, or of the gynaecologist or midwife witnessing the birth, and so on. Susan Martha Kahn describes how in an Israeli clinic run on Orthodox Jewish principles, the procedures must be monitored by Orthodox Jewish women, called *maschgichot*, or Halakhic (pertaining to the legal part of Talmudic literature) inspectors, who, as Kahn reports one of the women putting it, "make sure that Lichtenberg and Silberstein [their sperm] don't get mixed up" (Kahn, 2004, pp. 363–364). Sperm, egg, or cytoplasm function as the body of evidence. Susan Squier's detailed reading of the meanings of "babies in bottles" provides a wide range of examples of this visuality, and its prevalence and importance in narratives of reproduction. As Squier notes,

[i]f we spend a little time teasing out the implications of these images of babies in bottles, we can see they all enact the fantasy of

the womb as a see-through container for the previously invisible fetus. [Squier, 1994, pp. 2–3][5]

Ludmilla Jordanova's study of *Sexual Visions* similarly examines several examples of the ways in which vision is made to negotiate ideas of the penetration through levels and layers to a core of truth or nature, a "preoccupation with depth" (Jordanova, 1989, p. 55). Sarah Franklin sums up these issues when she writes that

> Visualizing and imaging technologies are critical to the technical and discursive apparatus of assisted reproduction. The development of a light source to enhance laparoscopic technique, for example, was a critical achievement in the realization of successful IVF. Scanning, screening, laparoscopy, x-rays, and powerful microscopic techniques are essential for both research and clinical technique in reproductive medicine. Hence the importance of feminist understandings of the patriarchal nature of the clinical gaze. [Franklin, 1995, p. 332][6]

Provable paternity is, therefore, in comments such as Bowlby's, constituted by this biology of the visual along with the model of the child witnessed as emerging from the maternal body. The sperm can now be witnessed to be the part of the body that the child emerges from. Where previously sperm might be seen as such, it could not be witnessed as the *right* sperm, the sperm of the legitimate father-to-be. In this way, we might say that the paternal biological or genetic body is finally born of the social and legal, and is defined in these kinds of arguments as the final answer to paternity and the own child. Anxieties around the possibilities of errors in the witnessing—the use of the wrong sperm, or the wrong egg—can be understood to be both produced by, and accounted for, in terms of the reliance of the own child on the correct and accurate witnessing. That, however, such a maternity and paternity of the body, with the attendant claimed final separation of the body from the legal and the social, is immediately problematic, and very difficult to sustain, is clear from the many conflicts around the ownership of eggs, sperm, and the babies of reproductive technologies. As philosopher Jacques Derrida comments:

> Paternity is induced from a judgment; maternity is observed in a perception. . . . But this schema . . . seems more fragile than ever.

Today less then ever we can be sure that the mother herself is the woman we believe we saw giving birth. . . . Techno-scientific capabilities . . . will no doubt accelerate a mutation in the father/mother relation in the future. But this will only be an acceleration . . . however spectacular or dreadful their effects may appear: the "mother", too, has always been a "symbolic" or "substitutable" mother, like the father, and the certainty acquired at the moment of giving birth was in my opinion an illusion. A very self-interested one, certainly, and the projection of a powerful desire, but an illusion. It remains one, for ever and more than ever. [Derrida & Roudinesco, 2001, pp. 40, 41][7]

Within the area of reproductive technologies, these conflicts themselves are composed of ongoing struggles around what constitutes the ownership of the child, or the child-to-be. Questions, for instance, of which biology of the visual is to take precedence is one manifestation of the difficulties. Is the egg donor or the surrogate mother to be the definitive biological maternity? Marilyn Strathern has commented in relation to surrogacy that

[t]here is no symmetry between the different types of mothers created through surrogacy arrangements. As Dolgin states . . . "mothers can be opposed to other kinds of mothers". Some come to represent culture, some nature (the commissioning or contract mother as opposed to the genetic and/or birth mother) . . . one can apparently "duplicate" motherhood by locating each in a different person. Yet there is no duplication of rights and claims. . . . Euro-Americans are uncertain as to how to "divide" motherhood. The difficulties that arose in the Ba[b]y M case testify both to the irreducibility of the elements involved and to the way in which till now they have been held to modify or supplement one another. [Strathern, 1992, pp. 157–158]

Here, Strathern is referring to a "contract" mother who is not also an egg donor: "the surrogate was also the genetic mother". In this case she sees the "two claims to motherhood [as] . . . irreducible. The former was based in law; the latter in biology" (ibid., p. 157). But in the case of egg or cytoplasm donorship, the opposing mothers can both, therefore, as Bowlby comments, be seen as the maternal body of visual biology, where the question is how and why one is to take precedence over the other, rather than being seen as different types of claim to motherhood. Several studies (Strathern, for instance, argues already in 1992 that "genetic origins and links [are] . . . taking an increasing hold in adjudications about procreative possibilities" (Strathern, 1992, p. 177)) have suggested that, in these cases, the "genetic" mother is (increasingly) favoured over the (non-genetic) surrogate, and this might be interpreted as the "genetic" being seen to constitute a stronger claim to ownership of the child or child-to-be. The genetic in such a case defines the maternal body, and, in this sense, the child may not be seen to emerge from the surrogate's body. The genetic may also be defined as in some ways "more" the witnessed emergence from the maternal body, either in terms of priority (conception before implantation), or in terms of the egg somehow being "closer" to the baby-to-be than the surrogate's pregnant body.

To put it differently, the surrogate may not be defined in terms of a "body" at all, but instead as a container, vessel, passage, or feeding-ground, for instance. Moreover, the witnessing of birth may be in such cases defined as a witnessing precisely of a separation between surrogate and baby, not as the establishment of a proven ownership. Ownership, too, might be constituted in a range of ways in turn. It might, for instance, rely on intention as the initiation of the production of the wanted child, as Stephen Levick's comments above implied. In this case, the surrogate is not seen to have wished for or wanted the child initially, although her later expression of a wish for the child may well have prompted the competition for priority. In both cases, intention and genetics, priority of ownership in terms of a process conceived of as temporal could be said to prevail. Bowlby's "vagueness", may be read, then, as a proliferation and dilution of maternity, or it may be read as another repetition ("duplication") of the retrospectively created past of a unified maternity—and a paternity modelled on a certain version of this unified maternity—in producing the own child. In other words, at issue here is whether reproduction, in terms of the own child, is read as confusion or as repetition.

Although it is not necessary to my overall analyses in this book, I would add the suggestion that, psychoanalytically speaking, reproductive technologies, in their central reliance on the own child, can be understood precisely to recapitulate femininity as constituted by penis-envy. Where Freud understands the baby, especially the boy child, to be cherished as a replacement for the absent phallus, reproductive technologies can be taken to be fully complicit in the claim that the *only* "solution" to femininity is the phallic baby, the baby that is a part of the maternal body; a part that has previously been always lacking, but suspected somewhere (see, for Freud's discussion of the fetish as the denial of the absence of the mother's penis, Freud, 1905d). This always lost penis that, for Freud, can never be replaced, but only supplemented through stand-ins, could be said to be insisted upon by reproductive technologies as *replacable*. This returns me also to Jacqueline Rose's noting of repetition as pointing to an underlying uncertainty, in terms of Freud's repetition compulsion as a repeated attempt at, and failure of, mastery. Where reproductive technologies insist on the own child, that insistence itself may raise the question of what must be denied, or what remains unmastered.

There are many texts, I have noted earlier, which do not address the issue of the own child as the child of reproductive technologies at all, and this raises pervasive difficulties for the important issues they wish to discuss, including disability. An example of this is the Institute of Ideas' volume *Designer Babies: Where Should We Draw the Line?* In her essay in *Designer Babies*, Agnes Fletcher defines her writing from a "disability equality perspective" as accepting that "every life is of value and that the variety of characteristics among humans, our diversity as a species, has innate value" (Fletcher, 2002, pp. 16–17). In discussing the work of disability rights advocate Adrienne Asch, Fletcher endorses Asch's belief

> that the decision to become a parent, if not based on the acceptance of parenting *any* child, fundamentally changes something about the parent's relationship with a particular child. If you expect to be able to determine certain outcomes, you may be deeply disappointed to find that life is full of vicissitudes and grief; that these are, quite literally, among the facts of life. [*ibid.*, p. 20, original emphasis]

Thomas Murray echoes this formulation when, in arguing against concepts of "non-directive" genetic counselling, he states that

> The more we come to see our children's characteristics as the product of choice, the more vulnerable we become to the likelihood—

indeed the near-certainty—of disappointment. Life is simply too
complex, its dangers too varied, and the wrenches of emotional
development, the search for identity, and the need for separation
and independence too certain. The desire to prevent hurt and
sadness intruding into our relationship with our children is a futile
fantasy at its heart. [Murray, 1996, p. 135]

A "life" that is unpredictable, various, and complex must include a
child that is also unpredicted and unpredictable, various, and
complex, otherwise an unwarranted "disappointment" will occur.

Except that, as with Wolf's and Greer's arguments, the "any"
child is here already not any child, as it is already accepted as a
"genetic" or "biological" child—a child born of parents either
through reproductive technologies, and/or with the use of pre-
implantation or pre-natal diagnosis and/or intervention. This child
is in any case not an adopted or fostered, or entirely unrelated, child.
Nor is it not a child anyway. A "parent" is here someone who has a
"relationship with a particular child", or, as Thomas Murray puts
it, "parents and children create value by their mutual caring and
maturation" (ibid., p. 135). (Murray uses the idea of "mutuality" to
try to address the problems of the polarities of "altruism" and "self-
ishness" in explicating the motivations for having children.) As with
Dion Farquhar's argument, as I read it, the idea of a free and open
reproduction with a liberality and multiplicity of outcomes is cut
across by the very relatedness she presupposes, but does not
acknowledge further. In Fletcher's discussion, similarly, "relationship" and "particularity" cut across the "any child". Parent and
child define each other, in terms of their relationship to one another,
here further specified in terms of the child's particularity. The not-
anyness of this child is, therefore, already part of the "determin[ing]
of certain outcomes" in terms of what any "genetic" or "biological"
aspect of reproductive technologies is held to entail, even before any
pre-natal or pre-implantation diagnostics are involved. Relationship,
whether understood as social, psychological, legal, biological or
genetic, implicates, and is implicated in, both parenthood and the
child. Therefore, as Louis Althusser argues, the child as "child"—
conceived of (in both senses of the term) as "child"—is already part
of "determin[ing] certain outcomes".

It is precisely the lack of attention to the issue that the child
within these discussions is always already not just "any child" or

even just "any thing", which affects fundamentally the continued debate in these important areas. Issues of social justice with regards to disability, for instance, or definitions and expectations of disability and its consequences, are addressed with more clarity than questions of why and how some babies are acceptable to parents, and others not, and how to negotiate this.[8] The determinations involved in the own child are exactly part of considering what investment parents are making in having a child of their "own" *at all*. If, as Greer and Mary Warnock suggest, for instance, the child would indeed be reproduced as a (to Greer narcissistic, to Warnock naturally desired) reproduction of the parental self, then disability, for example, could be understood as constructed as either the self or the not-self (depending on whether or not the parent(s) describe themselves as disabled), and desired or rejected on those grounds. (I have come across the situation of disabled parents particularly choosing to have a (similarly) disabled child mostly in relation to deaf parents choosing to use pre-natal or pre-implantation diagnosis to select a deaf child, where the deafness is due to genetic factors. I consider this issue further below.)

Fletcher, too, expresses concern that reproductive technologies "encourage a consumerist attitude towards children" (Fletcher, 2002, p. 19). As with Wolf, consumerism is here a money-exchange transaction, seen as inappropriate to the child, and it is here too connected to a dangerously unrestrained choice. The problem of "designer babies" specifically throws up repeatedly the danger of this unrestrained choice, whereby the struggle is over when, where, and why lines can be drawn in terms of what may be chosen and what may not. Often, this is described as a "slippery slope". I want to argue here, however, that the "own child" of reproductive technologies, assumed as beyond question, a self-evident and natural desire, even in discourses which are closely concerned with issues of discrimination and selection, has *pre-empted or pre-determined* the terms of this "slippery slope". In this sense, I would argue that *there is no slippery slope*. Where reproductive technologies are accepted at all, this acceptance rests on assuming that the choosing for the own child above others is either unchangeably, innately, determined, or that it is sufficiently valid and compelling for other reasons. These reasons include selection on the basis of eliminating genetic diseases or disability. The "own" of the own child trumps the option of "other" children, and the attempts to impose limits on the own child amount to efforts to close the stable door after the horse has bolted. The pleas of writers such as Wolf, Murray, Fletcher, and Asch for the acceptance of any child are undermined from the start by their tacit acceptance of the validity of choosing for the own child. In this way, they are already implicated in a language of ownership, choice, and selection. There is no slippery slope because, in this way, *the decision has already been taken.* Choice and selection have been accepted as justified and valid. Further debates can only fight rearguard and partial actions around redefining, restricting, or elaborating that own child, which has already been accepted and endorsed as the underpinning of reproductive technologies.

It is ownership, choice, and selection, which are also seen as part of a capitalist money economy in these arguments, which is constantly warded off, simultaneously establishing and negating the relationship. Writers such as Fletcher and Asch are making an important attempt to propose different understandings of disability, and the consequences of disability for the life of the disabled, their relatives, and a wider social world, but in accepting the privileging of the own child, they validate also the accompanying ideas of what it is seen to mean that this child is "own", and, moreover, a "child". Here, again, this is what "genetics" and "biology" are about with regard to reproductive technologies: they are to determine the child as both child and own. These paradoxes are contained in Fletcher's conclusion that "[t]he decision to end the relationship begun with a prospective, wanted child and to begin again, hoping for a different child, is clearly likely to be an agonizingly difficult one" (Fletcher, 2002, p. 21). The relationship of the parents to this child is determined by the child as they define it. What the parents want here is the product of their own desire, as I argued in the previous chapter. The desire is formulated in relation to an already defined object, which thereby is not a self-defining object, but a created object. Object and desire define each other, and the desire can therefore never be fully assuaged, as the object is never external to it, but constituted by it.

Therefore the relationship here is not present, but, as Fletcher's formulation struggles to accommodate, a prospective relationship with a prospective child, desired as possibility or potentiality. In this sense, the relationship is not with a child, but with the parents' own desire; with themselves. This desire is then seen to be temporarily stymied as its ostensible aim is defined as already inappropriate or inadequate to its ends. This is signalled by a shift from "a prospective, wanted child" to "hoping for a different child". The different child is defined in terms of the move from the initial child from being wanted to being unwanted, and from being prospective to no longer being prospective. It is an unimaginable child, imagined nevertheless as such. Hope is formulated on the basis of what is now not hoped for. Difference splits desire, and hope is first wanting and then not-wanting. Desire must then be set upon its path anew, pursuing its own ends, never sure whether its object can ever be attained, or is attainable, or even whether there is an object to attain at all. In any case, these vicissitudes of desire are founded upon the unimaginable child that is yet imagined as no longer wanted, that child against which the wanted child is defined as "different".

Dena Davis also focuses on disability (as well as gender) in relation to reproductive technologies, and proposes that "the concept of choice is at the heart of [my] book . . ." (Davis, 2001, p. 1). Davis wishes to negotiate the questions outlined above in relation to which choices may be made, and why, on the basis of her proposal (drawn from the work of philosopher Joel Feinberg (*ibid.*, p. 23)) that children have a "right to an open future . . . [p]arents ought not to make decisions about their children that severely and irreversibly restrict their right to an open future" (*ibid.*, pp. 5, 27). Davis engages with several of the points I have touched on above in arguing that

> The decision to have a child is never made for the sake of the child—for no child then exists. We choose to have children for myriad reasons, but before the child is conceived, those reasons can only be self-regarding. The child is a means to our ends: a certain kind of joy and pride, continuing the family name, and fulfillment of religious and societal expectations, among others. But morally the child is first and foremost an end in herself. Good parenthood requires a balance between having a child for our own sakes and being open to the moral reality that the child will exist for *her* own sake, with her own talents and weaknesses, propensities and interests, and with her own life to make . . . By closing off the child's right to an open future, they define the child as an entity who exists

to fulfill parental hopes and dreams, not her own. [*ibid.*, p. 34, original emphasis]

Davis, too, is clearly addressing important questions, but, as with the writers earlier, the difficulty lies in determining exactly how this statement of principle will play out in Davis's further arguments, and how unforeseen consequences may arise from certain assumptions. First, in the passage above, there is a child that does not yet exist, which is to become the child that does. Here it is conception and morality that mark the transition from a non-existent child to an existent child. The non-existent child, prior to conception and morality, is an assemblage of "self-regarding reasons", while the child that exists does so "for *her* own sake". The "reality" of the morality cannot reach the not-yet parent, at least not prior to conception. The existence of the child, in this sense, is a prerequisite to the existence of the "good parent", whose goodness consists of being able to acknowledge the existence of that child. As with Wolf, the child that exists and the good parent are defined in relation to each other: goodness is the ability to perceive autonomous presence.

Davis starts to become entangled further in the implications of this conception when she notes in a footnote to her "short discussion of harm", that with

> preconception decisions such as sex selection, the use of the term *right* becomes somewhat metaphorical. If, for example, little Jane is born as a result of her parents' use of sperm sorting to be sure that they have a girl, and if . . . that is morally problematic because it compromises Jane's right to a future that is relatively unconstrained by intense gender expectations, I can only mean that metaphorically. If Jane's parents took my advice and had a child without sex selection, that child (even if a girl) would almost certainly not have been Jane. [*ibid.*, pp. 36–37]

As before, conception marks a transition in terms of rights. "Existence" here is to do with particularity. Any existing child can only have been itself, and therefore cannot, for Davis, be said to have a right not to have been itself. "Metaphoricity" is brought in to negotiate a problem generated by the claim that the Jane produced by any other process than that occurred would ("almost certainly") not be Jane anyway. Jane, for Davis, has no rights not to be Jane, but she still wants to argue that the parents ought not to be permitted to select for gender, because it would harm the metaphorical rights of the metaphorical Jane. Jane is therefore both Jane and not Jane, or, to put it in the terms I have been following above, the child that exists is also the child that does not exist. The temporality, or advent of conception and morality that is to effect this transformation has not taken place yet for Davis in the case of "preconception decisions". Metaphor is part of her attempt, then, to define the good parent in relation to an existing child, even when that child, in this case, is seen by her not to exist (yet). Even the non-existent child, therefore, exists as child. The future child is, as child, prospectively allocated the real, which is understood as autonomy and particular existence.

Finally, it is, of course, not irrelevant that Davis proposes that sex selection ought to be avoided because Jane has a right "to a future that is *relatively* unconstrained by *intense* gender expectations" (my emphases). The "open future" is always limited, to Davis, by gender expectations, and it is only the degree of them that can be contained. As with the child, gender is assumed as an inevitable. The "open future" is already limited in its openness by childhood and gender: the (most) open future is male. Thus, openness is delimited in terms of what Davis assumes as inevitable and unavoidable against the optional and avoidable. In this sense, I would suggest that the child, as in the reading I offered of Farquhar's work in Chapter Two, intervenes in, or ends, argument in the production of a wish. The conclusions drawn are themselves, in this sense, the child that is wanted, not a child that can be proved through argument. The child is thus situated as itself part of the problem of proof: whether argument can be read as grounded in an ultimate point of origin, or fixed point of departure, or whether argument is to be understood as always departing from a wish.

Notes

1. See, for a discussion of some issues related to those I raise here also, Taylor, Layne, and Wozniak, *Consuming Motherhood* (2004); as Taylor writes:

Motherhood is supposed to be a special kind of relationship, uniquely important because uniquely free of the kind of calculating instrumentality associated with the consumption of objects. It stands for "love", in sharp contrast to "money"—a simple but persistent opposition that structures American middle-class cultural values concerning family, parenthood, and child-rearing. [Taylor, 2004, p. 3]

2. Alison Clarke's chapter, for instance, in Taylor, Layne, and Wozniak's volume, considers one version of such a foetus:

"things" emerge as the principle means by which women "make" (often far in advance of the anticipated birth) their babies and themselves as mothers: Through the buying, giving, and preserving of things, women and their social networks actively construct their babies-to-be and would-have-been babies, real babies and themselves as "real mothers", worthy of the social recognition this role entails. [Clarke, 2004, p. 57]

Lynn Morgan, too, provides a formulation of this issue in relation to the political problems around abortion in the USA:

Feminist philosophers . . . watch uneasily as the American public is distracted, enthralled, incited, and sometimes literally crazed by proliferating images of fetuses, increasingly depicted as free-floating, disembodied little babies at the mercy of their uncaring or vindictive mothers. Feminist philosophers rightly want to bring women back, literally "into the picture", to point out once more that "a fetus inhabits a woman's body and is wholly dependent on her unique contribution to its maintenance". [Morgan, 1996, p. 50]

Morgan continues by discussing several of the implications of these ideas, including assumptions around the body and the child, in a way related to several of my analyses in this book.

3. Both Jacqueline Rose, in *The Case of Peter Pan*, and analyses such as those of James Kincaid in *Child-Loving: The Erotic Child and Victorian Culture* (1992) point to the paedophilic implications of the desire for the child *as* child. I am not focusing on this aspect explicitly at this point, but it forms part of the overall implications of this argument, which I have also explored in "The psychopathology of everyday children's literature criticism" (Lesnik-Oberstein, 2000).

4. Thanks to Professor Bowlby for giving me a copy of this review.
5. Squier adds that "they differ in the meanings they attach to it [the images of babies in bottles], whether explicitly or implicitly" (Squier, 1994, p. 2), and I am, of course, reading a meaning of visuality in the specific context I am addressing here. Nevertheless, I do read Squier's study overall as a close and detailed elaboration of this visual own baby.

Another kind of study which considers aspects of a visuality of the own baby, is that on the roles of obstetrical ultrasound. Janelle Taylor is one example of several researchers who argue that one role attributed to these images (specifically in American culture in this case) is that of promoting and regulating "bonding" between mother and baby, and that

> The notion of ultrasound "bonding" equates pregnancy with the relationship between a woman and her newborn child. In this regard, it presumes a view of pregnancy as absolute, a relationship of unconditional maternal love for the developing fetus. At the same time, however, the ultrasound "bonding" theory suggests that this relationship forms through technologically and professionally mediated spectatorship, and even implies that it is the technology itself that in some sense "gives birth", to the fetus, construed as a child. [Taylor, 1998, p. 23]

As Taylor's comment suggests, this visuality has also been seen by many writers as introducing an "image of fetal autonomy, the strategic separation of gestating mother from fetus" (Squier, 1994, p. 134), but I am here focusing on reproductive technologies in terms of the production of the wanted or hoped-for child as the own child. That the ownness or ownership of the child is in turn contested and contestable in a range of ways I take to be part of this argument, not a contradiction of it.
6. Monica Konrad, referring to the work of anthropologist John Barnes, further specifies an increased separation between a professional, clinical, gaze and a "public" gaze, which is largely excluded from this new visuality:

> Since then, the advent of the new life technologies has made knowledge about the status of maternity less "macroscopic"—in Barnes's terms. Not only do laboratory technicians and others work routinely with the aid of microscopes and other new optical instruments such as *in vivo* nanoscopes, but life itself has become miniaturized and the assumed connections between

persons and body parts have become far less visible, far less ascertainable as certain knowledge. [Konrad, 2003, p. 122]

7. Many of my analyses can be read in the light of Derrida's comments here, as well as in his further works. With thanks to Stephen Thomson for giving me a copy of this essay.

8. See, for another example of a book that addresses issues of social justice and definitions of ability and disability, but not of the child or the wanting of the child, Joan Rothschild, *The Dream of the Perfect Child* (2005). Rothschild's arguments also provide further examples of the discourse / rhetoric / real confusions I analysed in the first two chapters of this book.

CHAPTER FOUR

The child that is wanted: kinship and the body of evidence

I n this chapter I want to look more closely still at how the "own" child that underpins and justifies reproductive technologies is defined. We started to consider in the previous chapter how the own child is understood in relation to certain ideas of biology. The idea of the "biological" child is ubiquitous in writings and discussions around reproductive technologies, and it has been pointed out by a number of anthropologists working in this area that the "biological" and the "own" are understood in a range of ways by those involved in reproductive technologies. Two areas that are key to ideas of the biological and the own are genetics and anthropological kinship studies.

I will return to a quotation from anthropologist Heléna Ragoné:

> [artificial reproductive technologies] have served to defamiliarize what was once understood to be the "natural" basis of human procreation and relatedness . . . as the Comaroffs so eloquently said of ethnography, "to make the familiar strange and the strange familiar, all the better to understand them both". [Ragoné, 1998, p. 118]

I mentioned this quote previously, in my introduction, to indicate ways in which reproductive technologies are seen to introduce new perspectives on "human procreation and relatedness". We saw a further specific example of this in Rachel Bowlby's review of Judith Butler's consideration of kinship. I suggested in relation to my discussion of Bowlby's comments that the innovation of reproductive technologies can, however, also be read, in terms of the own child, as not innovative, but as a self-figured repetition of a narrative of history. To be clear: I am not claiming that this reading is itself a repetition of a known historical "truth". Instead, I am arguing that the history of reproduction is itself written retrospectively—from the perspective of the present—as a history of stabilities and instabilities, socialities and biologies. In this sense, as in the previous chapters, I am following a Freudian or Foucauldian understanding of history as a production of the past in and by the present. (In this way, I am paralleling history to Freud's thinking around memory. Many commentators read Michel Foucault as anti-Freudian, but, as will be clear here, I do not. I take Foucault to be conceptualizing history as a production of the past in the present in a similar way to Freud's memory. It should be noted, too, however, that both Freud and Foucault's positions on these issues are not stable or singular, so that I am foregrounding a particular reading of moments in their arguments.) As anthropologist David Schneider comments, albeit in a slightly different context, in his study of American kinship,

> kinship is whatever the biogenetic relationship is. If science discovers new facts about biogenetic relationship, then that is what kinship is, and was all along, although it may not have been known at the time. [Carsten, 2004, p. 112]

Janet Carsten considers David Schneider's work at length in her recent work on kinship *After Kinship*. In considering how kinship has figured within the discipline of anthropology, and how it might go on to be considered, Carsten concludes:

> ... I would rephrase [Bruno] Latour's point about abandoning the nature–culture divide. Rather than moving away from this distinction, we need to make it the subject of proper scrutiny. It is precisely the ways in which people in different cultures distinguish between what is given and what is made, what might be called biological and what might be called social, and the points at which

they make such distinctions, that, without preconceptions, should be at the center of the comparative anthropological analysis of kinship. If we can manage to place side by side the ouija board and the Malay house, the sociality of anonymity and the Ecuadorean meal, or Tallensi personhood and organ donation in the United Kingdom, then we might be on the way to achieving a new kind of comparative understanding of kinship. [*ibid.*, p. 189]

I want here to take up Carsten's invitation, and consider precisely how in her own text distinctions between nature and culture are made, and at which points, in order to try to explain why I am going to disagree with Carsten's hopeful statement that she finds

> this sense of excitement afforded by the "sociality of anonymity" [of London egg donors in Monica Konrad's 1998 study] infectious. It suggests that assisted reproduction does not just raise concerns with which we were already familiar ... Nor are we necessarily entering an era in which the identity of persons is constrained by an ever-increasing concern for bounded individuals with discrete and singly owned body parts, whose genetic endowment has determined who they are even before birth. [*ibid.*, p. 183]

Like Dion Farquhar, Carsten clearly finds the possibility of a "geneticist" determination unsettling, and is happy to read in the formulations of kinship around reproductive technologies instead a liberation from constraint, and a possible proliferation or increasing diffuseness of relationship and identity.

If Farquhar draws her liberational model from a celebratory investment in an exuberance of the market, as well as a wished for "third way" of conceiving family, Carsten draws hers, I will argue, from two factors, one related to Farquhar's, and one somewhat different—at least apparently so. First, Carsten, like Farquhar, is open about an ethical investment in her work. Both these narratives, not coincidentally, I think, start out (as many do, as I have noted before) with an autobiographical fragment that works to introduce this investment as both a self-acknowledged and legitimized grounding for their studies. With Carsten, as with Farquhar, however, I will suggest that some implications of this investment are not fully within the control of their arguments. Second, unlike Farquhar, Carsten's readings rest on a residual retrieval of precisely what she is scrupulously putting into question: certain divisions between nature and culture, and, with this, certain definitions of genetics. Attendant on this ethical investment and the hope of an escape from an uncomfortably determining geneticism are ideas of metaphoricity and a complementary "literalness" to which I have referred before in discussing both Dion Farquhar and Janelle Taylor's writings in the previous chapter. I will look at each of these aspects to argue why I do not share Carsten's hopeful view of a liberation from constraint through reproductive technologies. Instead, I see this hope as precisely diagnostic of the own child as the definite product of reproductive technologies (whatever definitions of the "own" might be deployed). The insistence on the own child of reproductive technologies that I have been reading throughout may be wished away, but, as I have argued throughout, this to me is indeed a wish; a wish after the fact of the production and institution of reproductive technologies that rest entirely on the own child.

To turn first, then, to Carsten's use of biology and genetics. Throughout her book, Carsten closely reconsiders a history of anthropology in terms of an (retrospectively viewed) essentializing and subsequent de-essentializing of biology, nature, and gender. Reviewing a number of positions, Carsten concludes by discussing Judith Butler's writing on gender:

> [t]his more radically constructionist model dissolves the distinction between sex and gender; both are mutually constituted through the repeated enactment of appropriate gender performance. . . . While this position is apparently a logical one to take, it inevitably raises certain questions. . . . If the determinism of sex seems to have been replaced by the determinism of gender, it is paradoxical that bodies should still be on the agenda at all. Yet they figure largely (if somewhat abstractly) in Butler's follow-up to *Gender Trouble* (1990), entitled *Bodies That Matter* (1993) . . . This is a sophisticated rendition of a performative position, the central point being that the very act of referring to bodies actually helps to create them. As Busby . . . notes in her important critique, however, Butler's notion of performance is quite removed from actual everyday practice, and is grounded in linguistic and philosophical theory. . . . The determinism of the physical facts has been replaced by the impossibility of escaping "discursive iterations". [*ibid.*, pp. 65–66]

For Carsten, bodies should no longer be on the agenda, were Butler's position to be not paradoxical. This must constitute on Carsten's part an inability to conceive of the body as entirely discursive or performative, to use Butler's term. For how does the claim that the body is discursive lead to the body no longer being on the agenda at all? This seems to assume that bodies would be made invisible, ephemeral, or irrelevant in their discursivity. That assumption in turn must rely on a comparison with a maintained non-discursivity of relevance. That this is indeed Carsten's reading of Butler is confirmed in two further ways. First, by the formulation "that the very act of referring to bodies actually helps to create them". "Helps" indicates a partial role, rather than an entirety of discursivity or textuality that I—and Carsten herself in other statements—read in Butler's work. Second, by the comment in brackets that the bodies figure "somewhat abstractly", and this is in line with Carsten's general distrust, in her book, of the abstract and theoretical compared to an intimate, emotional, and felt experience of anthropology. Carsten several times makes comments to the effect that

> [w]hile fully acknowledging the importance of the value of individualism in the West, and its prominent expression in many legal, medical, philosophical, and religious discourses, it is important to recognize that Western notions of the person express other values too. These are present in very familiar and everyday contexts . . . In a game with her father, my then-four-year-old daughter grew tired of him playing the role of a crocodile: "No, no, stop being a crocodile, daddy," she admonished him, "be a person, be yourself, be a daddy." This succinctly phrased and utterly mundane demand makes clear how, for this small child (and, no doubt, most others), personhood, being "oneself", and being a father—in other words, being a relation—are quite intertwined. [*ibid.*, p. 97]

The familiarity and mundanity here are set against texts and narratives of the law, medicine, philosophy, and religion. Even if both can be seen to be allocated the status of discourse, none the less it is the function of the mundanity and the everyday to complicate the stability of the formal text. These are the "messier realities . . . as well as everyday experience" (*ibid.*, p. 16), while "legal history, philosophy, and theology . . . [give] a rather rarified view of what constitutes the person in Western contexts" (*ibid.*, p. 87).

It will be clear by now that I would not read it as accidental that it is the child who is at the heart of this vignette of the "very familiar"; a child, moreover, who is most exempted by definition—"(and, no doubt, most others)"—from the very individuality that is under question in the passage. If the Western individuality of the formal texts turns out to be as relational as the foreign in the everyday, then the child is not just relational, but every child or most children. The child is here, then, beyond doubt and, in this sense, beyond anthropology, as its being so is in brackets too.[1] This, paradoxically, in a volume which is highly and self-consciously theoretical. Nevertheless, this ultimate distrust of the formal, the abstract, and the theoretical, can be read too in Carsten's approval of Busby's comments. In noting that Butler's use of "performance" is "removed from actual everyday practice" Carsten relies on a notion of actuality and everydayness that operates throughout her arguments as a realm of nuance, differentiation, and complication in the face of theoretical clarities and rigidities, in a similar way to Janelle Taylor's view of the limitations of the theoretical in comparison to ordinary women's daily lives. A disruptive and multiplicitous actuality erupts into the nicely ordered realm of the abstract. However theoretical the body may be here, therefore, there is also a residually less abstract body, housed in the realm of the everyday and experiential. I should note here straight away that I do not find this residual body and its attendant residualities obviously or easily in Carsten's lucid and learned writing. That it is, nevertheless, there, and that it has important consequences, I will continue to argue.

The actuality and everydayness to which Carsten returns repeatedly also enters to address what she sees as the problem of the "determinism of the physical facts" having been replaced in Butler's work by the "impossibility of escaping 'discursive reiterations'". In order to achieve this interpretation of Butler, Carsten has to overlook in her discussion an aspect of the quotation from Butler that she uses: "sex is both produced *and destabilised* in the course of this reiteration" (*ibid.*, p. 66, my emphasis). In this sense, Carsten, in not addressing the claim to an inherent destabilization in reiteration, indeed reads Butler as "radically constructionist" (*ibid.*, p. 65), not deconstructivist (as I do). In these terms, this relates back to my discussion in the previous chapter, of the child as repetition, a repetition that I nevertheless read as an insistence that is not identical. As Heidegger formulates this:

Die Formel A=A spricht von Gleichheit. Sie nennt A nicht als dasselbe. Die geläufige Formel für den Satz der Identität verdeckt somit gerade das, was der Satz sagen möchte: A ist A, d.h. jedes A ist selber dasselbe. . . . Der Dativ ἑαυτῷ bedeutet: jedes etwas selber ist ihm selbst: zurückgegeben, jedes selber ist dasselbe—nämlich für es selbst mit ihm selbst. Unsere deutsche Sprache verschenkt hier gleich wie die griechische den Vorzug, das Identische mit demselben Wort, aber dies in einer Fuge seiner verschiedenen Gestalten zu verdeutlichen. [Heidegger, 1957, pp. 12, 14][2]

I read Butler, then, as I read Rose on the child, in the light of Heidegger's thinking around repetition as not being able to be a guarantee of the identical, but simultaneously, as Butler indicates, as the maintenance of instability.[3]

Carsten's residual body is co-extensive with a residually "scientific" understanding of genetics. I read this in the sections precisely where Carsten seeks to minimise any simple reliance on genetics as accounting for adoptees' efforts to contact their 'biological' parents. Carsten confesses that

[m]y own hesitancy about the research [into adoptees] that I was undertaking was well articulated for me by a colleague who prefaced her friendly enquiries about this work with the remark, "Oh, are they all terribly geneticist?" Indeed, the assumption that the motivations of adopted people seeking such meetings would reveal thoroughly "geneticist" views about kinship and personhood was a depressingly obvious one to make. The reality, which I am just beginning to tease apart, is of course somewhat different. [Carsten, 2004, p. 147]

This reality, for Carsten, is that she finds an

acknowledged importance of time and effort to the production of kinship . . . and a strong disavowal that in the absence of such sustained nurturance there is an automatic bond of kinship given by the facts of birth. [ibid., p. 149]

At the same time, these acknowledgements and disavowals "might be thought surprising in people who had committed considerable time and effort to discovering whom their birth relatives were" (*ibid.*, p. 149).

What I read here is an implicit defining of the depressingly "thoroughly 'geneticist' " as the holding of the view that *only* the bond of birth constitutes acknowledged kinship. As long as this is supplemented by a view that there is also a kinship of "time and effort", the depression of a "primacy" of the thoroughly geneticist view can be lifted for Carsten. But this leaves several questions, which, for me, emerge in some of Carsten's further comments on her adoptees' views. As one example of how "the assumption that these searches [for the birth parents] were predicated on a thoroughly geneticist view of human nature was not borne out" (*ibid.*, p. 150), Carsten recalls the case of an interviewee who

> had felt it necessary to establish the identity of her birth father by DNA testing, in spite of her own appraisal of his character as quite dishonest, and of the manifest impossibility of establishing a satisfactory relationship with him. The results of such a test would establish the truth—or as she put it, "stop the lies"—in the face of his persistent evasions, but clearly she would not by this stage have asserted very much beyond this physical tie to her birth father. [*ibid.*, p. 151]

The DNA testing is here Carsten's "thoroughly geneticist", and it is put alongside components of a psychological narrative of character and relationship. In the face of the latter being absent or unsatisfactory, Carsten sees the DNA test as being conducted "in spite of" this, and she is "struck by the apparent futility of the procedure" (*ibid.*, p. 104). Therefore, the DNA test can only be fully legitimate in this story had it provided the basis for a (more satisfactory) psychological kinship relationship, or the development thereof. Because the birth father was psychologically unsatisfactory and then died, the DNA test "would not by this stage have asserted much beyond this physical tie". But to whom is this a "physical tie", or, to put it differently, a physicality which is "not . . . much"? To the interviewee, as portrayed by Carsten, or to Carsten? I can read a different definition of the DNA test in the interviewee's narrative of the establishment of truth, or the "stop[ping of] . . . lies". This seems to me to define the DNA test in terms neither physical nor minimal, but precisely as a transcendent and absolute speaker of a truth of paternity. The DNA test can speak this truth *as* the father. The lying, persistently evasive father has been replaced by a father who can no longer lie by definition.

In this sense, the DNA test is the inevitably truthful revelation of origin, and, as such, the provider of a teleology of identity. As Marilyn Strathern suggests,

> the potential of genetic identification has created a new object of popular knowledge *for conceptualising* persons: genetic destiny. . . . Questions that the individual person once asked of him- or herself about origin and links need no longer be asked of kinship when they can be asked of the individual's genome. [Strathern, 1992, p. 178, original emphasis]

It is to be stressed that Strathern, as in my own argument here, is not herself accepting genetics as a teleology of identity (or as a "scientific" or "natural" kinship), but describing her readings of its being understood as such. It seems to me that Carsten first provides her interviewee's narrative of the DNA test as "stop[ping] the lies", and subsequently redefines the DNA test—and in so doing de-prioritizes it—as not much more than a physicality which is to be seen as minimal in comparison to a meaningful psychology of relationship.

This prioritizing of a psychological understanding of kinship over one understood as thoroughly geneticist is repeated, to my reading, in the next case that Carsten mentions:

> One woman described how, as a child, she had always been very much aware of her curly hair because her adopted parents and their families had straight hair. When she eventually met her birth mother, she realized the provenance of her curls. But in this case, as in many others, the relationship itself had not got onto a harmonious footing. While physical connections were often easy to make, emotional ties did not necessarily follow. [Carsten, 2004, p. 151]

The recognition of the curls is allocated by Carsten to an ease of "physical connections", but how is this necessarily "physical"? How might this not also, or instead, be read as itself an "emotional" tie, or indeed neither, but specifically the reading of the "biological", "genetic", "birth" or "own" which is negotiated in so many narratives of adoption, as Carsten herself notes? How otherwise to account for the interviewee's narrative including a description of how "very much aware" she had "always been" of her curls, as compared to the straight hair of her adoptive family? In precisely pre-empting the divisions according to her appropriate notion of genetics and the physical, and the psychological or emotional, Carsten also, I would argue, pre-empts precisely a more complex understanding of how the uses and meanings of genetics, biology, and the physical may have little to do with the "dictionary" definitions she seems to assume at these points. Carsten herself traces in her fifth chapter, the "Uses and abuses of substance", how

> [i]f we return to the dictionary definitions with which I began this chapter, however, it is notable that the meanings of *substance*, although they include corporeal matter and the consistency of a fluid, do not specify malleability, transformability, or relationality as inherent properties of substance. But these properties have been important aspects of the analytic work achieved by substance in the non-Western examples I have cited. [*ibid.*, p. 133, original emphasis]

In allowing the meanings of DNA tests and curls to be questioned and perhaps shifted accordingly, Carsten might, I would suggest, understand a different meaning for her interviewees than a simple thorough geneticism, divided off from a meaningful psychology and emotion.

In the interpretations she supplies, Carsten can escape the depression of the limitations of her understanding of genetics and the physical by supplementing it with a psychology, but she can no longer, I would suggest, read the possible meanings of the finding of psychologically unsatisfactory birth parents as anything other than a failure, or, at most, the retrieval of a minimal physicality. As Carsten writes, "[i]n just a few cases, my informants described being able to establish some kind of harmonious relations with his or her birth kin . . . such [are] positive outcomes . . ." (*ibid.*, pp. 148–149). Where she records the motivations of her interviewees' search for their birth kin as being most frequently "simply, 'to know where I came from', 'to be complete', or 'to find out who I am'. . . . answers . . . so formulaic that they suggested that the question itself was almost redundant" (*ibid.*, p. 147), I would note that these questions need not be taken as answered necessarily by "harmonious relations", however (more) positive such an outcome might be seen to be. Instead, an interpretation of the DNA test and curls as themselves, if you like, part of a psychology of origins and belonging, might account better for that sense of the search for the birth parents being "entirely obvious" (*ibid.*). This obviousness is the reading of "genetics", DNA, or physical resemblance, for instance, *as* the "roots" that are so ubiquitously assumed to be what adopted children lack, and that they must, in whatever way, find. It is also this interpretation that accounts, paradoxically, for a specifically cultural understanding of the meanings of adoption. For it is, according precisely to Carsten and many other anthropologists, a specifically Western (and specific historical) account of adoption that assumes these "roots" and their unquestionable and unquestioned centrality to the identity of the adoptee (and non-adoptees too).

Finally, my reading would also produce a congruence between Carsten and American anthropologist Kaja Finkler's accounts of their interviewees, rather than the disparity that Carsten tentatively notes:

> the assumption that [birth parent] searches were predicated on a thoroughly geneticist view was not borne out. And here there is perhaps a divergence from the American case where Kaja Finkler ... suggests that adoptees' searches for their birth kin are premised upon a quite thoroughly geneticized view of their health status, personalities, and kinship. [*ibid.*, pp. 150–151]

For although it is indeed the case that Finkler's interviewees use a language of genetic determinism, Finkler does not read this geneticism as necessarily conforming to a pre-determined "scientific" genetics, as Carsten does with her "thorough geneticism". Indeed, Finkler reads her interviewees' uses of genetics in turn as shifting along, or being composed of, a range of meanings:

> [c]onsider also that Kirsten confounds various facets of her person with genetics, including physical resemblance and political activism ... [her] emphasis on medical history anchors her person in her patienthood. Her biomedical understanding of genetic inheritance requires her even to be on annual recall schedule ... The medical history, by recapitulating genetic inheritance, turns into a kinship history and an ideological map of the past. Importantly too,

having her biological family's medical history affirmed for Kirsten her sanity . . . in this instance, a genetic medical history is equated with mental stability. [Finkler, 2000, pp. 125–126]

Instead, then, of Finkler accepting her interviewees' use of genetics as a depressing primacy of the merely physical that Carsten fears, she reads these genetics as, in turn, being about a range of meanings. It is only by adhering to a stable definition of genetics as the "truth" of a merely physical that Americanness could be, in this context, defined as the (greater) succumbing to a depressing materiality. (It may be noted that my rereading of this comparison between Americanness and Scottishness is in this respect not unrelated to my rereading, in the first chapter, of a disparity between Englishness and Americanness that Gay Becker suggests in comparing her interviewees with those of Sarah Franklin.) As Carsten herself notes elsewhere,

Schneider asserted that the primacy of biological ties in anthropological analyses of kinship arose from indigenous European and American folk assumptions. But it would appear that not all the natives adhere to these assumptions in the same way or to the same degree. And this might suggest that the primacy of biology was a product of a particular analytic strategy rather than straightforwardly imported from European folk models of kinship. [Carsten, 2004, p. 146]

I am making the same suggestion with regard to the non-primacy of the thoroughly genetic in Carsten's readings of her adoptees' search for their birth parents.

To turn to the other issue that I raised in relation to Carsten's work to begin with, I also link her residual body, with its attendant splits between the physical and psychological, the everyday and formal discourse, to the nature of the ethical commitment that Carsten professes. I analyse this ethical commitment as relying on this residuality, as if the non-residual body that Carsten understands Butler to be formulating would indeed evaporate or dissipate. Materiality, in this context, becomes a guarantor of a reality that is linked to the capacity for suffering or pain. (Compare this also to my analysis in Chapter One of the "speaking body" in Lay, Gurak, Gravon, and Myntti, 2000.)

As Carsten notes of her reading of Thomas Lacqueur,

[a]lthough Lacqueur considerably destabilizes the relation between biology and culture, and between sex and gender, he remains careful to maintain "a distinction between the body and the body as discursively constituted, between seeing and seeing-as" . . . Interestingly, he suggests that the reasons for not abandoning this distinction are, in the end, ethical and political. [Carsten, 2004, p. 65]

Judith Butler has commented on this type of rebuttal to her position that

Theorizing from the ruins of the Logos invites the following question: "What about the materiality of the body?" Actually, in the recent past, the question was repeatedly formulated to me this way: "What about the materiality of the body, *Judy*?" I took it that the addition of "Judy" was an effort to dislodge me from the more formal "Judith" and to recall me to a bodily life that could not be theorized away . . . restored to that bodily being which is, after all, considered to be most real, most pressing, most undeniable. . . . And if I persisted in this notion that bodies were in some way *constructed*, perhaps I really thought that words alone had the power to craft bodies from their own linguistic substance? Couldn't someone simply take me aside? [Butler, 1993, pp. ix–x, original emphasis]

In this way, I find it logical that I read Carsten's struggle with an ethics of materiality most clearly in a section on nationalism. Accompanying the notion of an ethics of materiality is a reliance on a notion of "emotional appeal" that Carsten, interestingly, hardly uses elsewhere in her book: "Why is it that the nation exercises such an extraordinary emotional appeal over its citizens? Why, in other words, are people prepared to lay down their lives for their country?" Where Carsten, again, precisely wishes to "scrutiniz[e] the 'blurred boundaries' between kinship, the nation, and religion more carefully" (Carsten, 2004, p. 155), her turn to emotional appeal has already split the nation apart from its citizens, necessitating its seduction of those citizens; a seduction, moreover, which is—appropriately to a narrative of romance—conducted in and through a realm of emotion. This formulation, of course, is also predicated on a very particular understanding of culture, but Carsten's text does not recognize or address this. It is relevant here that Carsten refers to nationhood and nationalism as "ideologies". I would refer back to my analyses of "ideology" as a particular kind of persuasive language in the writing of Gay Becker in the first chapter of this book: "'culture' [in Becker] . . . splits into several kinds of stories. Gender and normalcy are defined as 'ideologies' that function as constriction and coercion" (see Chapter One, pp. 11–12, referring to Becker, 2000, p. 29). In this part of Carsten's discussion, "ideology" also functions to split culture into several kinds of stories, where ideology is an external story that must, but also can, seduce the citizen.

Under pressure of possible impending warfare and death, Carsten feels that "calls to the fatherland or motherland in the name of the unity of the nation, or the solidarity of a brotherhood of fellow citizens, have a particular appeal" (Carsten, 2004, p. 158). The nation is here seen to be conflated with, or figured as, kinship by the use of terms such as "fatherland", "motherland", or "brotherhood", but its preconceived separation as an entity from the citizens, and the procedure of an emotional seduction, persist. This defines citizenship as a "particular" vulnerability to certain external factors, and in this sense therefore as already co-extensive with them. The citizen can be read, in this sense, as, for Carsten, already the kin of the state, even apart from any familial terminology. This unnoted kinship is further elaborated in a use of "metaphor" and the "literal", which, I would argue, is parallel to, or part of, the other residualities I have traced above. For, here,

> the violence of civil warfare . . . suggests that in certain negative circumstances the metaphors of kinship have the ability to take on meanings that are more literal than metaphorical. In such drastic moments of upheaval, commentators find themselves at a loss to account for the processes of destruction they witness. How is it possible for a war between "external" forces to become one that transforms longstanding neighbours into enemies? [*ibid.*, p. 158]

That Carsten here can, and does, revert to defining kinship as being composed of "metaphors" is part of the upholding of the residualities, and their attendant ethics, that I read as interwoven through Carsten's theoretical deliberations. Interestingly, the unnoted kinship of citizenship and nation would provide one account that Carsten sees as lacking of the enmity between neighbours. For the predication of this kinship, through "appeal", can be said to already have "internalized" what Carsten here calls "external" forces. Even in Carsten's own prior narrative, in other words, the neighbours were never entirely separate from forces that would otherwise need to corrupt them in order to "transform" them. The split between metaphor and literalness can, then, be read as relying on a world of the real, the everyday, and the material body, while metaphor constitutes a realm of a non-material textuality or language. Carsten writes,

> [t]he deployment of an imagery of kinship in ideologies of nationalism is apparently so conventional as to be hardly worthy of comment. It recalls H. W. Fowler's distinction between "live" and "dead" metaphors—between metaphors that are used with a conscious awareness of the substitution, and those whose use is so conventional that the metaphor has become almost indistinguishable from the literal referent. But Fowler's warning is apt: ". . . the line of distinction between the live and the dead is a shifting one, the dead being sometimes liable, under the stimulus of an affinity or a repulsion, to galvanic stirrings, indistinguishable from life. [*ibid.*, pp. 157–158]

(It is interesting that Carsten turns here to a guide to modern English usage, as she earlier turned to dictionaries in discussing her readings of "substance" in anthropology, to try both the anchor meanings, and then to move on from that anchorage.)

As I have analysed above in Carsten's work, a split is here both introduced and questioned, but persists nevertheless. What is at stake is what can be read as metaphor and what as literal, and the status accorded to these terms. For Carsten, after all, the metaphorical retains a secondariness and derivativeness in the face of the body, the everyday, and the violence of war. As Carsten concludes:

> [Veena] Das . . . reflects on the relation between bodily pain and its articulation in language and memory—both public and private. . . . The infliction of pain on the bodies of the victims is a means of actually making memories. And bodily experiences are not just an idiom for the *representation* of pain and trauma, or a kind of commentary upon it, but are part of that trauma. . . . Such events contradict the conventional wisdom that the occurrence of a language of kinship in political discourses of nationalism is

straightforwardly metaphorical . . . In the extreme, this particular metaphor may transform itself into a quite literal reality [and] we may begin to find an answer to Anderson's question about the emotional appeal of nationalism. . . . [H]ere the emotional power of kinship becomes quite "unfamiliar". It can apparently call forth acts that turn "the familiar person next door" into "a depersonalized alien". It is because such processes must concern us as social scientists, and as citizens, that we should understand the mechanisms of kinship on which they rely. [*ibid.*, pp. 160, 162, original emphasis]

Paradoxically, it is on maintaining a "quite literal reality" that all Carsten's careful attempts to dissolve metaphor as "mere[ly]" secondary and "a superficial phenomenon" (*ibid.*, p. 161) founder. The extremity that transforms metaphor into this literalness is then tautologous with the emotional appeal and the "unfamiliar" emotional power, rather than an explanation of it. Susan Merrill Squier makes a similar argument to my own, when she discusses Marilyn Strathern's comments on the use of the "Mandelbrot set" in a parliamentary debate in 1990, in Great Britain, on the authorizing of research on human embryos up to fourteen days old:

> . . . Strathern argues that the analogy between the Mandelbrot set and embryological development epitomizes the operation of modernist knowledge practices . . . Despite her awareness of the constructive function of analogies, however, Strathern dodges the full implications of the Mandelbrot set analogy when she characterizes "the metaphor so brilliantly summoned" as "an artificial graft, one that bore no intrinsic relationship to the subject of embryo development". Analogies are neither merely artificial grafts, nor wholly innocent. I suggest we would do well to reconsider the relationship between the analogies we make and the fields they are intended to illuminate. . . . Moreover, analogy is not a neutral scientific tool: "Analogy and primary referent are both altered in meaning as a result of juxtaposition". [Squier, 1994, pp. 25, 26]

Going even further, I am arguing that "analogy", "metaphor" and "referent" may themselves be "altered in meaning" and in status, as a result of interpretation.[4]

Moreover, the use of the "unfamiliar" creates a double effect for Carsten's theoretical considerations, for to whom is this emotional power of kinship "unfamiliar"? This can be read in Carsten's reference to "us as social scientists, and as citizens". On the one hand, as citizens "ourselves", the narration of the text locates the vulnerability to nationalist ideology also within itself and the group it takes itself as belonging to. On the other hand, the narration declares this group to be apart from, or innocent of, the experiencing of that power which is "unfamiliar". This power is only familiar to a nationalism "over there", so that the production through comparison of accounts of kinship that Carsten states she is striving towards is already split by an unfamiliarity produced by extremity, even as she finds liberating the idea of putting "the West into the same analytical frame as non-Western cultures" (Carsten, 2004, p. 189). In other words, any anthropological comparison such as this already predetermines the split between a " 'they' " and a " 'we' " (*ibid.*) which Carsten wants to trouble through her quotation marks, and is directed by it. What is at stake here again is the status and orientation of anthropological perspective, as I also discussed in the cases of Gay Becker, Kaja Finkler, and Lay, Gurak, Gravon, and Myntti in the first chapter of this book. Together with this, complex ideas of kinship not explicitly formulated in familial terms re-enter also, such as: is the anthropologist kin to his or her subject / object of study? In this context, I might say that the constitution of the area of study of anthropology *as* "object" or "subject" is part of the problem of kinship.

I have analysed the issues at stake in Carsten's text at some length, not only because Carsten is positioned as one of the theoretical innovators of anthropological kinship studies, but because it is these issues that I see as being fundamentally much more widely involved with the own child in, and of, reproductive technologies. If, as Marilyn Strathern, Sarah Franklin, Heléna Ragoné, Charis Cussins Thompson, Janet Carsten, and many other anthropologists and theorists suggest, reproductive technologies are, indeed, not only an important "new" area for anthropological kinship study, but may also affect retrospectively understandings of past anthropologies of kinship, then the issues I have investigated in Janet Carsten's work, are, I suggest, all bound up in the ways in which both the new theories are promulgated, and the ways prior theories are re-examined and reformulated.

It is not irrelevant, perhaps, that I read the chapter on assisted reproduction as the most uneasy part of *After Kinship*. (To repeat a clarification I have made before: I am not speculating on Janet

Carsten's views or feelings about her text, but reading certain aspects of the narration of *After Kinship* that I label "Carsten" for the sake of convenience.) That Carsten writes of being "infected" (Carsten, 2004, p. 182) by the excitement of Monica Konrad's conclusions about the "sociality of anonymity" (*ibid.*), of the London egg donors of her study seems to me to signal one of the ends of theory in this text. It is as if Carsten can turn with relief to not having a choice about the infection with this view. It fulfils her ethical preference for a not thoroughly geneticized world, in which an everyday anonymity prevails for the eggs donated over a more formal status of those eggs as genetic material with "inherent biogenetic properties" (*ibid.*, p. 181). But I am arguing here that, as I argued in relation to Dion Farquhar, a wish, although at the start of every argument, can not legitimately intervene at any other point to shift positions and outcomes. Neither can an ethics of material-ity function to prove a kinder, better world, in which the body is self-evidently a body of incontestable pain and suffering, above all demanding an appropriately ethical response. The own child is not necessarily the "ownness" of a strictly "biogenetic" genetics, but neither is that ownness dissolved or released by a "sociality of anonymity". For why, then, finally, should the egg donors donate eggs at all? Konrad's anonymity can not, after all, trump the status of the eggs *as* the body (part) which makes possible the production of the right child: as the baby witnessed as emerging from the body. In this context, the sociality of anonymity functions to uphold an idea of initially "unique, autonomous, and individualized" (*ibid.*) (not-"anonymous") bodies as merged into one indiscriminately, and this final body is the body of the woman to whom the eggs are donated. The eggs are released to be *her* body, in this case. Carsten, significantly for this analysis, writes:

> Donors see themselves as simply furnishing a means for "starting off" a process that the recipients will "finish" . . . Rather than talk-ing in terms of body-parts that are "owned", these women see themselves as being part of a joint effort to help infertile women conceive. [*ibid.*, p. 182]

To me, this strengthens, and does not weaken, precisely the priority and centrality of the own child. This own child, as I hope

I have demonstrated, is the product of the body of evidence on every level, and, indeed, as every level.

The child, then, is the seen and see-able. It is defined as a result, a consequence, an outcome. It is an object so sufficient unto itself that it does not require to be a subject of further analysis, as Jacqueline Rose argues. In reading the child of reproductive technologies as such a child, the child as utter presence, beyond the need for analysis, I would note too, as I have done elsewhere (see Lesnik-Oberstein (2002), that the child is rarely or minimally listed in indices of studies on reproductive technologies or kinship studies (or in other fields). It is not seen to be the subject or topic of most such studies, as I have suggested previously in this book, and proposed indeed as the reason for it. For, I am arguing, in entering a field instead as a self-constituted object, the child crucially underpins a residual objectivity that stymies some of the most sophisticated proposals for innovation in anthropological kinship studies, as indeed in other fields of theoretical endeavour. (I have argued extensively (also following Jacqueline Rose (1984)) in all my other writings how the child is an end of theory in a variety of contexts.) I am instead considering the child as an aspect of the production of many of the arguments of the texts I am reading.

What of the child, then, as a producer of anthropological kinship, and not the outcome of it? In this respect, I am agreeing with Kath Weston, who suggests in relation to the many declarations of kinship studies' innovation in the light of reproductive technologies:

Recent years have witnessed a concomitant gravitation back towards European and US constructions of relatedness (as evidenced, for example, in the attention given to procreation and parent–child ties). None of these scholarly preoccupations are, in and of themselves, wrong. All bear investigation. Yet it is worth sounding a cautionary note when "family resemblances"—the old baby making and the new baby making, so to speak—emerge in the midst of an avowed period of intellectual innovation. A cumulative focus on interrogations of biology and science, in the absence of an equivalent interest in connecting some different and less familiar dots, suggests that the new kinship studies is still indentured to kinship in the time-honoured sense of the term. [Weston, 2001, p. 153]

Judith Butler, in the light of Weston's query about the specificity of this focus, suggests that "[t]his question reopens the relation between kinship and reigning epistemes of cultural intelligibility, and both of these to the possibility of social transformation" (Butler, 2000, p. 24). Under question, therefore, is not just how kinship may be read, but why kinship is seen as an aspect or component of "reigning epistemes of cultural intelligibility", whether "Antigone's death signal[s] a necessary lesson about the limits of cultural intelligibility, the limits of intelligible kinship . . ." (*ibid.*, p. 29). Or, as Weston puts it,

> [w]hat happens, for instance, when investigation shifts from the issue of what makes a relative to the question of what relatedness makes? When political economy begins to organize topics broached as well as observations made? [Weston, 2001, p. 152]

In other words, why is kinship readable, and why is it kinship that is readable? Similarly, we can suspect relationships between the "possibility of social transformation" and the construction of the child as I have been reading it. In my terms, the child is again not, as I noted in the previous chapter in quoting Parveen Adams, an identity cleaving to a body, but a node of a range of discourses (see, for another extensive analysis of the child in this way, Lesnik-Oberstein and Thomson (2002)), including those of time, property, and the state, not just as the hoped-for-child-as, -and-of-, the-body, but as "the whole question . . . of what—in general—*can* survive, of what *is* endurance, perpetuity, and eternal worth" (Rose, 1984, p. 110, original emphasis), as Jacqueline Rose argues.

Butler echoes Rose too in her article "Is kinship always already heterosexual?": "one can see that the child figures in the debate [on gay adoption] as a dense site for the transfer and reproduction of culture, where culture carries with it implicit norms of racial purity and domination" (Butler, 2002, p. 22). I want to look at how the own child in Butler's argument might be read, as she grapples to address issues related to the ones that I noted in Carsten's work in *After Kinship*. Butler, in both this article and *Antigone's Claim*, is, first, investigating how kinship might be thought in terms of

> [t]he task . . . to take up David Schneider's suggestion that kinship is a kind of *doing*, one that does not reflect a prior structure but

which can only be understood as an enacted practice. This would help us, I believe, to move away from the situation in which a hypostatized structure of relations lurks behind any actual social arrangement and permit us to consider how modes of patterned and performative doing bring kinship categories into operation and become the means by which they undergo transformation and displacement. [Butler, 2002, p. 34]

So far, both Butler's reference to Schneider and her endorsement of his aims ally her with Carsten's alliances and aims, but Butler's formulations explicitly seek to avoid several of those residualities that I diagnosed in Carsten. This difference between them can be seen as summarized in Carsten's comments on Butler in *After Kinship*, as I discuss them above.

Second, Butler, as Rachel Bowlby points out, and like Dion Farquhar, wishes to dynamize further the

clearly salutary consequences, as well, of the breakdown of the symbolic order, as it were, since kinship ties that bind persons to one another may well be no more or less than the intensification of community ties, may or may not be based on enduring or exclusive sexual relations, and may well consist of ex-lovers, non-lovers, friends, community members. In this sense, then, the relations of kinship arrive at boundaries that call into question the distinguishability of kinship from community, or that call for a different conception of kinship. These constitute a "breakdown" of traditional kinship that not only displaces the central place of biological and sexual relations from its definition, but gives sexuality a separate domain from that of kinship, allowing as well for the durable tie to be thought outside of the conjugal frame, and opening kinship to a set of community ties that are irreducible to family. [*ibid.*, pp. 37–38]

Butler sees these salutary consequences as compared to the negative effects of

how quickly kinship loses its specificity in terms of the global economy, for instance, when one considers the politics of international adoption and donor insemination. For new "families", in which relations of filiation are not based on biology, are sometimes conditioned by innovations in biotechnology or international commodity relations and the trade in children. And there is the question of

control over genetic resources, conceived of as a new set of property relations to be negotiated by legislation and court decisions.
[*ibid.*, p. 37]

There is a struggle here over what the "specificity" of kinship is
about. It can be a liberation to lose it, but, at the same time, when
the specificity is lost "in terms of the global economy", this is a
negative loss. It seems that if kinship dissolves into the global economy of biotechnology, commodity relations, and the trade in children, this is a problem. At stake here is both the child as commodity
as a problem, and a definition of community. A positive loss of
specificity of kinship allows for its dissolving into the community.
Therefore, the loss of the specificity of kinship is either the child as
commodity, or the loss of the distinction between kinship and
community. The community is in this way separated out from a
contamination by the global economy. I am not sure if there is not
also an idea of location operating here implicitly. The dissolution of
the specificity of kinship in the global seems a dangerous diffusion
of location, or an insuperable distance, whereas community seems
to function as the knowable location of kinship.

I want to note first of all in relation to Butler's suggestions that
the specificity of the community and kinship are read somewhat
differently by, for instance, Jeanette Edwards and Marilyn Strathern,
who suggest instead how community may be already defined as
kin in relation to the "own":

> There is a moral propriety to the indigenous English concept of
> "ownership" which suggests that it is as natural (to want) to
> possess things, as part of one's own self-definition, as it is to be part
> of a community or to belong to a family. This gives rise to proprie-
> torial identity being claimed over a large range of animate, inani-
> mate, and quasi-animate entities, such as one's own past, the place
> where one lives, inheritance, family names, and so forth . . .
> Narrating such associations makes a chain out of them, and claims
> can travel along chains. . . . The concept of "belonging" has such an
> embracing (inclusive) effect in English that it can encompass any
> form of association, including narrational or logical association, as
> in stories or classificatory systems, and appropriations which draw
> any manner of human or non-human elements towards one . . .
> There is in this sense a constant interweaving of "family" and

"community" in Alltown talk. . . . Indeed, the analogy between community and family is common in English social commentary in general . . . A claim on the place entails a claim on those things that belong to the place. [Edwards & Strathern, 2000, pp. 149, 150, 151]

Here, the community of "English" as a language, a people, and things, forms an outer boundary of what may or may not belong, but within that boundary the concept of belonging "can encompass any form of association", "although the links through which they are brought into association may be diverse" (*ibid.*, p. 150). But Edwards and Strathern caution, too, that

The analogy between social and intellectual engagement (making connections) that strikes Strathern . . . is of a piece with the senti-mentalised view of sociality as sociability and of kinship ("family") as community that pervades much Euro-American commentary of an *academic* kind. Perhaps one counterpart to the romantic view of connections as benign and community as harmonious, or logic as satisfying for that matter, lies in a salient cultural fact of English and Euro-American kin connections: the significance of an emotion-ally binding core in the positive affect ("love") that links persons together. [*ibid.*, pp. 152–153, original emphasis]

Edwards and Strathern, differently than Butler, therefore, both read an economy as an aspect of community, and they, at the same time, question any simple acceptance of community as less prob-lematic in terms of being more desirable as, and than, kinship. Furthermore, and therefore, rather than seeing community and kinship as divided, but potentially merging into one another, they define community and kinship as already mutually implicated, or even, from the perspective of belonging, as co-extensive. To my reading, Butler's community of kinship, "ex-lovers, non-lovers, friends, community members", conforms exactly to Edwards and Strathern's diagnosis of the "significance of an emotionally binding core" in English and Euro-American kin connections. If, then, I am reading Butler as agreeing with Farquhar's wish to dissolve certain notions of kinship into a certain greater diffuseness of community, which "displaces the central place of biological and sexual relations from its definition" (Butler, 2002, p. 37), I am also reading Butler, like Farquhar, as overlooking the inhabitation of her argument by the child. For how does the child, including the own child of reproductive technologies with its special pertinence, by the way, to certain formations of gay reproduction, survive the dissolution of the family into the community of love? How is this community to be "irreducible to the family" in the presence of the child? Let me be clear that I am not asking these questions to resist Butler's vision of a liberation from coercive and normative (and in the context of her discussion, specifically heterosexist) notions of kinship through the enlistment of the child and family as identities to be necessarily defended or upheld. Instead, I am trying to understand the implications of Butler's arguments in terms of her location of the child within her arguments. In other words: can this child participate in the release from family and biology into the community? Are we to see this child, for example, as now being a friend instead? Or does the child remain a child not of family, but of the community of love?

This is, I think, why my reading is more akin to that of Edwards and Strathern, in that they and I depart from an interest in the "own" and its meanings. That "own", which Edwards and Strathern see as being so expansive, is, as they also note, simultaneously a boundary of power:

> We refer not just to the boundary that "our own" is supposed to throw up against outsiders, strangers, offcomers . . . and foreign families, but to the way the relatives can be disowned. For whatever reason, they cease to belong. [Edwards & Strathern, 2000, p. 153]

In this sense, Butler's division between the community and the global economy enacts, rather than disputes, such boundaries. As Edwards and Strathern conclude,

> [i]n the Alltown conversations in which Edwards participated there is an occasional metaphysical hint at the unity of humankind, but generally connections were made not in the abstract but through mediating human beings. . . . Limits are set by how far one wishes to claim—or own, or own up to—such connections. [ibid., p. 159]

(Edwards and Strathern, by the way, comment that they feel that "this self-limiting character is fruitfully regarded as part of kinship thinking. This is where our view parts company with Schneider's views on relatedness" (ibid., p. 158).)

The child, then, I am suggesting, inhabits Butler's discussion of gay marriage, its relation to ideas of the state, and the possible future directions of kinship, but its inhabitation is, it seems to me, not followed through in several ways. For not only does the child seem to me to be overlooked, or lost, in the community of love, defined in terms of a listing of relationships alternate specifically to "the conjugal frame" and the family, but the status of the child seems theoretically peculiar in terms of Butler's overall positions. For although I noted previously that Butler echoes Jacqueline Rose in understanding the child as "a dense site for the transfer and reproduction of culture", Butler later in her article modifies this claim:

> The relations of exchange that constitute culture as a series of trans-actions or translations are not only or primarily sexual, but they do take sexuality as their issue, as it were, when the question of cultural transmission and reproduction is at stake. And I do not mean to say that cultural reproduction takes place solely or exclusively or funda-mentally through the child. I mean only to suggest that the figure of the child is one eroticized site in the reproduction of culture, one that implicitly raises the question of whether there will be a sure transmission of culture through heterosexual procreation, whether heterosexuality will serve not only the purposes of transmitting culture faithfully, but whether culture will be defined, in part, as the prerogative of heterosexuality itself. [Butler, 2002, p. 35]

Keeping in mind Butler's response (quoted previously) to crit-ics who query her proposal of bodies that have no residual materi-ality as their reality-in-the-world, I am puzzled by the shift here from the child to the "figure of the child". Is Butler now after all disagreeing with my reading of Rose's proposal that the child is that which is the essential and enduring in and as culture? Or is Butler setting up an essential child-of-the-body as a possible misreading is order to reject it? But, in the latter case, how am I to misconceive this child which is not a figure as not "solely or exclu-sively or fundamentally" the means of cultural reproduction? Is the child-of-the-body not a construction precisely of the issue of culture? And fundamentally so, if I keep Rose's analysis in mind? In other words, I am not at all sure that the division that Butler sets up, perhaps to prevent misunderstanding, does not retrieve after all a residually unconstructed child that she rejects in her own theo-retical deliberations on the (adult) body.

Keeping in mind further Rose's (Lacan inspired) argument that the child rests on the repression of Freudian polymorphously perverse sexuality, which produces overall a precarious order of language and the conscious, I am also left wondering what definitions of sexuality are operating in Butler's claim here. (In keeping Rose's analysis of the child in mind in this way, I am not wishing to instate this as an ultimately correct version of the child, but to use it to query certain definitions of sexuality.) How are "the relations of exchange that constitute culture . . . not only or primarily sexual"? As with an essential child, am I to imagine that this is a warding off of a misreading in terms of a merely conscious, genital, sexuality as the preoccupation of the relations of exchange that constitute culture? But in her further own formulations, Butler seems to preclude my reading her relations of exchange, and culture as "a series of transactions and translations", as indeed the operations of an economy of desire. I think that issues of temporality or cause-and-effect may be contributing to my puzzlement here. The relations of exchange that I am not to see as only or primarily sexual "do take sexuality as their issue, as it were". If the relations of exchange appropriate as their child (issue) sexuality, then how are they not themselves implicated in that sexuality? Butler herself further addresses the way sexuality is at stake here when she adds that

> To call this entire theoretical apparatus into question is not only to question the founding norms of heterosexuality, but also to wonder whether "culture" can be talked about at all as a self-sufficient kind of field or terrain. . . . The relation between heterosexuality and the unity and, implicitly, the purity of culture is not a functional one. Although we may be tempted to say that heterosexuality secures the reproduction of culture and that patrilineality secures the reproduction of culture in the form of a whole that is reproducible in its identity through time, it is equally true that the conceit of a culture as a self-sustaining and self-replicating totality supports the naturalization of heterosexuality and that the entirety of the structuralist approach to sexual difference emblematized this movement to secure heterosexuality through the thematics of culture. But is there a way to break out of this circle whereby heterosexuality institutes monolithic culture and monolithic culture reinstitutes and renaturalizes heterosexuality? [*ibid.*]

The problem of how formulations of culture lay claim to the apparatus of reproduction as normalised heterosexuality is under question here. Butler turns for a solution to the kinship analyses of anthropologists such as Sarah Franklin to "no longer situate kinship as the basis of culture" (*ibid.*). Thus, she can break open the "conceit" of a monolithic and unified, self-sustaining culture through "conceiv[ing] it as one cultural phenomenon complexly interlinked with other phenomena, cultural, social, political, and economic" (*ibid.*). But I am not clear whether this solution is not, in fact, a displacement of the liberating diffusion of kinship into the community. I do not mean this here as a critique of Franklin's position *per se*, but as a querying of the way Butler turns to this position as a solution to the specific problems she raises. For I can read her use of Franklin as elaborating the foundational nature of kinship as much as I can read it as a release from it. The question is where divisions and unities are located: within or beside "culture", and in this sense we can see parallels here with my analyses of the location of story in the first and second chapters of this book. There, too, the definitions of culture depended on the dividing-up or re-uniting of stories of and about "culture".

I therefore wonder whether a return to Rose's understanding of the child could not offer another sort of solution, or, to put it differently, the same solution from a different perspective. For if the anthropologists Butler turns to offer her a release from culture as foundational, as the instigator of the culture of reproduction, then so does Rose's reading of the child. The child here is, after all, a cultural product too, but not a product from a foundation, but precisely from a non-foundation. That is, it is a formation out of the polymorphously perverse. It is a formation of stability and transparency that is to deny and control instability. Here, the child and heterosexuality (or any form of conscious, adult sexuality) function in the same way. In this sense it is ultimately certain uses of psychoanalysis that underpin Butler and Rose's difference of positions.

I read these questions and issues as recurring in another point in Butler's article, again specifically in relation to the child. In discussing some French responses to possible legislation on homosexual marriage, Butler addresses "how anxieties about biotechnology and transnational migrations become focused and disavowed" (*ibid.*, p. 36). She identifies two of these anxieties in the French writer Sylviane Agacinski's anti-gay marriage position: a fear about the "'Americanization' of sexual and gender relations in France", and a "fear that lesbians and gay men will start to fabricate human beings" (*ibid.*). Butler sees these fears as attesting to a desire to "keep these relations organized in a specifically French form, and the appeal to the universality of the symbolic order is, of course, a trope of the French effort to identify its own nationalist project with a universalist one" (*ibid.*). Butler formulates a rejection of the nature of these anxieties in two ways. First, she labels the fear of a homosexual fabrication of human beings as "exaggerating the biotechnology of reproduction", which, curiously, in terms again of Butler's overall theoretical commitment, moves the context of discussion from the diagnosis of anxiety to a dispute over the level of achievement ("exaggeration") of biotechnology. As if the dissolution of anxiety lies in an acknowledgement of its inappropriateness or unreal nature.

Second, Butler, I take it scathingly, asks:

> One might well wonder what technological forces at work within the global economy, or indeed, what consequences of the human genome project, raise these kinds of anxieties within contemporary cultural life, but it seems a displacement, if not a hallucination, to identify the source of this social threat, if it is a threat, with lesbians who excavate sperm from dry ice on a cold winter day in Iowa when one of them is ovulating. [*ibid.*]

Butler and the "one" here look with wonderment at the French, and at their hallucinated anxieties, although, on the other hand, the anxieties are also those of "the global economy" and "contemporary cultural life", albeit still not one that Butler and "one" participate in. From their perspective, it seems entirely inappropriate to see as a threat at all the "lesbians . . . in Iowa". But is Butler's perspective here the point, even in her own terms? Isn't her self-stated project to analyse the precise terms of Agacinski's homophobic rejection of gay marriage? Clearly, the Iowan lesbian is not a threat to Butler anyway, so how does her invocation operate in Butler's argument? Agacinski's anxieties are, on the one hand, analysed as demonstrating a convergance between debates on gay marriage and gay child-bearing or raising, with

issues of immigration, of what Europe is, and implicitly and explicitly, of what is truly French, the basis of its culture, which
becomes, through an imperial logic, the basis of culture itself, its
universal and invariable conditions [*ibid.*, p. 22],

but on the other hand dismissed as a "hallucination" in terms of the,
to Butler, non-threatening Iowan. But would the Iowan then not be
"American" to Butler's Agacinski? Is a specificity of the lesbian from
Iowa, or a particularity of the cold winter day, or a certain mundanity in the "excavation of sperm from dry ice", or even a certain physicality of the "when one of them is ovulating", to disrupt what
Butler diagnoses as French anxiety over Americanization? Am I to
read this as a bathos that simply deflates or ridicules the diagnosed
anxiety?

In other words: what anthropology precisely is Butler practising
here? Or is this a polemical supplement to anthropology? And if
so, again, what am I to make of it? If I am myself either homophobic,
French, or both, am I likely now, by this, to be persuaded of the
innocuousness of the Iowan? Or is this not precisely the figure of
my anxiety, as Butler herself was reading it just a few lines earlier?
In other words, the "exaggeration" which, in my reading, signals a
shift from analysis to correction, heralds a further shift from analysing kinship in anthropological—or comparative—terms, to leaving
behind such an anthropological—or comparative—stance altogether
in favour of a naturalized Americanness, which has the correct
perspective on, and knowledge of, the possiblities and impossibili-
ties of biotechnology, and the significant insignificance of lesbian
Iowans attempting artificial insemination. The French need not, after
all, hallucinate this baby as the American that will dilute and corrupt
the French, just as Butler seems to have previously dismissed the
child as the fundamental transmitter of culture. Finally, then, Butler
sets up a certain anthropology as providing a solution to theories
of foundational kinship through, and as, changing perspective,
which disperses monolithic accounts of culture into a multiplicity
of narratives, but as after all requiring a supplementary American—
but universalized—commonsense perspective to address the failings
of some French. (I take it as significant that Butler excludes this
section on the Iowan lesbians from the later version of the article
included in her book *Undoing Gender* (2004): perhaps this excision

has to do with what I read as a problematic status of this comment for Butler's overall arguments and positions?)[5]

Notes

1. I might note, too, that the crocodile is excluded from the intertwined-ness of categories that Carsten reads in her daughter's comments, although it is not clear why this should be so. That this is not an outrageous or niggling point is illustrated by Carsten's own discussion about drawing

> attention to the importance of analyzing conceptions of same-ness alongside of difference.... Gayle Rubin ... pointed out that although men and women are different, "they are closer to each other than either is to anything else—for instance, mountains, kangaroos or coconut palms" ... Rubin suggested that exclusive gender categories were in fact based on "the suppression of natural similarities". [Carsten, 2004, p. 71]

What is at stake in both these quotations is a self-evidence of what can be included and excluded from consideration as valid terms of comparison to read as similarity or difference. In this way, a kind of "common sense" is reinserted as suggesting an outrageousness indeed to including a crocodile, for instance, as also a term of relationship or identity compared to selves, persons, or daddies. But where, just to name two possible examples, would this leave Western accounts of astrology? Or Native American or Aboriginal totem identities? Or Gillian Beer's comment that Charles Kingsley's novel The Water-Babies reflects an interest in "the enlargement of kinship—the great family which must ... include the chimney-boy and the scientist, and which moralises the connections between plants, animals, and human life"? (Beer, 1985, p. 130). See also on ideas of kinship not ending with the "human" theorists such as Donna Jeanne Haraway (for instance in: Modest_Witness@Second_Millenium.FemaleMan©_Meets_OncoMouse™ Feminism and Technoscience (1997)). Interestingly, Carsten titles this section "On not being a crocodile, and posthumous conception" (p. 96). This seems to indicate that, in the title at least, Carsten can after all read the crocodile as implicated in identity formation, even if negatively so. She does not, however, discuss the crocodile further.

2. My translation into English is:

    The formula A=A speaks of equality. It does not take A as the same.
    The familiar formula for the sentence of identity therefore hides
    precisely that which the sentence would wish to express: A is A,
    that is to say, every A is the same to itself ... The dative ἑαυτῷ
    means: every self is to itself: given back, every self is the same—
    namely for itself with itself. Our German language, like the Greek,
    here has the advantage that it indicates the identical with the same
    word, but in the differing form in its declension.

3. This repetition, which is not identical, can also be seen in Marilyn
    Strathern's well-known formulation about "the domaining effect ...
    the ideas that reproduce themselves in our communications *never repro-
    duce themselves exactly*. They are always found in environments or
    contexts that have their own properties or characteristics" (Strathern,
    1992, p. 6, original emphasis). I am not using the specific idea of
    domaining here, however, as I wish to avoid the implications of bound-
    aries and levels—however qualified—that are included in the use of
    "domain". Finally, that repetition which is not the same can also be
    read to be the topic of Freud's *Beyond the Pleasure Principle* (1920g).

4. For a further extensive exploration of the reading of analogy, see my
    article 'The *Philosophical Investigations*' children" (Lesnik-Oberstein,
    2003).

5. I wonder, in turn, what such an analysis would make, for instance, of
    the French rules for the preservation of the French language, or the
    French actions to burn down MacDonalds' restaurants.

CHAPTER FIVE

The child that is wanted: reading race and the global child

Having argued throughout that an "own" child simultaneously underpins reproductive technologies, and on the other hand is often overlooked as and in doing so, I want to turn, finally, to the one area in terms of which own children are both seen and acknowledged to be fundamental to the status of reproductive technologies: this area is race. The questions of the desire for the child, and the child that is wanted, are widely seen to be determined by constructions of race as constitutive of repetition and the own, and, conversely, of difference and the "not own". As Claudia Castañeda for instance points out:

> In the United States, the nation with a total number of intercountry adoptions greater than that of all other countries combined, questions of the transnational adoptee's identity are informed by a long history of debate concerning transracial adoption. While in the US transnational adoption is differently located as compared to national adoption discourse ... the issue of racial identity carries through from the national to the transnational domain. [Castañeda, 2002, p. 85]

This race is closely bound up with understandings of the biological and genetic as we have already explored them. Charis Cussins Thompson describes how "[i]n donor egg in-vitro fertilization ... the overlapping biological idioms of blood and genes come apart" (Thompson, 1998b, p. 42). "Blood" and "genes" here form "parts" of the "own" which (pre-) determine the child as repetition. Similarly, Heléna Ragoné claims that it "is of fundamental importance to IVF surrogates to circumvent the biogenetic tie to the child" (Ragoné, 1998, p. 121) as this means to them that the child is then not "their own". She reports Lee, an IVF surrogate, as saying that:

> Yes, it's [the fetus] inside my body, but as far as I am concerned, I don't have any biological tie. The other way [artificial insemination], I would feel that there is some part of me out there. [*ibid.*, p. 122]

And Linda, a Mexican-American IVF surrogate pregnant with a Japanese couple's baby, is reported as saying that:

> No, I haven't [thought of the child as mine], because she is not mine, she never has been. For one thing, she is totally Japanese. It's a little hard for me. In a way, she will always be my Japanese girl; but she is theirs. [*ibid.*, p. 121, original insertion]

As Ragoné comments, a "surrogate ... thus creates a 'wanted child', who is, however, wanted by someone other than herself" (*ibid.*, p. 119), and for Linda, described as "Mexican American", the "Japanese" defines the child as "not mine", although she is "in a way ... my Japanese girl". The child is thus created as unwanted for the surrogate because it is "not own" in terms of being of a different identity and yet may be part of why the child is wanted as "own" by the commissioning couple. Race can be both a block on repetition or (part of) an enabling of repetition. Even in the respect in which Linda feels linked to the baby, it is still in terms of her difference.

In these terms, Ragoné puzzles over "popular conceptions about the connection between race and genetics" (*ibid.*, p. 126). She points out, as the flip side of Linda's separation from the "Japanese child", that "racial resemblance raises certain questions for [Carol, a gestational surrogate] about relatedness even when there is no genetic tie" (*ibid.*, p. 126). Ragoné concludes that the issue of likeness and difference is being played out in unique configurations ... Likeness or resemblance as a symbolic feature signifies more than just biological resemblance. It also signifies a type of identity with the self and separation between all that is a part of oneself and all that is not, although it is nonetheless problematic in families that utilize ARTs. [*ibid.*]

There are some questions here for me about shifts of perspective, for which knowledge attributes a "symbolic" and a "biological" resemblance? Do Ragoné's surrogate interviewees read genetics and the biological in such a way as to acknowledge them as the site of "true" resemblance, but then decide to reject them in favour of a "symbolic" resemblance? Or is Ragoné herself relying on the idea that "biological resemblance" is the "true" resemblance, compared to which perceptions of resemblance on the part of "social" parents must be "symbolic"? In terms of the "own child" as I have been reading it across a range of discourses, "scientific" accounts of genetics and biology can anyway not be stable or prevailing constitutions of the "own". In other words, the "own" cannot be seen as belonging ultimately to a genetics or biology either: in this sense, there are contesting constructions of the "own" child, in which no narrative necessarily prevails, as indeed the divergent, shifting, and competing legal judgments confirm. An added question may therefore be: what here constitutes "biological" resemblance? (This may be related to my discussion of Janet Carsten's adoptee with the curly hair in Chapter Four.) And, as a corollary to this: what, precisely, would a "symbolic" resemblance be? Presumably, Ragoné means to suggest by this a resemblance that is perceived, known to be "biologically" impossible—or not attributable to biological causes—but still used to attribute or constitute relationship. But I might argue that "biological" can be read in exactly the same way anyway: how is "resemblance" read as repetition and relationship at all? Ragoné somewhat changes the passages I am referring to here in a reprinted and modified version of "Incontestable motivations", where she seems to move towards addressing these questions herself, too, as when she adds the suggestion that resemblance has to do with "Euro-American kinship ideology [in which] the child continues to represent the symbolic fusion or unity of the couple" (Ragoné, 2000, p. 70). But note still the persistence of the "symbolic", joined by "representation", so that the child is confirmed as an existing object or subject somehow being used in a derivative or secondary sense to "stand for" a unity which is not itself.

Ragoné remarks further that "in the presence of unresolved needs to have a child, the manipulation of notions of racial identity is insufficient to prevent her [the surrogate mother] from wanting to keep the child" (Ragoné, 1998, p. 130, n. 11). Race can therefore here either be a primary identity, with childhood as secondary to it, or childhood can triumph over race. In the case Ragoné remarks upon, "unresolved needs to have a child" create the wanted child primarily as child, regardless of other identities that might be produced for it. Presumably the child here is "own" in the specificity of being the child that is wanted, whether or not it is perceived as racially the same or different. In the case Ragoné cites, where the baby was not genetically related to the surrogate, the child may have been constituted as "own" in terms of constructions we have encountered before, such as of pregnancy creating a tie through blood as connecting or creating bodies, or the maternal body as home (rather than guest-house or temporary vessel or container).

Race is read, then, as more or less powerfully implicated in the child as "own" or not "own". Race may trump the child, or child may trump race in determining race as a bar to, or an enabler of, ownness. I want to turn now to a broader context for these issues, as race is also read in relation to a global child. We have already seen, in Chapter Four, Judith Butler suggest that changes in ideas of kinship might liberate in terms of "allowing as well for the durable tie to be thought outside of the conjugal frame, and opening kinship to a set of community ties that are irreducible to family" (Butler, 2002, p. 38). This can be linked even more broadly to the widely noted ethical dilemma that, as Viviana Zelizer puts it, there are seen to be "persistently baffling contradictions between the private sentimentalization of our own children and the collective indifference to other people's children" (Zelizer, 1985, p. xiii), and the concomitant effort, as Claudia Castañeda describes it, to imagine "'global' humanity and 'global' family relations" (Castañeda, 2002, p. 88). Or, as Margarete Sandelowski tartly summarizes it from an inverse perspective: "Normally fertile couples who desire children neither forego, nor are they expected to forego, having their own children in the interests of adopting children already born and without parents" (Sandelowski, 1993, p. 39). In these comments, central questions can already be seen to recur: is the liberation from a narrow interest in the welfare only of the own child to be understood as a liberation from family, a displacement of family, or an expansion of family? And how and when does kinship coincide with family? We have already encountered a number of writers, including Germaine Greer, commenting on the relationships between the meanings and use of the expensive, time- and labour intensive (both on the part of medical professionals and the prospective parents) new reproductive technologies, and the large-scale neglect and suffering of "other people's children", either the poor or destitute within the own community (to whom Zelizer is referring), or in "other" countries. On the other hand, the "collective indifference" also has, as its corollary, (transnational) adoption. Race is formulated as one of the central factors in the constitution of children who are "own" enough to care for—where the child trumps race, or other comparable "difference"—and the cases where race trumps the child. I will continue here by examining the operations of these dynamic struggles between the child and race in the work of several writers on reproductive technologies.

I have examined previously, in Chapter Three, some aspects of Ann Anagnost's discussion of American adoption of Chinese babies. I will return to this now to elaborate further how Anagnost negotiates the child and the market as relationship in order to consider how the child as either adopted or "own", and as desired as such, is defined by the outer limits of theory in Anagnost's argument. These issues, I will argue, are crucial to further understanding how the child is conceived of as simultaneously a commodity and not a commodity, even in work that self-consciously sets out to analyse this very topic. Moreover, I will argue further, these issues have implications throughout discussions of the child of adoption as defining an "own" child, and vice versa, for, as we have seen, not only is the "genetic" or "biological" defined in relation to adoption (and vice versa), but the adopted child, as several writers point out, may also be, or become, an "own" child, albeit not necessarily in the genetic or biological senses we have already examined. As Kaja Finkler discusses in terms of a certain period of American adoption:

> According to Minow and Shanley, ". . . adoption did try to mirror the 'natural family' through efforts to match race and religion as well as to seal from view the adoptee's family of origin" . . . Dolgin states, ". . . For decades, however, the law continued to insist that adoption be structured 'in imitation of biology' ". [Finkler, 2000, p. 118, original emphasis removed]

As Finkler and many of the other anthropologists of kinship we have looked at argue, it is precisely these constructions of the "natural family", including constituents such as "race and religion" and "biology", against an adoption which could only "try" to "mirror" or "imitate" that family which open up questions about the very status of that family and its naturalness.

Anagnost comments that "we could perhaps suggest that all children are similarly constructed in terms of race and class that go unmarked because they are naturalized through the privileging of biological relatedness" (Anagnost, 2004, pp. 162–163, n. 8). Here, Anagnost reads race and class as always needing to be constructed or attributed, rather than automatically belonging, or adhering, to the biologically "own" child. (It may be noted that such a theoretical idea coincides with the view of many geneticists that, contrary to much popular usage, "race" is not a "genetic" category. As Steve Jones writes, "The genes do show that there are no separate groups within humanity . . . DNA bears a simple message; that individuals are the repository of most variation" (Jones, 2000, pp. 255, 263). Jones further remarks that in the popular sense "race" usually refers to appearance, such as skin colour, but he argues that, in terms of his field, this in turn is itself a construction of race, not a sign of further significant genetic differentiation or classification. In noting this agreement, I am not intending to assert a claim that Jones' position is therefore a "scientific truth" which can support this anthropological analysis, but precisely that a geneticist such as Jones must also be embroiled in the same difficulties around formulations of identity and the body that I am reading throughout.)

Anagnost therefore argues in this sense that the "ownness" of the child must be constructed as such, and that race and class, for instance, are aspects of this "own". I argued previously, in Chapter Three, however, that Anagnost ultimately still retrieves the child from construction as an autonomous being, separate, after all, from society and culture. Here, too, despite the suggested dissolution of the differentiation between the biological and adopted child in terms of race and class, Anagnost after all retains the child in a further way, which raises questions for the ways that the global child, and its relation to "own" children, may be thought about. Or, to put it differently, the retained transcendent child raises questions for if and how children may be thought as either global or own, or both.

The formulations in Anagnost's work also have to do with the body, as in several previous analyses I have offered, such as those of the writings of Lay and colleagues, or Janet Carsten. For, in Anagnost's writing, the child, as with several other identities, such as migrant labour, is minimally a body, just as it is minimally after all still also a child. Both the American and the Chinese baby are recognized from the American and the Chinese perspectives in the article as a child. Its variable "sub"-identity as either an American or Chinese child is dependent on a body:

> How are . . . economic and emotional investments in the child conditioned by the child's position within a larger political economy in which other bodies are recognized as having a lesser value? . . . Another way of posing this problem is this: If transnational adoption links together subjects inhabiting vastly different conditions of life, what sorts of transactions of value/power/desire enable infants to move across these "differentials"? . . . How in our analysis can we bring all these disparate determinations of value in relation with each other? [Anagnost, 2004, p. 140]

Without in any way wanting to elide Anagnost's very interesting and important questions about how transnational adoption operates, I do want to suggest that the child always recognized as such can be read as that very transnational "value" already, which Anagnost diagnoses as "disparately determine[ed]", and that the body is part of this in her argument. For it seems to be specifically inappropriate that it is "bodies" that are recognized as the unit of value when Anagnost is professing to rely on Gayatri Spivak's "frame of analysis" that

> value is . . . a concept metaphor that has "*no proper body*" of its own. It is, to use Karl Marx's word, *Inhaltlos* (without content, a form of

appearance). This is most evident in the inability to specify what value *is* or where it resides. [*ibid.*, p. 139, first emphasis is mine, further emphases are original]

For the child and the body travel across time and space in recognizable and recognized forms and ways, which do not just link "together subjects inhabiting vastly different conditions of life", but raise the question of how "vastly different" those conditions can be when all the "subjects" already know and recognize the child and its value and the child *as* value? In fact, it could be asked, are there then a time and space for the child to cross, or is this child the collapse of time and space?

The child and its value are, in this sense, the product again of a particular perspective, which can effect the recognition of the child as child, and the body as body, as well as assert the differences that they are supposed to transgress:

The role of the Chinese state must be emphasized in the creation of a global system of "stratified reproduction" in which the bodies of children embody a "value" that is caught up in transnational circuits of exchange. . . . How exactly do the determinations of the child's value in one site propel its passage to another? [*ibid.*, p. 144]

In other words, why do some Americans wish to adopt a Chinese baby, and why does the Chinese state, or do the Chinese people, allow those babies to be so adopted? Or to put it in terms that align these questions most obviously to the ones that this book is concerned with, I read Anagnost here as asking: what makes some Americans desire these children, and the Chinese not want them? What is a wanted Chinese baby? Or, to put it differently again, when can a Chinese person be recognized as a child, and then desired as such? Yet, in Anagnost's formulation, the global system is one in which, again, the "bodies" of children are not just "caught up", but "embody a 'value' ". The quotation marks around value here further indicate a value that is somehow not quite that, even though the earlier Spivak quote had foreclosed on diagnosing the site of value. Now the site of value is nevertheless located in the body of the child, and the child as body, and that body encapsulates, includes, or instantiates value. In doing so, it is nevertheless declared, willy-nilly, not to be value actually, which in turn insinuates an actuality of value elsewhere. Even if value has been declared as nowhere. The child's body halts—or absorbs—the circulation of value as a "floating" (*Inhaltloss*) term, by "embodying" it. The being caught up in "transnational circuits of exchange" confirms this reading: the body of the child is haphazardly snared in circuits where it is not at home.

In this sense I am arguing, as I did previously in relation to the writings of Dena Davis, Dion Farquhar, Janelle Taylor, and Janet Carsten, for instance, that what may be proposed as merely metaphor is not necessarily self-limiting or within its own control as metaphor. Anagnost's text, like that of several of the other writers, often demonstrates a complex awareness of, and engagement with, this issue, but the child is the "bottom line" for this theoretical self-consciousness. The child is constructed for Anagnost in terms of race and class, but not, after all, in terms of *child*. Before it is anything else it is a child, and a body. Bodies further are not just the child, but also the "migrant body", which is "cod[ed]". Anagnost explains that

> [v]alue, it would seem, is something that has to be added to bodies, through capitalized inputs of education and training. It is no longer something that inheres in the powers of the body itself through its capacity for labor. [*ibid.*, p. 144]

There once was a body, then, which was simply itself, and valued as such for its "powers". Now the body has to have "value" added to it. The body seems here to be both the minimal "blank page" (see, for a parallel analysis of the animal as a "blank page" to be constructed or inscribed with identity by others, Sue Walsh, 2002) on which, or out of which, identities are created by others, as well as the minimal unit of differentiation and perception, in terms of identity:

> For China's emergent middle class, this explains the intensity of parental investments in rearing their single child through education and through the consumption of commodities . . . that will ensure that their child will come to be recognized in the new economic order as "a body of value". [*ibid.*]

This activity on the part of the Chinese emergent middle class to me looks very similar to that described by the anthropologists, including Anagnost herself, for the American or English middle classes, for instance. Or, to put it differently, I can read a diagnosis on the part of Anagnost herself here not of a "vast difference" between the Chinese and the American with respect to the child, but a close similarity (at least with respect to the middle classes). This similarity, moreover, I am suggesting, rests not on the construction of an acknowledged "body of value" as a primary unit, but on the construction of the identity of "child". This child is transnational as child, and is value as child and child as value. I therefore propose that the child allows the American adoption to be primarily *not* "transnational", for what is being adopted is already recognized and recognizable as child above all to all involved.

I want to stress that by not understanding the child as inherent to a body, I am trying to maintain both child and body as "floating", also as value, not as Anagnost's congealing embodiment. As Jacqueline Rose puts it:

> Money relies on traffic. The value of a piece of money depends on what it can be exchanged for (goods) and what it can be compared with (more, or less, money). As a system, money can be compared with language where each unit is part of a web of complex relations. . . . A unit of money, like a word in language, never stands on its own or purely for itself. It is contaminated by association and exchange. Not so childhood. . . . Childhood is always a moment *before*—once it is contaminated it is lost. [Rose, 1984, p. 87, original emphasis]

I will continue to demonstrate that the child as construction or production leads to a different understanding of the issues of (transnational) adoption than presupposing the child as always already there, recognizable as such, and a container of value in that form. For the question may then be asked: when is a child a child, and when not a child? Or, in other words, may it be the case that Zelizer's "other people's children" are, speaking nationally and ethnically, for instance, not children at all? Or at least, not all the time? As Erica Burman argues, "The set of privileges and positions [childhood in modern industrialized societies] elaborates intersects with North–South relations so that Southern children who violate this Northern imagery appear as *unnatural* children" (Burman, 1995b, p. 125, original emphasis). Burman also argues what the consequences of this may be:

The problem is that when children (in the South or the North) violate these ideals then the penalty incurred may be that they are no longer accorded the indulgences and privileges associated with the status of childhood (few those these may be). [*ibid.*, p. 128]

Could, then, the value that Anagnost congeals in the child as embodiment instead continue to be read as a current or currency? I would refer back here to my previous discussion, in Chapter Three, of the writing of Parveen Adams and Valerie Walkerdine in this respect. As Adams argues: "It is only by examining the workings of particular practices that it can be shown that the concept of subject is inadequate to them" (Adams, 1990, p. 108). I do not find it coincidental in this respect that Anagnost precisely grounds her child not just as body, but indeed also as "Of course . . . not an object but a subject with its own possibilities of agency" (Anagnost, 2004, p. 150).

In fact, Anagnost's own project would be further supported by the "step back" to query also the child. As she writes,

In the adoption practices I am examining here, I am reading th[e] evocation of the gift as a disavowal, rather than a critique, of capitalism. . . . my intent is to open to question the division of labor between public and private domains within capitalist culture that constitutes the family as an interiority needing protection from the contaminations of the marketplace and capitalist culture. The necessity for this critique is to help us anatomize the structure of feeling that keeps advocacy for children contained within the family. [*ibid.*, p. 164, n. 24]

However much I sympathize in principle with Anagnost's aims here, I would add that it is precisely the child that here is read as the potential beneficiary of the release of advocacy from the limitations of the family. If, as Burman suggests, there are also "unnatural" children, indeed "unnatural" by virtue precisely, for instance, by their not being part of a correct family, then what are the implications of this? Which children qualify for advocacy, and how, even when released from the family? In this sense, this transnational adoption rests on the recognition of the child that is wantable: "Mothers describe how the small photo [sent prior to the adoption] is carried on their bodies, in a pocket, enabling frequent gazes at a tiny face, always 'beautiful' " (*ibid.*, p. 155). Anagnost's vision of an advocacy for children released from the family does not release advocacy from the child, or the child that is wantable. The wanted child defines the unwanted child, and vice versa. Releasing advocacy from the family leaves to one side the ways that the child is itself produced with the market that defines the non-market. If the child is a central guarantor of the family as privacy, intimacy, and the realm of non-monetary affect, so the appropriate child underpins advocacy itself. Unwanted children do not create families (or if they do, these are also "unnatural" families) or demand advocacy.

An anecdote in Anagnost's account again involves a construction of the child that trumps nationality and difference. Anagnost offers a description of the way adoptive parents discuss "the search for the ethnically marked commodity" for their child:

> A much more serious search, however, takes place for dolls with "Asian" features . . . as a supplement for what the parents cannot give: a surface that can mirror back to the child her or his "likeness" as a sign of the child's own difference. . . . Yet this search, which proves so very difficult . . . often founders with the child's own object choice. One mother reported that although her daughter identified with her Asian-featured doll with her own name, she still preferred her Pooh bear. [*ibid.*, p. 153]

The child is featured as being given a doll to "identify" with, but the child itself makes its "own object choice". The subject child of agency can make a choice for itself apart from society or culture. It is "*her* Pooh bear" that she chooses, even if she does not "identify" with it. The child recognizes the doll she is given as herself, but this self is not her own choice. Anagnost does diagnose a difficulty with this narrative, which she sees as the fact that "some of the parents who appear most avid in their pursuit for this inanimate double for their child do recognize that the doll is not only for their child but for themselves" (*ibid.*). But she does not read the anecdote's own constitution of the child and its play as for the parents themselves. Divided between an imposition on the child and the child's "own" choice, the reading of the mother rests on an idea of "identification" which is in turn triumphed over by the "own" choice. In other words, I can read this anecdote as constructing a child that freely chooses Pooh—also as American or English? In any case somehow not Asian-featured—despite the parents' own best efforts to give her difference to her through the doll that looks like her and has her name (there is no statement of who is supposed to have given the doll the child's name). Because Anagnost unquestioningly accepts the idea of the subject child with agency who can make its own free object choice, she accepts too that child as itself for itself, not as, I am suggesting, read by the parents for an affirmation of the child vanquishing or relinquishing its difference *in being above all child*, and doing so, moreover, of its own volition, in the face of their manifest efforts to provide her with her difference. My reading of the anecdote, then, provides also an additional suggestion to what Anagnost herself asks somewhat later:

> here the project [of replicating her or his class subjectivity in the child] is expanded by the addition of the successful negotiation of ethnicity as one of the duties of the responsible parent, an added bonus on which parental worthiness can be evaluated and appraised. However, we may also wish to consider how this plea-sure relates to the aestheticization of a cultural difference that appears unconnected to the history of racialized stratification in US society. Is there not a curious split here in which "culture" or "eth-nicity" signifies as an aestheticized difference, displacing race and class, which register as more unbridgeable frames of difference? [*ibid.*, p. 155]

Anagnost sees race and class as "more unbridgeable frames of difference", and is trying to locate in a shift to "culture or ethnicity" an "aestheticized" or watered down, superficial, or "surface" version of race and class. This seems similar to Claudia Castañeda's analysis of race in a Benetton advertisement as

> the child's race . . . imagined as a surface quality that can be detached, chosen, and finally rearranged in a different palet of colours. . . . the adoptee here is racially mobilized, made "available" for adoption, and for a broader vision of racial harmony [Castañeda, 2002, p. 103]

as against an understanding of race as "a signifier of specific histo-ries linked to contemporary social, political, and cultural worlds" (*ibid.*, p. 101). I am, however, reading the child as transcending dif-ference for the parents anyway, even where that difference is asserted to be acknowledged, confirmed, or even encouraged by the parents.

In this sense, I wonder whether race and class is most helpfully formulated as "diluted" in the contexts of transnational adoption as Anagnost and Castañeda analyse it, when the child can be argued, as Jacqueline Rose points out, always to have been an important healer or transcender of perceived chasms of culture, race, and class. Anagnost and Castañeda's discussion in this respect relies on notions of a "serious" idea of race, and a more superficial or "mutable" (see, for instance, Castañeda, 2002, p. 106) race. This is an important issue, as it involves precisely the difficult problem of potential positionings of a total determinism versus a meaningless relativism, as Castañeda points out:

> Incorporation . . . disallows race as a natural fact, something that means beneath the skin, but at the same time refuses it any historical or cultural significance. This is a relativizing, liberal mode of racialization, in which "race" is both empty and innocent. [*ibid.*]

As with Anagnost, Castañeda's serious efforts to negotiate these difficulties rely on an idea of "history", where "these histories are not simply 'available' for reappropriation, and children not simply 'available' for refiguration" (*ibid.*, p. 107). She therefore asserts that

> The ways in which global relatedness is imagined and sustained should be accountable to history or, to be more specific, to histories of racial domination and resistance. When global relatedness is figured through the child, this vision should also be accountable to the child, and to the history of adult uses of the child that I am attempting to describe in this book [*Figurations*]. [*ibid.*]

But there are some shifts here which point both towards the implications of the underpinning of argument by a wish, as I discussed in Dion Farquhar and Janet Carsten's work, for instance, and issues of hierarchy and perspective.

First, again, who is doing the imagining and providing the accountability here? Who is accountable to whose history? In the case of race, taking into account Castañeda's prior discussion of both black and white adoption specialists' deliberations around interracial adoption in the USA, all participants, both black and white, both supporters and detractors of interracial adoption, seem to be implicated in her desired accountability. What is notable about this, then, is that the history that Castañeda wishes them to be accountable to is one that she sees them as not necessarily producing, but produces for them as the appropriate history: "to be more specific, histories of racial domination and resistance". This, in and of itself, raises the very question of whether or not these histories are indeed "not simply 'available' for reappropriation", when who appropriates which, and whose, history seems precisely to be simultaneously part of Castañeda's investigation in a section she entitles "History as a technology of racialized reproduction: responses to [Elizabeth] Bartholet" (*ibid.*, p. 97).

Second, it is the adult who should account to the child for a global relatedness that it "figure[s] through the child", and also should be accountable to the "history of the adult uses of the child". There is a slipping here from an adult as someone who figures the child, to a child apparently separate from adult figuration, to a history of adult uses of the child which the contemporary adult can be separate from, and retrospectively accountable to. Finally, the "global relatedness" is a "vision", formulating a future that arises out of a contemporaneity to which history is past, and not a continuation of it in respect to the child as global relatedness. The questions I am raising are not, as ever, intended to elide the important analyses that Castañeda is making, but to suggest difficulties in making precisely the decisions that are themselves offered as solutions to further difficulties. For it is the wish to have a certain history and a certain child determine and receive a certain accountability from certain actors outside of that history and not of that childhood which pervades the problems that Castañeda herself also diagnoses in turn. The battle, therefore, becomes constituted as being over which history and which child will prevail to be accounted to and by whom. The wish, as with Farquhar, cannot pin down the correct history, or the correct child, or the uses to which they are put. Interestingly, Castañeda herself in some respects touches on these difficulties after making her wish, for at the end of the chapter she speculates after all that

> Perhaps the new world order poses new forms of inequality . . . that work . . . through change, through the power to change an other according to taste, or to become the other by appropriation. If so,

perhaps we must imagine a different kind of figuration that resists both naturalization and those forms of denaturalization—or deracination—that refuse relevant histories. Such an alternative figuration would also refuse the simple "availability" of children for adult visions of the future. [*ibid.*, p. 108]

Having read as "relevant" a history that is about race as not something that is about a surface appearance or colour that is changeable and mutable, Castañeda here contemplates the possibility of a shift into a new world order in which race and childhood are precisely that after all, although they are still also "other", and the changes are still motivated by "taste" or the wish to appropriate that other. "Figuration", too, persists, even if it is to be of a "different kind", not one vulnerable either to naturalization or to a too easy denaturalization. In other words, a past or history is confirmed in which the "other" of and as race and child could not be changed or appropriated in those respects, and in which figuration was either the difficulty or impossibility of change, or too easy and nonchalant a view of change. The future figuration nevertheless also seems to me still to coincide with one of the alternatives of the past figuration, that is, in its ease of change, as well as being coterminous with the past in terms of enduring inequality, albeit in "new forms". The asserted difference only seems to lie in change being entirely unlinked from relevant histories: they have become beyond the reach of refusal in the future figuration. Also, the child will be no longer about "adult visions of the future", although it is still recognizable as child in this vision, but perhaps meant to be seen as dissolved altogether in the future in its actuality as "new"? In any case the child of the figuration of history is also confirmed as the child of the present adult vision of the future. The contemporaneity of Castañeda's text, therefore, does not own its own vision of the future as invoking the child as available to be not available in the future of the future.

It is not clear to me whether I am to read this vision ironically or not. Does the text play on the involvement of its own present child in this future vision, or am I reading this implication of its own present child?[1] In not being able to decide this, I remain unsure whether this vision is utopic or dystopic for Castañeda, or whether the persistence of inequalities makes it more of the same, albeit in different forms and figurations. In any case, the future vision to her too after all closely resembles her past, for

> The mutability of the child figured as a body in process makes it eminently appropriable; not yet fully formed, it has no prior being that must be displaced and then re-placed. It has only to become, according to taste. Perhaps this is not the familiar, liberal individualism that it might at first appear to be. Perhaps the new world order poses new forms of inequality that do not work in terms of immutable, "natural" attributes. [Castañeda, 2002, p. 108]

These problems of how history, present, and future are both separated from each other and collapsed into each other, seem to me to be part of the issue that, as I commented briefly in Chapter Three, Castañeda from the start sets up a differentiation between a "category" child and "actual children and their experience of the world" (*ibid.*, p. 3) in order to define her "figuration" and the involvement of the child in it. She

> does not seek to offer an account of how these assumptions [about the "category" child] affect real children, although I am convinced that they do. Instead, [*Figurations*] is about the endurance of a particular configuration of the child as an entity in the making, and its prolific and multiple uses across disparate cultural sites . . . If the child appears not only where actual children's lives and experiences are at stake, but also where they are decidedly not, then how can we account for its pervasive presence across such disparate sites? . . . With what qualities or characteristics has the child been endowed to make this availability possible? [*ibid.*]

The child is both actual and a particular configuration, and Castañeda can tell which is which, and can accordingly diagnose the absence of the actual child and the presence of the configuration. The configuration is something that is produced by adding to the child "qualities or characteristics" that it does not have in actuality, but that enable a flexibility and range of usage. The actual child, therefore, is not prolific and available for multiple uses across such disparate sites. Nevertheless, Castañeda's stated aim is to

> convey a sense of the power generated in and through the child and its uses, without reproducing the problematically universalizing

or global claims that are so frequently made through this very category. [*ibid.*, p. 5]

If "universalizing or global claims" are then to be avoided, the fundamental separation between the actual child and the figurations "child" still does constitute, as I read it, a universal or global claim, and persists as such. One such persistence is, for instance, the child to whom the vision of global relatedness should be accountable. Similarly, it is why and how the decisions about relevant and non-relevant histories can be made, for actuality retrieved constitutes the knowledge of the relevant version. It is also there in the production of the child in and as history, as the repetition that cannot be evaded, even in visions of a futurity in which the child escapes history, and history the child. The actual child, departed from as merely residual in comparison to complex and wide-ranging figurations, continues to direct the arguments and analyses. It is in this sense the desire for the child that is the wish for a relevant history, as well as for a relevant future. In this way, perhaps the new world order that Castañeda suggests is one I read in one sense necessarily as both utopic and dystopic within Castañeda's narration: utopic at least in the proposed possibility of the escape of the child from an availability for adult visions of the future, but dystopic in my reading of that child as nevertheless inevitably the availability of the child for that vision of the future. Or, in other words, I read this future as a recapitulation and repetition of a past, and, in that sense, available neither as utopia or dystopia. The possibility of irony, then, is produced in the contrast between my reading of narration as proposing a perceived possibility, and my reading of that possibility as always already defeated.

In her concluding discussion of feminist theorists and figurations of the child, Castañeda comes to rest approvingly finally on Donna Haraway as offering a way of retrieving the child as in excess to (adult) knowledge, not fully knowable by the adult and as the adult. Yet, as I understand it, the central difficulty for this argument as a proposal in the service of an apparently felt need to redeem the child from an adult inhabitation is that the child is then fully knowable as not fully knowable, so that the adult, willy-nilly, reoccupies that from which the argument had hoped to evict it. In several respects Castañeda's reading of Haraway's work happens not to coincide with mine, but Haraway also does turn to a discussion of the child in relation to, as she puts it, "[r]ace, gender, sex, and kinship, [which] must be thought together" (Haraway, 1997, p. 309, n. 1), which I therefore here want to consider in its own right.

In a section in her book *Modest_Witness@Second_Millenium. FemaleMan©_Meets_OncoMouse(TM) Feminism and Technoscience*, Haraway sets out to consider

> the *missing* representations of fetuses and babies that must trouble anyone yearning for reproductive freedom. . . . From the point of view of a barely imaginable, desperately needed, transnational, intercultural, and resolutely situated feminism . . . questions about optics are inescapable. How is visibility possible? For whom, by whom, and of whom? . . . Here I want to explore one form of off-screen, out-of-frame positioning for the children of contemporary, expanding, marginalized populations. [Haraway, 1997, pp. 202–203, original emphasis]

This consideration, as with Judith Butler, is prompted by Haraway's being

> sick to death of bonding through kinship and "the family", and I long for models of solidarity and human unity and difference rooted in friendship, work, partially shared purposes, intractable collective pain, inescapable mortality, and persistent hope. It is time to theorize an "unfamiliar" unconscious, a different primal scene, where everything does not stem from the dramas of identity and reproduction. . . . I believe that there will be no racial or sexual peace, no livable nature, until we learn to produce humanity through something more and less than kinship. [*ibid.*, p. 265]

As with Ann Anagnost, I am in several ways in sympathy with the direction that Haraway here wishes for. All the more, however, am I also therefore puzzled by how she further proceeds to deploy the child as "missing representation" in her discussion of the work of anthropologist Nancy Scheper-Hughes in Brazil on child mortality and its causes. And specifically so in terms of the question of visibility. For to and from whom is the child seen to be missing, and how?

My puzzlement has to do with the invocation here of precisely the child to mobilize the questions of visibility and responsibility.

Why and how is it the "fetus" and "dead babies" that are "invisible"? And how would their visibility contribute to a humanity produced "through something more or less than kinship"? Haraway seems to be developing these ideas from her reading of a Bell telephone advertisement, in which, she discusses,

> The visual text showed a pregnant woman, who is undergoing ultrasonographic visualization of her fetus, telephoning her husband, the father of the fetus, to describe for him the first spectral appearance of his issue. The description is performative: that is, the object described comes into existence, experientially, for all the participants in the drama. Fathers, mothers, and children are constituted as subjects and objects for each other and the television audience. Life itself becomes an object of experience, which can be shared and memorialized. . . . The mother-to-be's voice on the phone and finger on the screen are literally the conduits for the eye of the father. . . . In the ad, reproductive technology and the visual arts . . . come together through the circles of mimesis built into communications practices in the New World Order. Life copies art copies technology copies communication copies life itself. Television, sonography, computer video display, and the telephone are all apparatuses for the production of the nuclear family on screen. [*ibid.*, p. 177]

This visualization relates to my previous discussion in Chapter Three of the witness and its role in the production of the own child in reproductive technologies. By my analysis of witnessing, on the other hand, does not necessarily relate to Haraway's proposal for a stance of a "modest witness" as she works it out in her text:

> My modest witness cannot ever be simply oppositional . . . s/he is committed to learning how to avoid both the narratives and the realities of the Net that threaten her world . . . S/he is seeking to learn and to practice the mixed literacies and differential consciousness that are more faithful to the way the world, including the world of technoscience, actually works. [Haraway, 1997, p. 3]

Haraway is developing an idea of how to witness, whereas I am trying to consider how witnessings and perspectives are produced in texts, including here the "modest witness".

Haraway further argues that "counting and visualizing are also essential to freedom projects", (*ibid.*, p. 202) and that

> Credible statistical representation is one aspect of building connection and coalition that has nothing to do with moralistic "standing in the place of the oppressed" by some act of imperialistic fantasy or with other caricatures of feminist intersubjectivity and feminist standpoint. Demanding the competent staffing and funding of the bureaus that produce reliable statistics, producing statistical representations in our own institutions, and contesting for the interpretation of statistics are indispensable to feminist technoscientific politics. Providing powerful statistical data is essential to effective public representations of what feminist and other progressive freedom and justice projects mean. [*ibid.*, p. 199]

In this sense, the role of witness is extended to a statistics that can somehow mobilize "freedom and justice projects", as long as the statistics are a "credible representation" and "powerful . . . data". But credible and powerful to whom, and, again, how? The production of the right kind of statistics already positions an entrapment in a statistical inadequacy, it seems to me. I read Haraway as being well aware of this is several ways, but not, after all, of the way in which I see the child as coming into her argument to be deployed as a corrective to the lack of power on the part of the statistics. Because, does this witnessing also usher in an extension of the own child? Is kin to be here extended, displaced, or liberated from? To whom are the dead babies and foetuses to be kin-ed? To Haraway, it is Scheper-Hughes who has fulfilled a role in terms of, as Haraway puts it,

> developing John Berger's image[.] Scheper-Hughes, an anthropologist, saw herself as a "clerk or keeper of the records"—listening, watching, and recording those events and entities that the powerful do not want to know about . . . For Scheper-Hughes, recording was the work of recognition and an act of solidarity. She attempted to count, to make statistically visible, the reproductive history, and especially the dead babies, of the poorest women in the Brazilian town. Moreover, she linked the existence and numbers of those dead babies to precisely the same global/local developments that lead their richer sisters . . . to seek the latest in prenatal care and reproductive medicine. Undercounted and on screen: Those were the two states of being under examination. [*ibid.*, pp. 203–204]

If the on-screen and off-screen child are the "two states of being under examination", the off-screen child can either be put on-screen, that is kin-ed, introduced into the narrative of the nuclear family, or it can be counted.

A number of issues arise here, it seems to me. First, who is the reader of Haraway's text? That is, to whom are the foetuses and dead babies being made visible, or for whom counted? Who is to witness? As I have discussed before, in addressing readership I am not speculating on some individual encountering Haraway's book, but thinking about how I read texts as producing a readership in terms of position and perspective. Is this reader "the powerful", then, to whom the foetuses and dead babies will finally be made visible, although they do not want this, by reading this? Or is it the already sympathetic reader, involved in Haraway's concerns of the feminist freedom and justice projects, at least potentially? And, if the latter, what is it that the dead babies are framed to be or do in this reading for that reader? Is this to be a final conversion? A lesson in mobilization? Second, how exactly are the foetuses and dead babies uncounted? They are not counted here in Haraway, they are innumerable, indeed uncountable, dead babies and foetuses:

> ... my last image springs from a missing gaze, I have no picture to print, no reprinting permission to seek. In the demographers' language, this nonimage is of human "reproductive wastage", that is, of the dead babies and fetuses, the *missing* offspring, who popu-late the earth's off-screen worlds in unimaginable numbers in the late twentieth century. These are fully "modern" or "postmodern" fetuses and babies, brought into invisible existence within the same New World Order that ordains bright lights, genetic gymnastics, and cybernetic wonders for the public fetuses of the better-off citi-zens of planet Earth at the end of the Second Christian Millennium. ... The missing images, and what they represent, are precisely contemporary with and embedded in the same networks as the all-too-visible on-screen fetal data structures. [*ibid.*, p. 203, original emphasis]

Scheper-Hughes is credited already as the counter, the "clerk or keeper of records" for those who did not know previously, including the powerful who did not wish to know, but knew, too, what and that they did not wish to know. Haraway cannot print a picture, a picture that would be an image of "human 'reproductive wastage'", that is signalled by the quotation marks, I take it, as inappropriately designated as waste by "the language of the demographers", read against a human which seems to refer to the desired "human unity and difference" that validates the human as constructive, not destructive and reductive, not divided into repro-ductive preciousness and reproductive wastage. It is the pictures of dead babies and foetuses, not human reproductive wastage, which would accomplish this human, had they been available. Presumably, as I read it, Haraway's piece is to produce as visible to the reader the invisible foetus as invisible, but now visible as such. It is notable to me that just a bit later Haraway refers also to over-population as a threat not just to "the long-term survival of ourselves" but also of "incomprehensible numbers of other species" (*ibid.*, p. 205). "Ourselves" know the other species as well as the dead babies and foetuses as unimaginable and incomprehensible in their numbers. This can be read as simply an incontrovertible assessment of a lack of knowledge of precise numbers, but it never-theless is marked to me that it is the non-human and the child that are specifically available to be imagined as the unimaginable, and most of all as the final object and subject of a self-announcing pathos: an unimaginable *loss*. (See, for a suggestion that the "miss-ing child" is a "dominant structure of feeling [of the late Twentieth-Century]", Morgado, 2002.)

Why is the "non image" of "dead babies *and fetuses*"? If the "dead babies" are the objects that speak to subject-viewers of pathos, the victims of a corporate capitalism that thrives on its lack of accounting, then why also "fetuses"? Are they accepted as included in the devastation of reproductive freedom for poor Southern peoples as a self-evidently significant differentiation from the dead babies? Why I am disturbed by an overlap I read with the language of the politics of abortion, in which the anti-choice move-ment portrays lackadaisical women as nonchalant disposers of foetuses as nothing more than non-human "wastage"? And whose preferred strategy, as we have considered, centres on producing the foetus as human in its visibility in photos or in echograms? As Lauren Berlant argues, "the anonymity of the fetus becomes a necessary precondition to the form of useful empathy constructed by the pro-life movement" (Berlant, 1997a, p. 143). (Berlant reads the foetus and visuality in ways which relate to aspects of my discussion here throughout her chapter "America, 'fat', the fetus".) Is Haraway evoking this in order to align anti-choice discourses and the operations of affluence in feeding off the poor? Haraway, as with a number of the writers we have looked at, proposes that the invisible foetuses and dead children are produced against the wanted child, the child of "all-too-visible on-screen fetal data structures". Kinship is constituted as the wanted child divided off from the non-kin unwanted child, and visibility and recording establish this. If visibility and invisibility, then, are both the dividing line between kin and non-kin, and the way in which a joining, as and in a parasitic relationship between the North and the South, is produced, then how does Haraway's own deployment here of visibility and invisibility either evade that debt or re-view it?

Somehow, still, here the invisible foetuses and dead babies have been proposed as a supplement or corrective to invisibility. They are not to be seen on screen, or in a picture, but made visible textually: not seen, but written, which is here therefore both visual and not visual. One point here for me, then, is how and why Haraway is using Scheper-Hughes' counting. It is her work that carries the count in Haraway's discussion, yet Scheper-Hughes's numbers are nowhere supplied. I take it that Haraway is framing Scheper-Hughes's counting as a way to extend her argument about the relevance of the stories that statistics tell, although I have already suggested that, as such, I read Haraway's tale as necessarily constituting itself as a supplement to an inadequacy of the statistics after all. For why had not then Scheper-Hughes's counting already accomplished visibility in and of itself? And if so, then why are Scheper-Hughes's numbers precisely absent, reconverted to unimaginable numbers of dead babies and foetuses? Is the child to accomplish what Scheper-Hughes's counting after all cannot? The questions then arise, too: is a number a picture, but a picture not a text here? Are the visible and the visual here the same, or different, and which "visual"?

Haraway notes these issues in some respects when she acknowledges that

> Of course, images of hungry babies and children, if not fetuses, periodically fill our television screens. The *mode* of presence and absence changes for differently positioned citizens in technoscientific public

reproductive visual culture more than absolute presence or absence. The visual icons of hungry infants do not perform the same semiotic work as the icons of the highly cultivated on-screen fetuses favored by Bell telephone. [Haraway, 1997, p. 203]

The interjection "[i]f not fetuses" compounds my puzzlement around my reading this language as implicated in the discourse of the anti-choice movement, for it is in that area where, I might say, I precisely encounter images of foetuses on "our television screens". (Lauren Berlant, for instance, asks "why the most hopeful national pictures of 'life' circulating in the public sphere [of the United States] are not of adults . . . but rather of the most vulnerable minor or virtual citizens—fetuses, children, real and imaginary immigrants—persons that, paradoxically, cannot yet act as citizens" (Berlant, 1997b, p. 5).) "Our television screens" too confirms the reader as the kin of Haraway, the Western watcher of these Southern visibilities and invisibilities as they are visible in Haraway's account of Scheper-Hughes's account, making of Haraway a counter of counters, but not, in fact, a counter of foetuses and dead babies according to herself uncountable. Nevertheless Haraway relies on "mode" to differentiate perspective from perspective: the hungry infants are "icons", as the highly-cultivated on-screen foetuses are "icons", and these icons "do not perform the same semiotic work".

Iconicity, then, is a performance of semiotic work, which produces modes of "presence and absence". The child as icon has meanings, and these meanings differ, although in very determinate ways: the hungry child is not "highly cultivated", while the Bell child is. But are the dead babies and foetuses also icons even if not cultivated at all? Or are they here, after all, a non-iconic child, neither the child offered up as self-speaking pathos to the view of the potentially charitable individual viewer, embedded in a capitalist order which isolates charity as an always insufficient corrective to that necessarily parasitic relationship, nor the iconic child whose pathos is to mobilize the Bell telephone consumer? In other words, am I to read Haraway's dead babies and foetuses as, for once, exempt from a certain performance of a certain semiotic work? Or precisely as part of a performance that I should already be recognizing? Here again I return to my reader, for mode and performances of semiotic work constitute a certain predictability of reading, a certain knowledge of what the child here is to be. Without reverting to unhelpful vaguenesses around reading as open to any interpretation, I nevertheless am not clear on how Haraway can be so sure of her modes and semiotic performances. I, at any rate, am one confused reader, whereby I do not, again, wish to reinsert myself confessionally as a reader of singular relevance, but want to reflect on my impossibility of locating a reader's perspective in this text that would make sense to me of what I as reader am to read, and how. Or perhaps my confusion is the confusion of reading the child here after all as, in a sense, one mode, and therefore not a mode at all, in the examples that Haraway gives for her local arguments in this section. (I would want to emphasize here that I am not referring necessarily to other ways in which Haraway analyses the child and/or the foetus in other (sections of) texts, although I would not necessarily be comfortable with "mode" in any context.) The risk of the child, as Stephen Thomson formulates it (Thomson, 2003), is that the child is presumed here as able to be that "absolute presence or absence", which Haraway wants then to see as mediated by a "mode": the question here for her is not if there is a child present or not as such, but *how*, and that how is "mode". But to read the "child" as able to be absolutely present or absent institutes the child as a real presence prior to mode. The introduction of degree ("more") and iconicity can not ward off this problem. If the reader is to produce the appropriate child, then the child must be recognized as the right child by the reader.

Haraway acknowledges and positions Scheper-Hughes as being "responsible for my missing visual text as I follow her through her search in the municipal records offices and *favelas*, or slums" (Haraway, 1997, p. 203). In this formulation, Scheper-Hughes's text does put Haraway in the picture then, and the visual text is both present and absent, already supplied, but needing to be "followed through". Haraway therefore explicitly sets herself up as retracing Scheper-Hughes, and repeating her work with and for her, as and in a reading of her work. In this way, the reader in Haraway's text is presumably to follow Haraway's following of Scheper-Hughes. This framing, Haraway further proposes,

> besides drastically reducing the complexity of accounts in her book, my sketch adds analogies, renarrativizes, and uses parts of her

story in ways she did not. But we are enmeshed together in webs
spun by yearning and analysis. [Haraway, 1997, p. 203]

Haraway and Scheper-Hughes are separate texts in certain
ways, but they are nevertheless sufficiently bound together, caught
in the same yearning and analysis, for Scheper-Hughes presumably to be authorized by Haraway as forgiving her framing. In all
of this, most significant, because not accounted for, it seems to
me, remains the conversion of the originally valued counting into
uncountable dead babies and foetuses, and, as a corollary, the
text which is not a picture, but which is "visual", and must make
"visible".

Haraway maintains Scheper-Hughes's counted as "one form" of
"children of contemporary, marginalized populations" being positioned as "off-screen, out-of-frame", although it remains to me
unclear how they are here "off-screen, out-of-frame" when they are
precisely in the frame as out-of-frame, besides already being
counted previously after all. They are both pictures and not-
pictures, with the text supplementing the lack of the work the
pictures do. The dead children and foetuses are produced here as
the non-picture to be pictured. This is to explain why statistics
count. Haraway notes that there is a great deal of counting going
on by "demographers and population specialists", but nevertheless
it is the "clerk of the records—working out of the traditions of
Catholic liberation theology, socialist feminism, medical anthropology, and risk-taking ethnography [who] was still needed to count
missing children in the biopolitical age" (*ibid.*, p. 205). It is the right
kind of counter who can count the "missing children", who previously were also the "*missing* offspring" (Haraway, 1997, p. 203, original emphasis), not any counter at all. This counter knows what is
there to count. The missing are known to be missing to her, and can
be retrieved by her counting: it is the counting of liberations and
resistances in and to the "biopolitical". And this counter is
"needed", but, again, by whom? Does the counter liberate the South
from the North, or extend its relationship to it, and, in fact, dependency on it? I relate this to Erica Burman's arguments, referring in
turn to the work of Pat Holland:

The representation of lone black children in aid appeals works
frequently to pathologise their families and cultures, positioning

these as failing to fulfil their duties. Colonial legacies blend into humanitarian concern, where in order to qualify for "help", parents are either invisible or infantilized as incapable. ... To quote Pat Holland again: "The aim is for recognition of differences that do not lead to conflict, but this is precisely where the limit of childhood runs up against its limits. Childhood is sought as that space beyond conflict, before those rigid differences have taken hold, as a point where 'humanity' aspired to an impossible escape from 'society' ". [Burman, 1995, pp. 23, 33]

I note that Haraway proceeds in her piece to argue that both the Brazilian child of reproductive technologies and the dead babies are the products of capitalist transformations of breastfeeding practices through the introduction and propagation of powdered milk, as well as through maintaining working hours that are prohibitive to breastfeeding. However, in my reading, this elaborates, rather than negating, the problems that Burman and Holland note of "infantil-ising" Brazilian parents in important respects: these parents are constructed in Haraway's texts only as entirely vulnerable to, and embedded both socially and culturally, within lethal impositions. This is not to say that I read Burman and Holland as proposing a "correct" or "true" parent that could be known, or that I am propos-ing this myself, but that I can read Haraway's narration as setting against each other certain North American parenthoods against certain Brazilian parenthoods, in which issues of knowledge, action, the body, and identity are configured differently.

My point here is not somehow callously to ignore the disastrous rates of infant death due to contaminated water and malnutrition, but to question whether Haraway's constructions of Brazilian child-hood and the Brazilian family here are compatible with her own "yearnings" as declared in the text, and with her own attempts to pre-empt certain difficulties. For, in a footnote, Haraway asserts that "Chic resistance talk will get one nowhere; material-cultural analysis might have a chance to provide consequential insight" (Haraway, 1997, p. 307, n. 39). I take this straining for an *effective-ness* (as with the longed for "credible" statistics and "powerful data") to be a measure of her frustration at a powerlessness that the child is invoked here to heal. But, and this is the problem of kinship and the child, the "other" child, the unnatural child, the non-child to be retrieved as a child to be owned, and therefore only a child in so far as it is belatedly recognized as such, never does speak itself, or heal the powerlessness that the witness of unimaginable death is producing. I am reading this section of Haraway's work, if only this section perhaps, as falling back into the classic position of the powerless liberal, and it is the advent of the child, the dead babies and foetuses, that heralds this collapse. As they say in the movies: "never act with children and animals". The danger is not just that you will be out-cuted, but, or as an extension of this, that you will be out-acted by those who precisely need not act, but just "be". As Joe Kelleher writes of children in film:

> We might say, a certain fantasmatic child labour is put into operation, whereby surplus value is returned to adults in terms of symbolic capital, as our own heuristic investment. The child's work is to carry, unwittingly, the burden of signification. [Kelleher, 1998, p. 29]

I do not think it is accidental, in the light of Haraway's slipping through visualities, that it is Kelleher's discussion of the child specifically in film that comes to my mind here. In his discussion of Tarkovsky's *Ivan's Childhood*, Kelleher further suggests that

> in the film's final fantasy sequence . . . in which Ivan reappears, alive, in another time and place from the historical scene of war given by the film's narrative, as a child playing happily on a beach. . . . the figuring of the *child* as the (dis)appearance of terror into the context of history [gives us] the outlines of a significant trope of *film* history—and of film *as* history—that situates the image of the child as a problematic hinge between the discrepant technologies of cinematic narrative and the *mise-en-scène*. [*ibid.*, pp. 36, 37, original emphases]

And, Kelleher concludes, the child

> is a site for the locating of experience *between* the image and the narrative of the image; that is to say, the figure of the child in the cinema is a site for the locating of experience in a space that passes between the real and the represented, the Real and the Symbolic. . . . Any symbolic appropriation of the child figure comes up against the problem that in the cinema the child returns as precisely that, a *child*. [*ibid.*, p. 39, original emphases]

Similarly, Stephen Thomson writes of literary criticism, "the loss and recovery of a child, and the loss and recovery of a meaning, seem to coincide" (Thomson, 2002, p. 110).

I read kinship, then, as inescapable in terms of these anchorings in and of the child, despite Judith Butler's and Donna Haraway's professed desires to be released from kinship, and in terms of their seeing the release from it as a possible liberation into a kinder, more inclusive world. The difficulty for this release from kinship, as Jacques Derrida suggests, is that

> there will always be, not THE family, but *something of* a family, some attachments, some sexual differences, some "sexual relation" (even where there is none, as Lacan would say), some social bond around childbearing in all its forms, some effects of proximity and the organization of survival—and some law [du droit]. But this persistence of an order produces no *a priori* determinable figure of any particular familial model. [Derrida & Roudinesco, 2001, pp. 38–39, original emphases; insertion Fort's]

Derrida's interest here is not in specificities of familial configurations, but in "this persistence of an order", an order in, *and as*, language. It is in this sense too that I read the child, and kinship with it, persisting in the arguments above, and directing those arguments in "being there". Kinship continues to pivot around the presence of the child as either to be the salvation for, and as, a global child in its extensions and elaborations or displacements, or as lethal in its exclusions and limitations. In any case kinship is neither dissolved nor transcended as the central question with respect to the child remains, in the serious sense: who cares?

Note

1. In this consideration, I am indebted to Sue Walsh's thinking on irony (oral communication).

CHAPTER SIX

Conclusion: coming to grief in theory

Having analysed the implications of several personal statements concerning reproductive technologies in works
I have read in this book, perhaps it is no more than appropriate to introduce this conclusion with an anecdote of my own, not
as simply some sort of a psychological confessional, but, as with the
ways I have analysed those other statements, to offer another way
of locating my motivations and commitments in terms of what and
why I hope I have argued in this book. My written research in this
area, after even longer-term informal thoughts, readings, and
discussions, was prompted by a number of factors, one of these
being a kind invitation to write a paper on childhood for, and to
speak to this paper at, a "writers' workshop" on "Indeterminate
bodies". (I am grateful to Professor Naomi Segal, Ms Lib Taylor, and
Dr Roger Cook, the organizers of the workshop, for this invitation,
and for publishing my paper in their subsequent volume,
Indeterminate Bodies (2003). "Representations of the indeterminate
body: a writers' workshop" took place at the University of Reading,
19–21 March 1999.) Besides my previous work on childhood, readings in critical anthropology and reproductive technologies
prompted me to formulate some of my initial ideas about the

constructions of the own child in this area, and became the basis for my arguments in this book. As part of the workshop, small-scale groups were organized in which the contributors' papers were discussed and provided with feedback. Crucial for me was the fact that several of the participants in the group at which my paper was considered commented on what they saw as my neglect of attention to the pain of infertility. I ought, they explained, to write about this emotional pain. And this intrigued and challenged me, because I thought this was exactly what I was writing about. My analysis was, to me, an attempt at understanding better what and why the own child is seen to be such that it generates almost unquestioned and unquestioningly—when "natural" reproduction is seen to fail—the highly complex range of efforts of financial, organizational, medical, legal, psychological, and personal kinds, together called reproductive technologies (which may include, in certain interpretations, adoption, including transnational adoption, as we saw in Chapter Five in the arguments of Claudia Castañeda, for instance). Why did this child matter so much, when, as I have discussed in the previous chapter, the "not own" child, or, as Erica Burman puts it, the "unnatural child" (Burman, 1995b) matters so little, or at the very least so much less? And why is all this effort to produce the own child "natural", while efforts on behalf of the "not own" child are so often judged as exceptional, extraordinary, self-sacrificing, heroic, whether on the part of adoptive or fostering parents, teachers, medical or legal professionals, or aid workers? It seemed and seems to me that this *is* the "emotion" around which infertility and reproductive technologies are constructed. But, somehow, to some of my fellow discussion-group members, my analysis was not about, or appropriate to, emotion.

I understood their comments to be part of views that emotion, indeed, is, and should be, resistant to analysis; that analysis in this arena is an invasive and "cold-hearted" instrument of dissection and anatomization that does not understand emotion, but negates or restrains and disciplines it. I had often encountered this response to analyses of the child as construction in my previous work, too. Yet I have always read the child and emotion as mutually implicated in this way: that the child underpins certain Western definitions of emotion: the family, sexuality, and romance as contracts of, and as, affect, and humanity as an identity and value resting on that affect of the family. As Margarete Sandelowski writes of a shift in the late 1980s and early 1990s in studying infertility and reproductive technologies to

> Rediscovering the individual and, more significantly, the "universal singular" . . . researchers and clinicians in a variety of disciplines, especially those involved in a category of inquiry often labeled qualitative, have recently emphasized the need to privilege the narrative efforts of their subjects and patients: to return the "suffering, afflicted, fighting human subject[s]" to the center of consideration and inquiry where they rightfully belong . . . This new narrative focus in scholarship is part of a larger turn in the social and behavioral sciences towards interpretive methods and away from conventional research strategies that fail adequately to represent personal meaning and the varieties of reality. [Sandelowski, 1993, p. 2]

In these comments, what was previously being failed to be "adequately represented" were "personal meaning and varieties of reality". Realities may be various, but they are what are to be "represented" to do justice to the centrality of the suffering human subjects. Suffering and the human subject are already constituted as a source.

In this sense, my approach rests on a particular understanding of the role and status of analysis, drawing broadly from my understandings of both psychoanalysis and certain philosophical attitudes both referred to and worked out in this book. I do not, for instance, see analysis as antagonistic or inappropriate to emotion. This goes together with not seeing emotion as the self-evident, spontaneous, *sui generis* and authentic realm of expression of a private and privileged internality: as the most "real" of the *a priori* human subject. This is why and how I have focused throughout on the ways that, in a range of arguments, analysis is seen to be aligned to, or the same thing as, "theory" or the "theoretical", in opposition to an alignment of the child, the family, and emotion, with the everyday, the mundane, the practical, and the unpredictable of, and as, "life", even in works that are themselves self-consciously theoretical. Not, indeed, as I hope I have made clear throughout, because I deny views of, and investments in, emotion as such a thing precisely, or even because I could evade being absolutely implicated in such accounts myself. But I do indeed see these never-theless as particular culturally and historically situated narratives. I see myself, and my self, too, as a product of such narratives, and as not able to divest myself simply of them by choice, in the same ways as I read Judith Butler, for instance, as arguing for a body that is both entirely constructed, but not, therefore, somehow related to, or based on, a non-constructed body, however residual. As I argued in my discussion of Lay, Gurak, Gravon, and Myntti on reproduc-tive technologies, or Janet Carsten's work on kinship, it is only when emotion and the body continue to reside as a residual "real" that their attendant construction becomes, after all, secondary and derivative; insubstantial.

Perhaps implicated in the dispute over appropriate analysis, too, are disciplinary issues, not unrelated to those that Sandelowski mentions above, for the participants at the workshop were largely literary and historical scholars interested in the body, rather than anthropologists, and it was in anthropology that I found analyses more compatible with my own than in the fields of literature or history, with due regard to the very significant exceptions that I have noted in this book. As I have argued elsewhere extensively (see, for this particularly, Lesnik-Oberstein, 1994, 1998, 2000, 2002, and Lesnik-Oberstein & Thomson, 2002), literature and history seem to be, in disciplinary terms, perhaps particularly implicated and invested in the child as unquestionable, by virtue of a history, however contested in other ways, of constituting as and in them-selves narratives of the human and its (in)humanity. Yet the own child seemed to me to be retained nevertheless too in the anthro-pological studies of reproductive technologies, all the more notice-ably because of what I see as the analytic fruitfulness of these studies otherwise. The question I have tried to raise here is: why?

I have tried to pursue this question without simply acceding to one side or another of an opposition: either a confirmation of a determinist innateness of a desire for an own child, or a revelation of such a desire as social, cultural, or historical in which history, culture, and society are constituted as secondary, derivative, and therefore ultimately disposable. Instead I have tried to work seri-ously with the idea that, in this sense, the notions of experience and emotion are neither inevitable and fixed, but neither are they secondary, derivative, and mutable simply by choice. In these terms, my deepest debt is to psychoanalysis, which establishes a response to this dichotomous debate by conceiving the unconscious and meaning as neither fully internal nor fully external, as neither fully determined nor entirely voluntary, neither the automaton nor pure free will. The child, as I have read it, is implicated in the negotiation of these intersections, and intervenes in them at every turn. It does so in my own writing inevitably, too, but I hope at least to have created some further questions where previously I read not answers, but the unquestionable.

Therefore this book, while questioning the own child, and offering analyses of it, has not been about being able either to dispose of the own child, or of the reproductive technologies that are dedicated to producing it and are produced by it. As Jacqueline Rose argues in relation to children's literature in her seminal analysis of childhood as a cultural construction in *The Case of Peter Pan or: The Impossibility of Children's Fiction,*

> My questioning does not bring with it some ideal form of writing which I am wishing to promote for the child. It is a questioning of language itself as the means through which subjective identity, at the level of psychic and sexual life, is constituted and then imposed and reimposed over time. [Rose, 1984, p. 140]

Just as Rose does not see her diagnosis of children's literature as a production of an adulthood producing both itself and its childhood as resolvable by either "some ideal form of writing" which would truly be able to be for a real or actual child, or by the stopping of writing for children, so I do not see my analysis of the own child of reproductive technologies as resolvable simply either by stopping such technologies, or by proposing ways in which they could be used that would evade their inherent reliance on the "own" and its myriad consequences. Analysing the child and the need for it, as constructed within certain discourses, does not make it simply evaporate, or the myriad concomitant practices that, more or less obviously, participate in its construction.

REFERENCES

Adams, P. (1990a). Mothering. In: P. Adams & E. Cowie (Eds.), *The Woman in Question. M/F* (pp. 315–327). London: Verso.

Adams, P. (1990b). A note on the distinction between sexual division and sexual differences. In: P. Adams & E. Cowie (Eds.), *The Woman in Question. M/F* (pp. 102–109). London: Verso.

Adams, P., & Cowie, E. (Eds.) (1990). *The Woman in Question. M/F*. London: Verso.

Althusser, L. (1971). Ideology and the state. In: *Lenin and Philosophy and Other Essays* (pp. 127–186). B. Brewster (Trans.). New York: Monthly Review Press.

Anagnost, A. (2004). Maternal labor in a transnational circuit. In: J. S. Taylor, L. L. Layne, D. F. Wozniak (Eds.), *Consuming Motherhood* (pp. 139–168). New Brunswick, NJ: Rutgers University Press.

Ariès, P. (1960). *Centuries of Childhood: A Social History of Family Life.* R. Baldick (Trans.). New York: Vintage, 1962.

Barker, M. (1989). *Comics: Ideology, Power, and the Critics.* Manchester: Manchester University Press.

Barrington, J. (1980). Why children? In: S. Dowrick & S. Grundberg (Eds.), *Why Children?* (pp. 144–165). London: Women's Press.

Becker, G. (2000). *The Elusive Embryo. How Women and Men Approach New Reproductive Technologies*. Berkeley, CA: University of California Press.

Beer, G. (1985). *Darwin's Plots: Evolutionary Narrative in Darwin, George Eliot, and Nineteenth-Century Fiction*. London: Ark Paperbacks.

Berlant, L. (1997a). America, "fat," the fetus. In: *The Queen of America Goes to Washington City. Essays on Sex and Citizenship* (pp. 83–145). Series Q. Durham, NC: Duke University Press.

Berlant, L. (1997b). *The Queen of America Goes to Washington City. Essays on Sex and Citizenship*. Series Q. Durham, NC: Duke University Press.

Bialosky, J., & Schulman, H. (1998). Introduction. In: J. Bialosky & H. Schulman (Eds.), *Wanting a Child. Twenty-Two Writers on their Difficult but Mostly Successful Quests for Parenthood in a High-Tech Age* (pp. 3–8). New York: Farrar, Straus and Giroux.

Bowlby, R. (1993). *Shopping with Freud*. London: Routledge.

Bowlby, R. (2003). The constancy of kinship. *The Cambridge Quarterly*, 32(1): 77–80.

Burman, E. (1994). *Deconstructing Developmental Psychology*. London: Routledge.

Burman, E. (1995a). The abnormal distribution of development: policies for southern women and children. *Gender, Place and Culture*, 2(1): 21–37.

Burman, E. (1995b). Developing differences: gender, childhood and economic development. *Children & Society*, 9(3): 121–142.

Butler, J. (1990). *Gender Trouble: Feminism and the Subversion of Identity*. London: Routledge.

Butler, J. (1993). *Bodies that Matter: On the Discursive Limits of "Sex"*. London: Routledge.

Butler, J. (2000). *Antigone's Claim: Kinship Between Life and Death*. New York: Columbia University Press.

Butler, J. (2002). Is kinship always already heterosexual? *Differences: A Journal of Feminist Cultural Studies*, 31(1): 14–45.

Butler, J. (2004). *Undoing Gender*. London: Routledge.

Carsten, J. (2004). *After Kinship*. Cambridge: Cambridge University Press.

Castañeda, C. (2001). The child as a feminist figuration: towards a politics of privilege. *Feminist Theory*, 2(1): 29–53.

Castañeda, C. (2002). *Figurations. Child, Bodies, Worlds*. Durham. NC: Duke University Press.

Chodorow, N. (1978). *The Reproduction of Mothering: Psychoanalysis and the Sociology of Gender*. Berkeley, CA: University of California Press.

Clarke, A. J. (2004). Maternity and materiality: becoming a mother in consumer culture. In: J. S. Taylor, L. L. Layne, & D. F. Wozniak (Eds), *Consuming Motherhood* (pp. 55–72). New Brunswick, NJ: Rutgers University Press.

Cocks, N. (2000). Reading repetition and difference in the boy's school story. University of Reading, unpublished PhD thesis.

Cocks, N. (2004). The implied reader. Response and responsibility: theories of the implied reader in children's literature criticism. In: K. Lesnik-Oberstein (Ed.), *Children's Literature: New Approaches* (pp. 93–118). London: Palgrave.

Cooper, S. L., & Glazer, E. S. (1998). *Choosing Assisted Reproduction. Social, Emotional and Ethical Considerations.* Indianapolis, IN: Perspectives Press.

Davis, D. S. (2001). *Genetic Dilemmas. Reproductive Technology, Parental Choices, and Children's Futures.* Series: Reflective Bioethics. New York: Routledge.

de Marneffe, D. (2004). *Maternal Desire. On Children, Love, and the Inner Life.* New York: Little, Brown.

Derrida, J. (1967). *Of Grammatology.* G. C. Spivak (Trans.). Baltimore, MD: Johns Hopkins University Press, 1974.

Derrida, J., & Roudinesco, E. (2001). Disordered families. In: J. Derrida & E. Roudinesco. *For What Tomorrow . . . A Dialogue* (pp. 33–47). Jeff Fort (Trans.). Stanford, CA: Stanford University Press, 2004.

Deveraux, L. L., & Hammerman, A. J. (1998). *Infertility and Identity. New Strategies for Treatment.* San Francisco, CA: Jossey-Bass.

Diamond, R., Kezur, D., Meyers, M., Scharf, C. N., & Weinshel, M. (1999). *Couple Therapy for Infertility.* The Guildford Family Therapy Series, London: Guildford.

Diepenbrock, C. (2000). God willed it! Gynecology at the checkout stand. Reproductive technology in the *Women's Service Magazine,* 1977–1996 (pp. 98–121). In: M. M. Lay, L. J. Gurak, C. Gravon, & C. Myntti (Eds.). *Body Talk. Rhetoric, Technology, Reproduction.* Madison, WI: University of Wisconsin Press.

Dowrick, S. (1980). Why children? In: S. Dowrick & S. Grundberg (Eds.), *Why Children?* (pp. 67–76). London: Women's Press.

Dowrick, S., & Grundberg, S. (Eds.) (1980). *Why Children?* London: Women's Press.

Dutton, F. (1980). Why children? In: S. Dowrick & S. Grundberg (Eds.), *Why Children?* (pp. 117–131). London: Women's Press.

Dyson, S. (1993). *The Option of Parenthood.* London: Sheldon.

Edelman, L. (2004). *No Future. Queer Theory and the Death Drive*. Series Q. Durham, NC: Duke University Press.

Edwards, J. (2004). Incorporating incest: gamete, body and relation in assisted conception. *Journal of the Royal Anthropological Institute*, 10(4): 755–774.

Edwards, J., & Strathern, M. (2000). Including our own. In: J. Carsten (Ed.), *Cultures of Relatedness. New Approaches to the Study of Kinship* (pp. 149–67). Cambridge: Cambridge University Press.

Ettore, E. (2002). *Reproductive Genetics, Gender and the Body*. London: Routledge.

Farquhar, D. (1996). *The Other Machine: Discourse and Reproductive Technologies*. London: Routledge.

Felman, S. (1977). To open the question. In: S. Felman (Ed.), *Literature and Psychoanalysis. The Question of Reading: Otherwise* (pp. 5–11). Baltimore, MD: Johns Hopkins University Press, 1982.

Finkler, K. (2000). *Experiencing the New Genetics: Family and Kinship on the Medical Frontier*. Philadelphia, PA: University of Pennsylvania Press.

Fletcher, A. (2002). Making it better? Disability and genetic choice. In: E. Lee (Ed.), *Designer Babies: Where Should We Draw the Line?* (pp. 15–29). Series: Debating Matters. London: Hodder & Stoughton.

Franklin, S. (1995). Postmodern procreation: a cultural account of assisted reproduction. In: F. D. Ginsburg & R. Rapp (Eds.), *Conceiving the New World Order. The Global Politics of Reproduction* (pp. 323–345). Berkeley, CA: University of California Press.

Franklin, S. (1997). *Embodied Progress: A Cultural Account of Assisted Conception*. London: Routledge.

Franklin, S. (1998). Making miracles: scientific progress and the facts of life. In: S. Franklin & H. Ragoné (Eds.), *Reproducing Reproduction: Kinship, Power, and Technological Innovation* (pp. 102–117). Philadelphia, PA: University of Pennsylvania Press.

Freud, S. (1905d). *Three Essays on the Theory of Sexuality*. S.E., 7: 125–249. London: Hogarth.

Freud, S. (1916–1917). Symbolism in dreams. In: *Introductory Lectures* (Parts 1 and 2). S.E., 15: 149–169. London: Hogarth.

Freud, S. (1920g). *Beyond the Pleasure Principle*. S.E., 18: pp. 3–67. London: Hogarth.

Freud, S. (1933a). Anxiety and instinctual life. *New Introductory Lectures on Psycho-Analysis*. S.E., 22: 81–112. London: Hogarth.

Gay, P. (1984). *The Bourgeois Experience: Victoria to Freud*. Vol. 1: *Education of the Senses*. Oxford: Oxford University Press.

Geertz, C. (1973). Ideology as a cultural system. In: *The Interpretation of Cultures* (pp. 193–233). New York: Basic Books, 2000.

Geertz, C. (1983). Common Sense as a cultural system. In: *Local Knowledge. Further Essays in Interpretive Anthropology* (pp. 73–93). London: Fontana, 1993.

Gilbert, S., & Gubar, S. (1979). *The Madwoman in the Attic: The Woman Writer and the Nineteenth Century Literary Imagination.* New Haven, CT: Yale University Press.

Goodison, L. (1980). Why children? In: S. Dowrick & S. Grundberg (Eds.), *Why Children?* (pp. 30–41). London: Women's Press.

Greer, G. (2003). Afterword. In: J. Haynes & J. Miller (Eds.), *Inconceivable Conceptions. Psychological Aspects of Infertility and Reproductive Technology* (pp. 207–216). Hove: Brunner-Routledge.

Hall, S. (2002). Two women given wrong embryos in IVF mix-up. The *Guardian*, 29 October, p. 2.

Haraway, D. J. (1991). *Simians, Cyborgs, and Women: The Reinvention of Nature.* London: Routledge.

Haraway, D. J. (1997). *Modest_Witness@Second_Millenium.FemaleMan©_ Meets_OncoMouse™ Feminism and Technoscience.* London: Routledge.

Heidegger, M. (1957). *Identiteit en Differentie/Identität und Differenz.* Two-language edition (German/Dutch). S. Ijsseling (Trans.). Amsterdam: Boom, 2001.

Hewlett, S. A. (2002). *Creating a Life. Professional Women and the Quest for Children.* New York: Talk Miramax.

Hrdy, S. B. (1999). *Mother Nature: Natural Selection and the Female of the Species.* London: Chatto & Windus.

James, A., & Prout, A. (1997). Introduction. In: A. James & A. Prout (Eds.), *Constructing and Reconstructing Childhood: Contemporary Issues in the Sociological Study of Childhood* (second edn) (pp. 1–6). London: Falmer.

Jones, S. (2000). *The Language of the Genes. Biology, History and the Evolutionary Future* (revised edn). London: Flamingo.

Jones, S. (2003). *Y: The Descent of Men.* London: Abacus.

Jordanova, L. (1989). *Sexual Visions. Images of Gender in Science and Medicine between the Eighteenth and Twentieth Centuries.* London: Harvester Wheatsheaf.

Kahn, S. M. (2004). Eggs and wombs: the origin of Jewishness. In: R. Parkin & L. Stone (Eds.), *Kinship and Family. An Anthropological Reader* (pp. 362–378). Series: Blackwell Anthologies in Social and Cultural Anthropology. Oxford: Blackwell.

Kelleher, J. (1998). Face to face with terror: children in film. In: K. Lesnik-Oberstein (Ed.) *Children in Culture: Approaches to Childhood* (pp. 29–56). London: Macmillan.

Kincaid, J. (1992). *Child-Loving: The Erotic Child and Victorian Culture*. London: Routledge.

Kohlstedt, S. G., & Longino, H. E. (2000). Foreword. In: M. M. Lay, L. J. Gurak, C. Gravon, & C. Myntti (Eds.), *Body Talk. Rhetoric, Technology, Reproduction* (pp. ix–xi). Madison, WI: University of Wisconsin Press.

Konrad, M. (2003). Gifts of life *in absentia*: regenerative fertility and the puzzle of the "missing genetrix". In: J. Haynes & J. Miller (Eds.), *Inconceivable Conceptions. Psychological Aspects of Infertility and Reproductive Technology* (pp. 120–43). Hove: Brunner-Routledge.

Lancaster, R. N. (2003). *The Trouble with Nature: Sex in Science and Popular Culture*. Berkeley, CA: University of California Press.

Lay, M. M., Gurak, L. J., Gravon, C., & Myntti, C. (2000). Introduction. In: M. M. Lay, L. J. Gurak, C. Gravon & C. Myntti (Eds.), *Body Talk. Rhetoric, Technology, Reproduction* (pp. 3–26). Madison, WI: The University of Wisconsin Press.

Layne, L. L. (2004). Making memories after pregnancy loss. In: J. S. Taylor, L. L. Layne, & D. F. Wozniak (Eds.), *Consuming Motherhood* (pp. 122–139). New Brunswick, NJ: Rutgers University Press.

Lesnik-Oberstein, K. (1994). *Children's Literature: Criticism and the Fictional Child*. Oxford: Clarendon.

Lesnik-Oberstein, K. (1998a). Childhood and textuality: culture, history, literature. In: K. Lesnik-Oberstein (Ed.), *Children in Culture: Approaches to Childhood* (pp. 1–28). London: Palgrave.

Lesnik-Oberstein, K. (Ed.) (1998b). *Children in Culture: Approaches to Childhood*. London: Palgrave.

Lesnik-Oberstein, K. (2000). The psychopathology of everyday children's literature criticism. *Cultural Critique, 45*: 222–242.

Lesnik-Oberstein, K. (2002). *Holiday House*: grist to *The Mill on the Floss*, or: Childhood as text. In: K. Lesnik-Oberstein (Ed.), *Yearbook of English Studies* (pp. 77–94). Special Section on "Children in Literature", vol. 32. Leeds: MHRA.

Lesnik-Oberstein, K. (2003). The *Philosophical Investigations'* children. *Journal of the Theory and Philosophy of Education, 35*(4): 381–394.

Lesnik-Oberstein, K. (2005). The owned child and commodification. *New Antigone, 1*(1): 20–27 (see also at: http://www.newantigone. com/oscommercedownload/reproductive%20technologies.pdf)

Lesnik-Oberstein, K., & Thomson, S. (2002). What is queer theory doing with the child? *Parallax, 8*(1): 35–46.

Levick, S. E. (2004). *Clone Being. Exploring the Psychological and Social Dimensions*. New York: Rowman and Littlefield.

Lyotard, J.-F. (1992). *The Postmodern Explained to Children. Correspondence 1982–1985*. J. Pefanis & M. Thomas (Trans). London: Turnaround.

Mauss, M. (1950). *The Gift. The Form and Reason for Exchange in Archaic Societies*. W. D. Halls (Trans.). London: Routledge, 1990.

Miller, J. (2003). Mourning the never born and the loss of the angel. In: J. Haynes & J. Miller (Eds.), *Inconceivable Conceptions. Psychological Aspects of Infertility and Reproductive Technology* (pp. 47–60). Hove: Brunner-Routledge.

Mitchell, J. (1974). *Psychoanalysis and Feminism*. Harmondsworth: Penguin.

Mitchell, J. (2000). Introduction. In: *Psychoanalysis and Feminism. A Radical Reassessment of Freudian Psychoanalysis* (pp. xv–xxx). New York: Basic Books.

Morgado, M. (2002). A loss beyond imagining: child disappearance in fiction. In: K. Lesnik-Oberstein (Ed.), *Yearbook of English Studies* (pp. 244–259). Special Section on "Children in Literature". Vol. 32. Leeds: MHRA.

Morgan, L. M. (1996). Fetal relationality in feminist philosophy: an anthropological critique. *Hypatia: A Journal of Feminist Philosophy, 11*(3): 47–70.

Murray, T. H. (1996). *The Worth of a Child*. Berkeley, CA: University of California Press.

Plato (1949). *Timaeus*. B. Jowett (Trans.). New York: Liberal Arts Press.

Raphael-Leff, J. (2003). Eros and art. In: J. Haynes & J. Miller (Eds.), *Inconceivable Conceptions. Psychological Aspects of Infertility and Reproductive Technology* (pp. 33–46). Hove: Brunner-Routledge.

Ragoné, H. (1998). Incontestable motivations. In: S. Franklin & H. Ragoné (Eds.), *Reproducing Reproduction: Kinship, Power, and Technological Innovation* (pp. 118–131). Philadelphia, PA: University of Pennsylvania Press.

Ragoné, H. (2000). Of likeness and difference. How race is being transfigured by gestational surrogacy. In: H. Ragoné & F. W. Twine (Eds.), *Ideologies and Technologies of Motherhood. Race, Class, Sexuality, Nationalism* (pp. 56–76). London: Routledge.

Robertson, J. A. (1994). *Children of Choice. Freedom and the New Reproductive Technologies*. Princeton, NJ: Princeton University Press.

Rose, J. (1984). *The Case of Peter Pan or: The Impossibility of Children's*

Fiction. Series: Language, Discourse, Society. London: Macmillan.

Rose, J. (1986). *Sexuality in the Field of Vision.* London: Verso.

Rose, H., & Rose, S. (Eds.) (2001). *Alas Poor Darwin: Arguments Against Evolutionary Psychology.* London: Vintage.

Rothman, B. K. (2004). Motherhood under capitalism. In: J. S. Taylor, L. L. Layne, & D. F. Wozniak (Eds.), *Consuming Motherhood* (pp. 19–31). New Brunswick, NJ: Rutgers University Press.

Rothschild, J. (2005). *The Dream of the Perfect Child.* Bloomington, IN: Indiana University Press.

Rousseau, J.-J. (1762). *Émile.* B. Foxley (Trans.). London: Dent, 1989.

Sandelowski, M. (1993). *With Child in Mind. Studies of the Personal Encounter with Infertility.* Series: Studies in Health, Illness, and Caregiving. Philadelphia, PA: University of Pennsylvania Press.

Sedgwick, E. K. (1994). Epidemics of the will. In: E. K. Sedgwick (Ed.), *Tendencies* (pp. 130–143). London: Routledge.

Segal, N., Taylor, L., & Cook, R. (Eds.) (2003). *Indeterminate Bodies.* London: Palgrave.

Shabi, R. (2004). Baby chase. The *Guardian.* Weekend section, 26 June, pp. 14–23.

Shanner, L. (2000). Bodies, minds, and failures. Images of women in infertility clinics. In: M. M. Lay, L. J. Gurak, C. Gravon, & C. Myntti (Eds.), *Body Talk. Rhetoric, Technology, Reproduction* (pp. 142–160). Madison, WI: The University of Wisconsin Press.

Squier, S. M. (1994). *Babies in Bottles. Twentieth-Century Visions of Reproductive Technologies.* New Brunswick, NJ: Rutgers University Press.

Stanworth, M. (1997). Reproductive technologies: tampering with nature? In: S. Kemp & J. Squires (Eds.), *Feminisms* (pp. 482–487). Oxford: Oxford University Press.

Stern, D. N. (1995). *The Motherhood Constellation. A Unified View of Parent–Infant Psychotherapy.* New York: Basic Books.

Strathern, M. (1992). *Reproducing the Future. Essays on Anthropology, Kinship and the New Reproductive Technologies.* Manchester: Manchester University Press.

Taylor, J. S. (1998). Image of contradiction: obstetrical ultrasound in American culture. In: S. Franklin & H. Ragoné (Eds.), *Reproducing Reproduction: Kinship, Power, and Technological Innovation* (pp. 15–45). Philadelphia, PA: University of Pennsylvania Press.

Taylor, J. S. (2004). Introduction. In J. S. Taylor, L. L. Layne &

D. F. Wozniak (Eds.), *Consuming Motherhood* (pp. 1–17). New Brunswick, NJ: Rutgers University Press.

Taylor, J. S., Layne, L. L., & Wozniak, D. F. (Eds.) (2004). *Consuming Motherhood*. New Brunswick, NJ: Rutgers University Press.

Taylor, L., & Taylor, M. (2003). *What are Children For?* London: Short Books.

Thompson, C. C. (1998a). Producing reproduction: infertility clinics. In: S. Franklin & H. Ragoné (Eds.), *Reproducing Reproduction: Kinship, Power, and Technological Innovation* (pp. 66–101). Philadelphia, PA: University of Pennsylvania Press.

Thompson, C. C. (1998b). Quit sniveling, cryo-baby. We'll work out which one's your mama! In: R. Davis-Floyd & J. Dumit (Eds.), *Cyborg Babies. From Techno-Sex to Techno-Tots* (pp. 40–66). New York: Routledge.

Thompson, C. C. (2005). *Making Parents: The Ontological Choreography of Reproductive Technologies*. Series: Inside Technology. Cambridge, MA: MIT.

Thomson, S. (2002). The adjective, my daughter: staging T. S. Eliot's "Marina". In: K. Lesnik-Oberstein (Ed.), *Yearbook of English Studies* (pp. 110–127). Special Section on "Children in Literature". Vol. 32. Leeds: MHRA.

Thomson, S. (2003). Derrida and the Child: Ethics, Pathos, Property, Risk. *Oxford Literary Review*, 25, 337–59.

Thomson, S. (2004). The child, the family, the relationship. Familiar stories: family, storytelling, and ideology in Philip Pullman's *His Dark Materials*. In: K. Lesnik-Oberstein (Ed.), *Children's Literature: New Approaches* (pp. 144–168). London: Palgrave.

Thornton, S. (1998). The vanity of childhood: constructing, deconstructing, and destroying the child in the novel of the 1840s. In: K. Lesnik-Oberstein (Ed.). *Children in Culture: Approaches to Childhood* (pp. 122–151). London: Macmillan.

Walkerdine. V. (1990). *Schoolgirl Fictions*. London: Verso.

Walsh, S. (2001). Untheming the theme: the child in wolf's clothing. Unpublished doctoral thesis, University of Reading.

Walsh, S. (2002). Animal/child: it's the "real" thing. In: K. Lesnik-Oberstein (Ed.), *Yearbook of English Studies* (pp. 151–162). Special Section on "Children in Literature". Vol. 32. Leeds: MHRA.

Warnock, M. (2002). *Making Babies: Is There a Right to Have Children?* Oxford: Oxford University Press.

Weston, K. (2001). Kinship, controversy, and the sharing of substance:

the race/class politics of blood transfusion. In: S. Franklin & S. McKinnon (Eds.), *Relative Values. Reconfiguring Kinship Studies* (pp. 148–175). Durham, NC: Duke University Press.

Wolf, N. (2001). *Misconceptions. Truth, Lies, and the Unexpected On the Journey to Motherhood.* New York: Anchor, 2003.

Zelizer, V. A. (1985). *Pricing the Priceless Child. The Changing Social Value of Children.* Princeton, NJ: Princeton University Press.

INDEX

abortion, 114, 171
Adams, P., 2, 37–38, 50–53, 74, 81, 136, 159, 185
adoption, xii, xv, xvii–xviii, xx–xxi, 62, 100, 108, 125, 127, 153–154, 159, 180 *see also*: child, adopted
  gay, 136
  transnational/racial, 91, 137, 149, 153, 155, 158–159, 161–163, 180
Agacinski, S., 144–145
Althusser, L., 78, 108, 185
Anagnost, A., xiv, 91, 153–162, 167, 185
Antigone, 95–97, 99–100, 136
Ariès, P., xiii–xiv, xxiii, 13, 22, 185

Barker, M., 38, 185
Barrington, J., xv, 185
Becker, G., xxii, 11–24, 26–28, 30, 32, 35, 37, 55, 69, 84, 128, 130, 133, 186
Beer, G., 146, 186

Berlant, L., 171, 173, 186
Bialosky, J., 9–11, 13–15, 35, 186
birth
  father, 124
  kin, 126–127 *see also*: kinship
  mother, 105, 125
  parent, 124, 126–128
Bowlby, R., vii, 83, 87, 99–106, 115, 118, 137, 186
Burman, E., vii, 91, 158–159, 175–176, 180, 186
Butler, J., xxiv, 31, 37, 95–97, 99–101, 118, 120–123, 128–129, 136–146, 152, 167, 178, 182, 186

Carsten, J., 118–134, 136–137, 146, 151, 155, 157, 162, 182, 186
Castañeda, C., 79–80, 85, 149, 152, 161–166, 180, 186
child *see also*: genetics, child
  adopted, xii, xvii–xviii, xx–xxi, 57, 62, 108, 123–128, 153, 155, 161

own, vii, xiv, xvii–xviii, xx–xxi,
26, 33–34, 43, 45, 57, 62, 87,
93, 97–99, 102–104, 107,
109–110, 115, 117–118, 120,
133–134, 136, 139, 149,
151–155, 168–169, 180,
182–183
childhood, xiii, xix, xxii, xxiv, 14,
64–65, 77, 79–80, 83, 113, 152,
158–159, 163–164, 176, 183
Chodorow, N., 2, 40–41, 45–55, 64,
67–69, 72–74, 187
Clarke, A. J., 114, 187
Cocks, N., viii, 38, 65, 187
coercion, 12, 15–22, 40–41, 46–47,
67, 130, 140
commodification, 44, 81, 87–88,
91, 93
commodity, child as, 79, 81–82,
84, 87–89, 93, 95, 97, 137–138,
153, 160
conception, xi, xxi–xxiii, 6, 22, 34,
56–59, 61–62, 66, 78, 84, 87,
98, 102, 106, 108, 111–113,
119, 121, 134
conscious(ness), 7–8, 36, 40–41,
46, 49–50, 59, 69–72, 142–143,
168 see also:
unconscious(ness)
consumer choice, 87, 92
consumption, 89–92, 114, 157
contraception, xiv, 6, 13, 34, 37
Cook, R., vii, 179, 192
Cooper, S. L., xv, xviii, 10–11, 13,
21–26, 28, 30, 35–36, 42, 55,
64, 187
Cowie, E., 37–38, 185

Davis, D. S., 111–113, 157, 187
de Marneffe, D., 73, 187
dead babies, 168–173, 175–177
Derrida, J., viii, xxiv, 104–105, 116,
178, 187
"designer baby", 79, 109
Deveraux, L. L., xvi, 187
Diamond, R., 36, 187

Diepenbrock, C., 29, 32, 34–35,
187
disability / disabled child, xiii, 79,
98, 107, 109–111, 116
DNA, xviii, 127, 154
test, 124–127
donor(s), xi, 87, 98, 105, 137, 150
egg, 103, 105, 119, 134, 150
Dowrick, S., xv–xvii, 187
Dutton, F., xvi, 187
Dyson, S., 13–14, 22, 188

Edelman, L., 78, 188
Edwards, J., 74–75, 138–140, 188
embryo(s), xii, xvii, xxii–xxiii, 10,
59, 61, 78, 81, 132 see also:
foetus(es)
erotism
anal, 70–71
genital, 71
oral, 70–71
ethnicity, xiii, xxiv, 28, 35, 161
Ettore, E., 38, 188
expectation(s)
cultural, 12
gender, 112–113
of fatherhood / motherhood,
xiii, 1, 23–24, 78
societal, 12, 41–42, 111

Farquhar, D., xx, 43–45, 53, 87–89,
92–94, 96, 102, 108, 113,
119–120, 134, 137, 139, 157,
162–163, 188
fatherhood, 23 see also:
motherhood, parenthood,
paternity
Felman, S., 72–73, 188
femininity, xvi–xvii, 27, 31–32, 40,
48–49, 51–52, 54–55, 58, 60,
69, 72, 106–107
feminism / feminist views, xv,
xxii, 2, 19, 31, 38, 40, 49, 75,
87, 104, 114, 166–167, 170, 175
fertility, xv, 10, 21, 36, 57–58, 65
treatments, 27, 33

Finkler, K., 18, 127–128, 133,
   153–154, 188
Fletcher, A., 107–110, 188
foetus(es), 75, 90–91, 114, 169–175,
   177 *see also*: embryo(s)
Foucault, M., 118
Franklin, S., vii, xv, xviii, 20, 42,
   73, 102, 104, 128, 133, 143, 188
Freud, S., 47, 50–51, 54–55, 64,
   68–72, 74–75, 78, 83, 89, 95,
   106–107, 118, 142, 147, 188

Gay, P., 37, 189
Geertz, C., 36–37, 189
gender role(s), 40, 50, 53–54 *see
   also*: social role(s)
genetic(s), xi, xiii, xv–xviii,
   xx–xxii, xxiv, 25–26, 38,
   66–67, 98–99, 104–106,
   108–110, 117, 119–120,
   123–128, 134, 138, 150–154,
   170
   child, 11, 108
   continuity, 25–26
   inheritance, 18, 127
Gilbert, S., 60, 189
Glazer, E. S., xv, xviii, 10–11, 13,
   21–26, 28, 30, 35–36, 42, 55,
   64, 187
Goodison, L., xvi, 189
Gravon, C., 26–35, 55, 128, 133,
   155, 182, 190
Greer, G., 68, 70, 81, 85–87, 94, 98,
   108–109, 153, 189
Grundberg, S., xv, xvii, 187
Gubar, S., 60, 189
Gurak, L. J., 26–35, 55, 128, 133,
   155, 182, 190

Hall, S., xxiii, 189
Hammerman, A. J., xvi, 187
Haraway, D. J., 36, 146, 166–178,
   189
Heidegger, M., 79, 123, 189
Hewlett, S. A., 3–5, 7–8, 189

Holland, P., 175–176
Hrdy, S. B., xviii, 4–9, 36, 46, 85,
   189

infertility, xi, xv–xvi, xxi, 10–12,
   16–18, 21–25, 30, 34, 36, 39,
   42, 44, 56–64, 67, 98, 134, 180

James, A., xiii, 114, 189
Jones, S., 74, 154, 189
Jordanova, L., 104, 189

Kahn, S. M., 103, 189
Kelleher, J., 177, 190
Kezur, D., 36, 187
Kincaid, J., 114, 190
kinship, 92, 95–97, 99–103,
   117–119, 123–125, 127–133,
   135–141, 143, 145–146,
   151–154, 167–170, 172–173,
   176, 178, 182 *see also*: birth kin
Klein, M., 64, 69
Kohlstedt, S. G., 23, 26, 190
Konrad, M., 115–116, 119, 134, 190

Lancaster, R. N., xviii–xix, 6, 190
Lay, M. M., 26–35, 55, 128, 133,
   155, 182, 190
Layne, L. L., 91, 113–114, 190, 193
Lesnik-Oberstein, K., xiii, 14, 38,
   114, 135–136, 147, 182,
   190–191
Levick, S. E., 86, 97–98, 106, 191
Longino, H. E., 23, 26, 190
Lyotard, J.-F., 65, 191

Mandelbrot set, 132
Marx, K., 87, 155
maternity, 68, 100, 102–106, 115
   see also: motherhood,
   parenthood
Mauss, M., 70, 191
Meyers, M., 36, 187
Miller, J., 56–65, 67–68, 72, 74, 81,
   86, 191
miscarriage, 59, 74–75

Mitchell, J., 49–53, 69, 71, 74–75, 191

Morgado, M., 171, 191

Morgan, L. M., 91–92, 114, 191

motherhood, xv, xvii, 4, 15, 23–24, 34, 41, 45–46, 48–49, 51–52, 64, 73, 88–90, 92–93, 99, 105–106, 114 *see also*: fatherhood, parenthood

Murray, T. H., xvi–xvii, 83, 86, 94, 98, 107–108, 110. 191

Myntti, C., 26–35, 55, 128, 133, 155, 182, 190

narcissism, 98, 109

normalcy, 12–22, 30, 35, 69, 130

object relations, 47, 49–51, 69

objectivity, 17, 135

parenthood, xvii, 12–13, 21–22, 25, 68, 82, 84, 86, 88, 98–99, 108, 111, 114, 176 *see also*: fatherhood, motherhood

paternity, 99–101, 104, 106, 125 *see also*: fatherhood, parenthood

penis envy, 51, 55, 64, 69–70, 75, 106–107

Plato, 1, 191

pregnancy, xvi–xvii, 23–26, 30, 33–34, 43, 54, 60, 89, 115, 152

Prout, A., xiii, 114, 189

psyche, 56, 58, 61

psychic, 48, 50–51, 53–54, 95, 183 reality, 47, 51, 53 *see also*: social reality

psychoanalysis, 47, 49–50, 66, 72–75, 106, 143, 181, 183

psychology/psychological, xii–xiii, 23, 28, 40–41, 45, 47–48, 51, 55, 63, 67, 73, 86–87, 91, 108, 124–128, 179–180

Ragonè, H., xii, 117, 133, 150–152, 191–192

Raphael-Leff, J., 60, 64–69, 72, 78, 85, 191

reproduction, xvi, xix–xx, 6–8, 10–14, 24–26, 28–29, 41, 43, 45, 52, 55, 57–58, 64–67, 79, 87–89, 91–93, 97–99, 103, 106, 108–109, 118, 136, 143–144, 156, 163, 167, 180
  assisted, xxii, 21, 25–26, 104, 119, 133
  cultural, 141–143
  third party, 22

reproductive technology(ies), xi–xii, xvi, xix–xxiii, 1, 10, 13, 19–23, 26, 33–34, 37–39, 41–44, 47, 55, 61, 68, 72–73, 77–78, 83, 87, 90, 94, 97–120, 133, 135, 140, 149, 153, 168, 176, 179–183
  assisted/ARTs, xxii, 22, 24–26, 35, 42, 44–45, 57, 61, 74, 93, 98, 151
  in-vitro fertilization/IVF, xi, xv, xxiii, 42, 63, 73, 104, 150

Robertson, J. A., 98–99, 102, 192

Rose, H., 36, 192

Rose, J., xiii, xxiv, 38, 107, 114, 123, 135–136, 141–143, 158, 162, 183, 192

Rose, S., 36, 192

Rothman, B. K., xvii, xxiii–xxiv, 93, 192

Rothschild, J., 116, 192

Roudinesco, E., 105, 178, 187

Rousseau, J.-J., 4, 192

Sandelowski, M., 44, 152–153, 181–182, 192

Scharf, C. N., 36, 187

Scheper-Hughes, N., 167, 169–170, 172–175

Schneider, D., 118, 128, 136–137, 140

Schulman, H., 9–11, 13–15, 35, 186

Sedgwick, E. K., 46–47, 192

Segal, N., vii, 179, 192

self, 16, 23, 26–28, 31, 39, 48, 64, 68, 71, 94, 98, 109, 151

sexual/sexuality, xi, xiii, xviii, 6,
    57–58, 67, 71, 79, 95, 100, 137,
    139, 141–144, 167, 178, 180,
    183
  emotions/feelings, 4–5, 22
  hetero-, xvii, 36, 48, 52, 59, 66,
    97, 99, 101–102, 136, 141–143
  homo-, 36, 48, 99, 136, 140,
    143–145
  identity, 45
  intercourse, 66
  polarity, 67
Shabi, R., 97, 192
Shanner, L., 32, 192
social reality, 47, 51, 53 see also:
    psychic reality
social role(s), 53 see also: gender
    role(s)
Spivak, G., 155–156
Squier, S. M., xxiii, 103–104, 115,
    132, 192
Stanworth, M., 43–44, 92–93, 192
Stern, D. N., 73, 192
Strathern, M., vii, 7, 42, 103,
    105–106, 125, 132–133,
    138–140, 147, 188, 192
subjectivity, 18, 35, 91, 161
surrogate, 98, 105–106, 150–152

Taylor, J. S., 89–92, 94, 96,
    113–115, 120, 122, 157, 193
Taylor, L., vii, xvi, 13–14, 22, 77,
    179, 192–193
Taylor, M., xvi, 13–14, 22, 77, 193
Thompson, C. C., xxi, xxii, 37, 42,
    78, 81, 133, 150, 193
Thomson, S., viii, 36, 116, 136, 174,
    178, 182, 193
Thornton, S., viii, 83, 193

unconscious(ness), 8, 36, 40–41,
    47–50, 53, 64–72, 75, 95, 167,
    183 see also; conscious(ness)

Walkerdine. V., 80, 159, 193
Walsh, S., viii, 35, 157, 178,
    193–194
Warnock, M., xvii–xviii, xx–xxi,
    109, 194
Warnock Report, The, xv, xvii, 1
Weinshel, M., 36, 187
Weston, K., 135–136, 194
Wolf, N., 81–82, 84–87, 93–95, 98,
    108–110, 112, 194
Wozniak, D. F., 91, 113–114, 193

Zelizer, V. A., 83, 89, 152–153, 158,
    194